Inner Animalities

gROUNDWORKS

ECOLOGICAL ISSUES IN PHILOSOPHY AND THEOLOGY

Forrest Clingerman and Brian Treanor, *series editors*

Inner Animalities

Theology and the End of the Human

Eric Daryl Meyer

Fordham University Press | *New York 2018*

Fordham University Press gratefully acknowledges financial assistance and support provided for the publication of this book by Carroll College.

Fordham University Press also publishes its books in a variety of electronic formats. Some content that appears in print may not be available in electronic books.

Visit us online at www.fordhampress.com.

Library of Congress Cataloging-in-Publication Data available online at https://catalog.loc.gov.

Printed in the United States of America
20 19 18   5 4 3 2 1
First edition

to Carolyn, Lupine, and Avery

Contents

Introduction

What kind of animal is a human being? Is a human being an animal at all? Do politics or prayers set human beings apart from other animals? The "yes-and-no" answers that each of these questions elicit are a symptom of the fact that in the West, the discourses through which human beings have endeavored to understand themselves set humanity and animality in an ambiguously oppositional relationship. Whereas Aristotle regards the human being as a "political animal," every six-year-old knows the political force of a command to "stop acting like an animal."[1] We suppose that we are the animals who are supposed to be something other than animals.[2]

The story has been told often: human beings come to understand ourselves through comparisons and oppositions.[3] We come to know who we are by talking about who we are not, observing those who we perceive as different—across edges of ethnicity, nationality, sexuality, species, and so on—in order to triangulate a sense of ourselves. Moreover, the contours of power always guide the discourses of difference and collective self-discovery so that subordination, exploitation, and resistance are written into competing narratives of identity and exclusion. Most of the ways that we think and talk about nonhuman animals function in this way. Of course, no oppositional comparison is a blank slate; we always bring some nascent sense of difference and some rudimentary sense of ourselves to our interactions with one another. And so, through a perversely circular form of confirmation bias, moderately functional but inaccurate prejudices tend to be confirmed. We think and act in a feedback loop where the perception of our encounters with animals reinforces our self-understanding, while our self-understanding constrains us to interact with animals in particular ways.[4]

This book orbits our efforts at self-definition vis-a-vis animality with a very specific focus: What happens to the parts of ourselves that we think we hold in common with other creatures—what I call our human animality—when we obsessively differentiate ourselves from them? Could we come to think differently about our common animality?

All the prevalent Western forms of human self-understanding arise from some version of a categorical distinction between human beings and other animals. That is to say that humans and all other animals are supposed to be discontinuous in at least one way, no matter how many other continuities are acknowledged. Because these persistent, undeniable continuities between human beings and other animals always remain, any categorical distinction between humanity and animality necessarily also cuts across the interior of human life. Categorical distinctions between human beings and all other animals "out there" correlate with interior distinctions between some core of humanity-within-the-human and human animality.[5] Classically, human beings are thought to be rational while all other animals lack rationality, a demarcation line that simultaneously sets up an opposition between human reason (as the fulcrum of our exceptionalism) and human desire, emotion, and embodiment as sites of a common animality.[6] The differences that we use to set ourselves apart from all other animals also form regulatory boundaries that govern and subordinate aspects of our lives.

To what degree is our subjectivity, our selfhood, located in our common animality, if at all? Our self-understanding remains deeply conflicted around questions of animality, no less in theological anthropology than in other discourses. This book brings sustained theological analysis to the endlessly looping feedback between the outward cut that divides humans from other animals and the inward cut that divides our humanity from our animality.[7]

The Problem of Human Animality

The mainstream of the Christian theological tradition has been committed to some version of a categorical distinction between human beings and all other animals, as described above. When this longstanding commitment collides with two other thoughts—the undeniable commonalities of human and nonhuman life, and the

Christian commitment to the fundamental unity of the human being—Christian anthropological exceptionalism generates what I call the "problem of human animality." In the long history of the Christian theological tradition, the effort to hold these three convictions together coherently has produced a multitude of strategies that control and contain human animality, competing solutions to a common problem. The manifest commonality of human life with the lives of other animals in embodiment, nutrition, mortality, and reproduction is obvious enough, but a few more comments may elucidate the dogmatic Christian commitment to the fundamental unity and integrity of the human being as a creature.

Leaning on Greco-Roman philosophy, the Christian tradition is replete with anthropologies that divide up human beings into parts. There have been contentious arguments over the boundaries between human soul, spirit, body, concupiscence, reason, and passion, among others. Some of these parts have been more closely associated with animality than others. Nevertheless, for all their talk of parts, Christian theologians have generally affirmed the ultimate integrity of the human being. The human being whom God saves is the *whole* human being, no matter how many subdivisions have been conceptually generated. Theologians who have tried to sustain a fundamental division in the human person (so that, for example, the human body is a temporary provision and only the human soul spends eternity with God) have been strongly censured.[8] Internal divisions within the human being function within Christian theology as heuristic devices or means of exhortation, rather than a fault line along which a human being could hypothetically be divided. Thus, although proper humanity and human animality can be distinguished within theological anthropology, most Christian theologians are committed—at least in principle—to holding them together in accounts of creation, redemption, and eschatological transformation.

Maintaining that human beings are categorically unique among God's creatures in the face of this commitment to the integrity of the human being and the manifest commonality of human life with the lives of other animals requires careful conceptual navigation, particularly around human animality. Any theology that has generated a concept of humanity by means of contrast with nonhuman animals must tread lightly around questions of human animality so that the experiences of creaturely life that human beings share with other animals do not undermine anthropological exceptionalism. A theologically validated difference-in-kind between human beings and other animals is simple enough: despite the characteristics that human beings share with other creatures, God sets human beings apart in some way (an immortal or rational soul, for example) so that human beings can be neatly separated out from all the others. The conceptual boundary between humanity and animality *within* a human being, however, is never quite so tidy. To illustrate, if human beings are taken to be uniquely rational, then the irrational aspects of human life (particularly irrational urges or behaviors *shared* with other animals) seem to undermine anthropological exceptionalism and require some discursive strategy of explanation or management.[9] These strategies render animality peripheral and inessential to human life so that the theologically underwritten uniqueness remains the most important thing about being human. Human animality is variously explained, ignored, sublimated, obscured, sacrificed, or negated in order to preserve humanity's unique status before God and basic creaturely integrity. The problem of human animality is an abyss over which theological anthropology has been trained to leap. The leap has been made so many times that we often fail to recognize it. Human animality is the abjected remainder of the human being, the shadow of proper humanity's ascent to the glory of God. Carefully tracking the movements of human animality within theological anthropology, in other words, reveals constitutive tensions and contradictions in theological discourse that otherwise remain invisible.

The intrahuman division between humanity and animality is, of course, laden with judgments of value. *Humanity* names a set of cherished and accepted behaviors, values, and traits; while *animality* names a corresponding set that is generally subject to discipline and restriction. In most accounts, God's grace works to amplify the humanity of human beings and, simultaneously, to attenuate human animality. *Proper humanity* does not just designate one part of the human being; by expressing what is truly or authentically human, it also provides a normative ideal. *Animality,* then, designates the subordinate aspect of human life that must be modulated, controlled, or redirected in order to conform more fully to proper humanity. In the following chapters, I use the terms *humanity* and *proper humanity* to refer to this regulatory conception of authentic humanness. I use the term *human beings* to refer to the psychosomatic creatures whose lives are regulated and formed by humanity.

This book approaches the problem of human animality with two goals in mind. First, I seek to analyze and expose the ways in which dealing with the problem of human animality has left constitutive contradictions and tensions in the fabric of Christian theological anthropology. The maneuvers that sideline human animality are often hastily executed along the way to loftier ideas, so that animality returns in some unnamed way to play an unrecognized but essential role in a theologian's account of humanity. Second, and more constructively, I want to demonstrate that anthropological exceptionalism is unnecessary for Christian theology. In other words, I want to resolve the problem of human animality, not with a newer and better strategy for subordinating and managing our common creatureliness, but by offering a theological account of human life centered the aspects of creaturely life that human beings share with nonhuman neighbors, that is, an account that abandons the categorical distinction between human beings and all other animals.[10] In fact, at the very point where most theological anthropology disavows and subordinates animality, there are often openings onto different paths, opportunities to think differently about our common creatureliness. It is possible to start over, beginning again out of the irresolvable tensions that result from efforts to cut off humanity from animality in order to go a different route. In this way, the constructive work of the book grows out of the critical work that precedes it.

The innovation here is primarily formal. Insofar as proper humanity and human animality have been distinguished and described in a thousand different ways (but almost always along the lines of the same basic hierarchical subordination of animality beneath humanity), I am less invested in any particular notion of humanity or animality than in the possibility that God's work in creation elevates animality, however described, rather than giving divine ratification to anthropological exceptionalism.

Reconsidering Human Animality as an Approach to Ecological Theology

At the level of the trees, this book is about the relations between humanity and animality in Christian theology—what might be called the "textual ecology" of Christian theological anthropology. At the level of the forest, it is about ecology in a broader sense, a search for some adequate way to respond to the catastrophic degradation of the earth's ecosystems. The question that gave rise to the project as a whole is this: What prevents Christianity from generating sustained and effective resistance to ecological degradation? The longer I mulled the question, the more deeply I became convinced that the answer lay in the deep narratives of theological anthropology, where narrow ideas about the image of God, sin and redemption, and the eschatological destiny of the redeemed generate and sustain forms of human self-understanding that separate and subordinate animality. Insofar as the conceptual relationship between proper humanity and human animality comes to structure concrete interactions between human beings and other animals (and, by proxy, nature/creation as a whole) the problem of human animality is a knot at the center of Christianity's inadequate resistance to anthropogenic ecological degradation in its myriad forms (climate change, mass extinction, loss of biodiversity, pollution).[11] Research into the problem of human animality not only promises a new line of analysis for theological anthropology, but also a novel approach to ecological theology.

Nor are the questions at the heart of this book an intramural discussion for insiders to the world of Christian theology. The commitment to a categorical distinction between humanity and animality in our global political and economic systems derives—more than from any other source—from a sustained Christian investment in anthropological exceptionalism. Christian theology takes up anthropological exceptionalism from Greco-Roman philosophy (particularly the Stoics), amplifies it with theological and scriptural reasoning, and then, at the dawn of the era of European colonial expansion, passes it into the secularized exceptionalism of Enlightenment humanism.[12] Christian theological anthropology, then, remains the historical foundation beneath the secularized anthropologies of humanism, liberalism, and global capitalism.

The human animal distinction is foundational to the opposition between culture and nature; the two distinctions map more or less directly on to one another (humanity/culture stands over against animality/nature). Even in seemingly incompatible deployments of the idea of nature—as the nostalgic site of primal purity or as stockpile of natural resources awaiting human use—the opposition between humanity and animality is at the core. And this conceptual separation of human culture from all other earthly life is arguably the central problem to which the environmental movement responds.[13] The pervasive conceptual arrangement in which humanity and human culture are "other" than nature, receives its primary validation from the conviction that human beings can be categorically distinguished from other animals, and must become properly human in distinction from their own animality.

In turn, the opposition between culture and nature generates and sustains human irresponsibility with regard to the politics of creaturely life. Despite four decades of clear warnings from the popular environmental movement that the planet's ecosystems cannot absorb the effects of the Euro-American bourgeois lifestyle as it is intensified domestically and adopted globally, patterns of irresponsible consumption and despoilment have changed only superficially. Western modes of human self-understanding instill a sense of entitlement to "nature's" ecosystemic goods in a manner wildly incommensurate with ecological stability. An ecologically sustainable economy cannot even enter the range of common-sense plausibility because its adoption would require forgoing many esteemed cultural goods—the "fulfillment of our humanity," much of what "makes us human." Instead, the response to ecological degradation focuses on tolerable but inadequate changes—conscientious consumerism and individual ecological piety. All of this would indicate that human irresponsibility in creation is not primarily a function of conscious human choices—between, for example, a sustainable lifestyle and an unsustainable one—but a function of the profound structures of identity and self-understanding.

Of course, at the level of ethics and activism, animal advocacy and environmentalism are two divergent, and occasionally conflicting conversations. Heated arguments divide groups working on these issues. For example, on questions of culling invasive species, ecologists place the integrity of an ecosystem over the interests of particular living creatures, while animal rights activists insist on the inviolable integrity of every living creature. There is no easy resolution of these tensions. However, at a level conceptually prior to ethical questions—in cosmology and fundamental human self-understanding—the two conversations are inexorably linked. The wager of this project is that reconsidering the relationship between humanity and animality gets back to a hinge point at which the pressing concerns of animal advocacy and environmental activism can be addressed. Therefore, I am less interested in adjudicating specific ethical issues than in exploring, mapping, and reconfiguring the terrain in which the ethical questions of human-animal relations and ecological responsibility arise.

The earth's capacity to sustain diverse and stable communities of living creatures faces no greater threat than the human habit of exempting ourselves from fundamental relationships of interdependence. Layer upon layer of economic, political, military, and industrial destruction stand, ultimately, on questions of basic human self-understanding—they stand on questions of the relationship between humanity and animality. Insofar as Christian theological anthropology is deeply implicated in current forms of human self-understanding that separate and subordinate animality, Christian theological anthropology also represents an appropriate discourse for reconsidering our cosmology and self-understanding.

One potential point of confusion must be addressed at the outset. Although this project seeks to destabilize the opposition between humanity and animality, it persists, from beginning to end, in using these terms. It remains essential to remember that the human-animal distinction collapses the unimaginably complex frontiers of difference between earthworms, gorillas, squid, sloths, condors, and human beings into a single, simple cut. Every time it is uttered, the term *animal* is a false promise that all the differences among nonhuman creatures can be neatly contained so that human beings can rise above them all.[14] Nevertheless, the fault-line of the human-animal distinction runs so deeply within the structure of Western thought, that one cannot avoid, avert, or overturn it through changing one's linguistic habits.[15] The word *animal* and the constitutive conceptual opposition between humanity and animality don't lose their power when someone stops using the terms. Like a fault between tectonic plates, one may study it carefully, and one may seek to understand the tensions and pressures involved, but one should not be under any illusions that one can bury the fault, cover it over, or remove it altogether with the tools at hand.

The division between humanity and animality is not an accurate way of perceiving living creatures so much as an almost impossibly powerful idea deeply embedded in Western accounts of subjectivity, sociality, culture, and politics. The operation of powerful ideologies cannot be effectively resisted by denying that they exist, or by directly refuting them with rational discourse; ideology's logic of assent does not rely on intellectual agreement. Calling attention to the bumps, hitches, and internal grinding of ideology disrupts its smooth, largely invisible quotidian function, and exposes the mechanisms of its operation. Anyone who tarries with the contradictions embedded in the human-animal distinction will find that this boundary appears with alarming frequency in daily conversation, in the deep structures of moral reasoning, in emotions like disgust or anger, in one's own self-regard, and in basic patterns of self-understanding.

In retaining the terms *animal* and *animality* throughout the project, I do not endorse the simplistic categorical distinction that they presume and perpetuate. I hope instead to transform the categories, to repeat them with a difference that undoes their power. To shift metaphors slightly, the term *animal* is a window framed into the very structure of human understanding—we know who we are by reference to those creatures that we are not (however inaccurate our ideas about them may be). Rather than looking out *from* humanity onto "the animals" as if there were obviously a wall separating them from us, this project seeks to look *in* through the window at the human who incoherently presumes coherence for his categories. What if there is no wall, only a window frame? Who are *we* when we presume to already know, without really asking, who animals are? What truths about *us* do our fictions reveal? I use the term *animality* as a window onto humanity and, wherever possible, I bind human life to our (mis)conceptions of animality in order to provide a different way of thinking about humanity and, I hope, the seeds of a different way of *being* human.

A Comment on Method and Overview

In order to reconsider the role of animality in Christian theological anthropology (and, concomitantly, to imagine a novel theological response to ecological degradation), I approach the problem of human animality both historically and constructively. A few comments regarding the method(s) peculiar to my approach may be of service, since I see the historical and constructive work as being integrally linked together. The historical work in the first three chapters represents a theologically focused response to Matthew Calarco's call for a "historical and genealogical analysis of the constitution of the human-animal distinction and how this distinction has functioned across a number of institutions, practices, and discourses." For Calarco, "not only would this project further desediment and denaturalize the human-animal distinction, but it would also help to uncover alternative ways of conceiving of human beings and animals that have been ignored, covered over, and distorted by dominant discourses."[16] Not only does this historical work demonstrate that Christian theological anthropology is pervasively shaped by the problem of human animality, as Calarco suggests, it also "denaturalizes" our most familiar conceptions of humanity and animality, and opens up imaginative space to reconsider ourselves in relation to nonhuman animals. Attending to the problem of human animality at the fourth-century roots of Christian theological anthropology exposes the parochiality of present-day views by way of an encounter with the (no less parochial, but differently so) ideas of humanity and animality at work in the theological anthropology of Gregory of Nazianzus and Gregory of Nyssa.

I have chosen to focus on fourth-century figures to do this work for several reasons: First, the fourth century is a uniquely influential period of Christian thought. Following the conversion of Constantine and the establishment of Christianity as the majority religion of the Roman Empire, Christian teaching hardens into dogmatic form across any number of important subjects. Paradigmatically, this dogmatic hardening occurs around trinitarian questions at the councils of Nicea and Constantinople, but the theological reflections of fourth-century authors such as Athanasius of Alexandria, Basil of Caesarea, Gregory of Nazianzus, Gregory of Nyssa, Evagrius of Pontus, John Cassian, Jerome and Augustine have an outsized impact on the following millennia's theological reflection regarding a range of questions other than the trinity—theological anthropology no less than other areas. Second, stretching the project's historical perspective from the present back to the fourth century helps to support a large claim about the pervasiveness of the problem of human animality within Christian theological anthropology as a whole. I am not undertaking the kind of massive genealogical effort that would be required to trace lines of influence exhaustively and diachronically, but I am persuaded that the problem of human animality is embedded so deeply in the structure of Christian theological anthropology that similar analysis could be carried out in almost any other geographical or historical location.

The historical portion of the project—comprised of two chapters on fourth-century authors and a survey of the problem of human animality in contemporary theological anthropology—critically diagnoses the tensions and contradictions written into Christian theological anthropology around the problem of human animality and provides leverage for the constructive reimagining of human life in relation to animality. Where ancient authors' accounts of humanity and animality strike our ears as strange, they also provide alternatives that allow us to examine our own understandings of humanity and animality more closely. Furthermore, close attention to the points in theological anthropology at which animality is disavowed, sacrificed, and subordinated highlights places where constructive thought can imaginatively return to reverse the polarity of these hierarchical schemes, so that animality takes a central role. In these ways, the constructive chapters in the second half of the book grow out of the historical work in the first half.

Chapter 1 focuses on two orations from the fourth-century bishop and theologian Gregory of Nazianzus. For Gregory, human animality is associated most strongly with human corporeality and the necessary limits of the body in mutability, passibility, and mortality. The most properly human activity for Gregory is the intellect's rational contemplation of God through which the human being is graciously assimilated to the light of divine life. Drawing out and amplifying several tensions within these two orations, I make two claims: first, that rational contemplation ultimately depends upon animal mutability, and second, that the form of subjectivity described in the highest reaches of rational contemplation is fundamentally indistinguishable from the form of subjectivity that Gregory attributes to simple animals whose behavior is determined by instinct. In these ways, human animality turns out to be integral to the proper humanity which is defined over-against it; or, put otherwise, wherever Gregory seeks to establish a domain of pure humanity, it is always already contaminated with animality.

Chapter 2 examines Gregory of Nyssa's homilies on the Song of Songs. The text of the Song of Songs is full of animal imagery and Gregory's homilies make abundant use of these creaturely analogies. Nevertheless, at the beginning of his series of sermons, Gregory sets out hermeneutical rules for himself and his listeners that make an effort to totally humanize the text. Wherever the text's erotic scenes and animal imagery would seem to lead the reader into passion, uncontrolled desire, or base thoughts, Gregory argues, it must instead be understood in a spiritual sense that transforms these erotic energies into the compelling force that leads a person into union with God. The animal reading, then, is the false and vicious reading that leaps to conclusions based on the superficial appearances of the text's bare letters. A more subtle, spiritual allure rises from beneath the surface of the text and generates an authentically human reading that draws the properly attuned listener to God. In Gregory's exposition, then, animality appears at both the upper and lower limits of rationality and language—though Gregory only recognizes it explicitly at the lower end. One can fail to be properly human by being mired in a subrational fixation on naked corporeal beauty, but one is also lead beyond the capacities of human language and reason to comprehend the incomprehensible God through an (animal) desire attracted to the display of divine beauty manifest in the very same images of the text. Nudity, beauty, and animality are thus doubled back on themselves in Gregory's homilies in a manner that undermines his effort to hermeneutically refine animality out of the text of the Song of Songs.

Chapter 3 functions as a hinge or transition between the historical portion and the constructive portion of the project. I offer a survey of contemporary theological anthropology covering a diverse range of significant works from the twentieth and twenty-first centuries in order to demonstrate that the same pattern of differentiation and disavowal that operated within the texts of the ancient authors still operates in contemporary theology. After examining eleven other theologians much more briefly, I examine the theological anthropology of Karl Rahner and Wolfhart Pannenberg in order to explore in greater detail the particular contours of the tensions and contradictions surrounding human animality in contemporary theology. The chapter establishes that the problem of human animality has persisted in Christian theology from antiquity to the present, but it also helps to establish the need for a constructive theological anthropology with a relationship to human animality other than disavowal or sublimation, moving the book toward the constructive chapters that follow.

Chapter 4 begins the project's constructive work, with three chapters of theological anthropology devoted to the three major narrative moments of Christian theology: creation, sin and redemption, and eschatological transformation. Each chapter takes up moments at which animality has traditionally been disavowed and subordinated within theological anthropology in order to reimagine animality at the center of God's work among human beings. This first constructive chapter describes the creaturely identity of the human through the complex politics of creaturely life rather than through the logic of contrast and sovereign exceptionalism. In the same way that relational accounts of personal human identity ground individual formation in the concrete social politics in which each person lives, this chapter seeks to expand the frame of reference for theological purposes to suggest that personal human identity is grounded in the concrete relations of ecological politics—even though we typically regard our relationships with other animals as functionally irrelevant to our identity. I argue that Jesus's teaching in the gospels and the story of Nebuchadnezzar in the prophetic book of Daniel ought to turn Christian understandings of the image of God toward ecological relations of interdependence rather than sovereign differentiation.

Chapter 5 reconsiders animality in sin and redemption by offering creative rereadings of two touchstone scriptural texts on these theological themes—Genesis 2–3 and John 1. Drawing on the work of Louis Althusser, Giorgio Agamben, and Judith Butler, I propose thinking about *humanity* as an iterative ideological structure that forms human beings by demanding the performed repetition of maneuvers of differentiation relative to animality. Subsequently, I seek to link this ideological structure with the concept of original sin, supporting this connection with a critical rereading of Genesis 2–3 as an account of the disastrous origin of the categorical difference between humanity and animality. If the narrative of the fall also tells the story of human beings asserting their difference-in-kind from animals, then the traditional theological devaluation of animality relative to humanity begins to look suspect. Turning to the prologue of John's gospel, the chapter confronts another traditional site of the assertion of categorical human uniqueness. Insofar as the *Logos* becomes incarnate as a human being, many theologians have taken the incarnation as license to claim that God is more specially concerned with human beings than any other creature. My reading of John's prologue disrupts this claim by suggesting that the incarnation may be an attempt to deconstruct humanity from within for the sake of the integrity of the whole creation, rather than an endorsement of human pretensions to transcendence above the other animals. The movements of both sin and redemption on this picture, then, turn on the relationship between humanity and animality—sin being the constitutive disavowal of animality that forms humanity as we know it, and redemption being a deep transformation that returns human beings to the animality that they have disavowed.

Chapter 6 considers eschatological transformation and the resurrection from the dead. While the Christian tradition has, from a very early date, strongly affirmed the resurrection of the whole human body with all its organs intact, theologians have argued with striking regularity that physiological functions such as digestion and sexual expression will be absent from resurrected human bodies. I argue that digestion and sexual expression are a kind of condensation of animality within the human body inasmuch as these physiological functions are often the most obvious and undeniable reminders of the continuity of human life with the lives of other animals. Attempting to overcome the traditional exclusion, this chapter sets both digestion and sexual expression at the very center of the eschatological communion between God and all God's creatures. Where human animality is no longer excised from the life of the new heavens and new earth, all the other creatures come to play constitutive roles in the Spirit's perfection of creation. Thus, the chapter argues that the eucharist, the resurrection of the body, the messianic banquet, the new heavens and new earth, and unbroken communion with God should be understood within the context of ecological relationships. The sacramental sharing of divine life and love is multiplied through all the dimensions of creaturely diversity rather than restricted to the rarified economy of proper humanity.

Finally, the conclusion takes the argument of the project regarding human animality in Christian theological anthropology and labors to make the ecological stakes of this argument as explicit as possible. An adequate response to anthropogenic ecological degradation, I maintain, must address the conceptual and structural differentiation of proper humanity from human animality—especially insofar as it is this formulation of human uniqueness that is reconfigured and secularized in enlightenment philosophy and undergirds the entitled human appropriation of nature in global capitalism. Nothing less than a fundamental shift in human self-understanding relative to creation and other creatures is necessary. While Christian theological anthropology is at least partly culpable for the structure of human self-understanding in the West, it also retains the disciplinary and discursive tools to address the widest frame in which human beings understand themselves. As a whole, then, this project seeks to set out the trajectory—within the discourse of Christian theology—for a resistance to proper humanity and an effort to place human self-understanding within the politics of creaturely life—for the good of human animality and all our creaturely neighbors.

PART I

Critical and Historical Animalities

1

Gregory of Nazianzus: Animality and Ascent

The Moon gives the beasts fearless speech [parrhesia]; the Sun rouses the human for work.

—*Gregory of Nazianzus*[1]

A bishop in late antiquity could be measured by the fulfillment of two prominent vocational criteria: first, the practice of *mystagogy*, leading Christians in spiritual ascent by means of ritual, instruction, and personal example; second, the practice of *parrhesía*, bold and fearless speech that stands up to powerful forces on behalf of the poor and the vulnerable.[2] Bishops such as Ambrose of Milan, Basil of Caesarea, and Gregory of Nazianzus practiced parrhesia by confronting emperors and governors on behalf of their flocks.

By daylight, both mystagogy and parrhesia are paradigmatically human activities for Gregory of Nazianzus, marks of the categorical difference between human beings and nonhuman animals. Humanity is almost angelic in proximity to God; animals are earthbound, filthy, passion ridden, and associated with idolatry. Under the gentler light of the moon however, wild animals emerge from between the lines of the text practicing a parhessia and a mystagogy of their own. And although Gregory will not grant episcopal authority to the lunar endeavors of the beasts, this chapter demonstrates that the daylight of Gregory's texts presses on toward an evening, opening onto the light of the moon and the boldness of animals in speech and mysticism of their own. In Gregory's theological anthropology, human animality fares much the same. With his pen, Gregory violently excludes animals and animality from theological knowledge and spiritual practice, and yet human animality remains essential—even if unacknowledged—for the transformation of the redeemed.

The problem of human animality produces fault lines in Gregory's theology. Gregory's theological anthropology stands conflicted on its own terms. Human animality is radically and violently disavowed, yet simultaneously plays an indispensable role in human salvation. The movements of human transformation in Gregory's theological anthropology rely on fundamentally conflicted depictions of nonhuman animals and animality to generate movement from dissolute fallenness toward a renewed and elevated human nature. Gregory's text transgresses the terms of his own categorical cut between humanity and animality in order to describe God's redemption of the whole human being. On the one hand, Gregory's spirituality of purification (*kátharsis*) operates with a logic of sacrifice. Gregory's discourse violently subordinates nonhuman animals to make the point that human animality must be either silenced or slaughtered for the sake of spiritual union with God. On the other hand, however, Gregory's explicit disavowal of animality falters where animals also provide images of a redeemed and perfected humanity living out an elevated instinctual bond to God. Humanity's genuine repentance, vocation to worship, and perfected subjectivity all absolutely depend on qualities that Gregory associates with animality, but by the time he discusses these points, animality has been forcefully removed from the frame of reference.

This chapter begins by mapping the major elements of Gregory's theological anthropology—mind, flesh, logos—onto the division between humanity and animality. The bulk of the chapter is then devoted to analysis of two of Gregory's homilies—Oration 39 and Oration 28. Although these orations respectively address the mystery of baptism and the knowledge of God, taken together they present a complete anthropological narrative, from primordial origins to eschatological transformation, taking stock of the pitiable state of humanity between. These two texts offer an excellent synopsis of Gregory's theological anthropology,[3] but they are also two texts in which animals appear quite frequently at the margins, inhabiting the edges of Gregory's theological anthropology. Nonhuman faces appear momentarily in imagery and exhortation, but rarely linger long since these texts are overwhelmingly concerned to carve out space for an authentic and proper humanity. I will follow these animal apparitions closely to trace out the complex relation between humanity and animality in Gregory's texts.

Gregory's Paradoxical Anthropology: Mind, Flesh, and Logos

Like most ancient thinkers, Gregory divides the human being into conceptual parts, allocating and measuring the humanity and animality of each. While Gregory follows Origen in conceiving of a human being as the tripartite composition of flesh, soul, and mind (*sárx, psyché,* and *noūs*),[4] he much more frequently presents the human being as a paradoxical dipolarity between mind and flesh (*noūs* and *sárx*).[5] Gregory obviously and persistently devalues flesh: "Flesh is shoddy in comparison with soul, as everyone with a good understanding should agree."[6] Flesh is material, corruptible, mortal, dense, obstructive, unspiritual, distracting, and riddled with pain and passion (*páthos*)—qualities associated with animality. Mind (*noūs*) is immaterial, immortal, light (both luminous and ethereal), spiritual, and active—qualities associated with angels and proper, normative humanity. The division between mind and flesh aligns precisely with an intrahuman division between proper humanity and human animality.[7]

Within the interior geography of the human, the seeing and speaking subject resides in the mind—the proper site of freedom, subjectivity, and knowledge.[8] Gregory's "I" or "We" speaks from the position of the mind while the flesh is an intimate alterity, an object or obstacle to be managed and overcome: "This bodily 'murkiness' stands between us and God just like that ancient cloud stood between the Egyptians and the Hebrews, and again like that 'darkness [God] set as his covering,' namely our density, through which only a few spy ever so briefly."[9] When Gregory urges members of his congregation to confess, pray, contemplate, or reform their lives, he addresses their minds and counsels them to go to work upon their flesh. The mind faces the challenge of the flesh's passion and takes responsibility for the flesh's purification.

Gregory persistently worries over the animality of human flesh: The animality of the flesh must be tamed and put to good use or it will surely run wild and overcome the human mind. The passions (which reside particularly in the flesh), "wickedly feed upon and consume the inner human being."[10] The inner work of the mind consists of "driving out," keeping tight reins upon, but not "violently strangling" the life of the flesh.[11] A steady reliance on metaphors of domestication and capture bind animality and flesh together in Gregory's anthropology.

In addition to harboring untamed animality, Gregory also complains that the flesh has a deadening effect on the operation of the mind. Norris notes, "As Gregory sees it, full knowledge of God's nature is impossible for humans since their view is obstructed by their fleshly condition. The problem is not one of language or attitude, but one of mental power, for such knowledge is beyond even those prepared by contemplation."[12] The flesh is a thick curtain or a lead blanket which impedes contemplation in two ways. It obscures the ability of the contemplative mind to see the divine light but also impedes transformation toward a more ethereal mode of life.[13] The mind naturally strains to see great distances and rises in affinity with the divine and angelic natures, but flesh blocks its vision and drags it downward: "By fear they are rectified, purified, and (so to speak) rarified in order to rise up to the heights. For where fear is, there is heeding of commands. Where heeding of commands is, there is purification of flesh—that cloud eclipsing the soul, not allowing it to see the beam of divine light in purity. But where purification is, there is illumination."[14] God's incomprehensibility is only partly a function of divine transcendence and mystery. It is also the density of the flesh that prevents a more adequate knowledge of God by impeding the mind's efforts to rise to God's unsearchable heights: "There is no way for those in the body to become fully present with intellectual things apart from corporeal things. For something of our embodiedness always intrudes if the mind strives to attend to connatural and invisible matters—even though the mind completely divorces itself from visible things and more fully realizes its nature."[15] For Gregory, flesh marks off distance and difference from God. It is the thick veil through which the human mind labors to peer and the dissolute animality that drags the mind away from spiritual concentration.

While the flesh marks off human distance from God, the mind is the site of a deep affinity between discursive creatures (the *logikōn*—angels and human beings) and the divine Logos. Discursive beings would have a profound and transformative knowledge of God were it not for the density and impurity of the flesh. Logos is the substance or content upon which a mind operates and the bond of perception and expression between one mind and the next.[16] Through creation, incarnation, and redemption, the divine Logos anchors an intellectual fellowship; a relation of special continuity between God, humanity, and angels that Gregory frequently describes with metaphors of light and illumination:[17]

> [Angelic nature] is nearly incorporeal; at any rate, it is exceedingly close. You see how our heads spin around this discourse (*perì tòn lógon*)! We do not have a way forward, some means great enough to know angels and archangels, thrones, dominions, magistracies, authorities, brilliant lights, ascents, mindful powers or minds, pure and authentic natures—all immovable (or very difficult to move) toward inferiority, always dancing around the First Cause. Illumined as they are by the purest of light from that origin—or else each [illumined] with the light fitting for its nature and position—how should someone hymn them!? They are so thoroughly formed and molded in beauty that even as they become lights, they are able also to illumine others by their own influx and communication of the first light.[18]

Reading such passages, one scholar goes so far as to claim that, for Gregory, God is a "great Mind."[19] In the same way that flesh links humanity to animals/animality, the mind links humanity to God and the angels.[20]

Despite proposing an equally hierarchical anthropology, Gregory does not follow Origen in linking the human fall into sin with the union of human mind and flesh. It is not human flesh that is responsible for the fall, but the immaturity of newly created minds. Using a medical term, Gregory describes the immaturity of the human mind as a *protopath*—a leading indicator or symptom of a disease that will get much worse.[21] An immature mind is not a problem in and of itself, but through its confusion the entire human may be led astray. The mind is the linchpin, in other words, to spiritual health, and once it has been struck blind (as the devil well knows) a human being may be led into every form of vice to which the animal flesh was already prone.[22] The fleshy corporeality of human life is not the origin of the predicament of sin, but once an undisciplined mind allows the flesh room to go astray, the flesh becomes the site of all manner of wickedness.[23] Overcoming the sinful condition of humanity, then, requires a two-fold strategy of purification and illumination. Stripping away the burdensome distractions of the flesh through a rigorous program of cathartic purification opens the way for the reunification of the human mind with God and the angels, a destiny toward which luminous human minds naturally yearn.

The purification of the flesh is a precondition for the union of the mind with God. For that reason, Gregory's twofold strategy for overcoming sin also describes a trajectory of development that moves from animal entanglement toward a rarified proper humanity centered in the intellect. Even though purification is an operation that takes place *within* a human being—an action of the mind upon the flesh—it is simultaneously a task that divides humanity from animality, inscribing this familiar boundary within the interior geography of the human for the sake of self-reflective discipline. Insofar as the flesh obscures the mind's spiritual vision and encumbers its spiritual progress, Gregory describes the spirituality of purification as a sacrifice—not of the flesh itself, but of the animality of the flesh—carried out by the mind as it strives toward God. In what follows, I offer a reading of Oration 39 that traces out the contours of Gregory's spirituality of purification followed by a reading of Oration 28 that tracks the ascent of the mind toward union with God. In both cases, Gregory's theology cannot finally afford the success of its own sacrificial strategy because fleshly animality remains silently indispensable to the logic of Gregory's account of human salvation.

What Kind of Animal Is a Purified Human?

Gregory delivered Oration 39, traditionally entitled "On the Holy Lights,"[24] shortly after Emperor Theodosius legitimized Gregory's claim to be the Bishop of Constantinople by exiling Demophilus, his anti-Nicene rival.[25] It is a baptismal homily given at Epiphany, and Gregory preaches to a group of catechumens whom he has not catechized, but whom, nevertheless, are to be baptized the following day. In fact, they have been catechized by his opponent and predecessor, Demophilus.[26] To put it mildly, Gregory is not terrifically confident of the theological rectitude of those he will shortly initiate into full participation in the church. Undertones of trinitarian politics resound through the themes of idolatry, purgation, repentance, and illumination. The oration moves from the rejection of pagan idolatry, to purification by fear and obedience, to the true knowledge of the trinity, and finishes by insisting on the necessity of repentance and divine mercy for true illumination.

Gregory's purification specifically targets idolatry, heresy, and passion—all three of which are strongly associated with animality.

For example, passion and vice "wickedly feed upon and consume the inner human being."[27] Idolatry too drags human beings away from God by encumbering their minds with animal thoughts:

> I will leave off speaking of the veneration of snakes and wild animals, of the eager honor of their formlessness—each having for itself an initiation and a festival, though demonic lunacy is common to them all. As if it were completely necessary to defile themselves and fall away from the glory of God, they dragged themselves down to idols, crafted works, hand-made creations. Those in possession of a mind could ask for nothing worse than to revere such things! As Paul says, "They ought to receive the recompense necessary for their aberration"—by means of the things they worship! They do not so much honor the objects of their worship as degrade themselves through them. They are revolting in their aberration, and more revolting yet in the cut-rate objects of their prayer and worship. They may be more senseless than even the things they honor, as exceedingly mindless as the objects of their prayer are cheap![28]

Gregory begins by driving away these animal thoughts, then announces that his discourse (logos) has purified the assembly hall and prepared the way for genuine knowledge of God.[29] All the encumbrances of the flesh and every thought of lizards and leopards must be cast aside in order to prepare for baptismal illumination: "By fear they are rectified, purified, and (so to speak) rarified in order to rise up to the heights. For where fear is, there is heeding of commands. Where heeding of commands is, there is purification of flesh—that cloud eclipsing the soul, not allowing it to see the beam of divine light in purity. But where purification is, there is illumination, and illumination is the fulfillment of yearning for those longing for great things, the greatest thing, or what lies beyond greatness."[30] Purification prepares the way for illumination. Gregory describes illumination as an ascent beyond the cheap and grimy thoughts of the flesh, beyond association with senseless beasts, and into pure divine light.[31] In an oration delivered the following day, Gregory makes the link between baptismal illumination and the transcendence of animality explicit: "Of those who fall short [of baptism], there are some who are completely akin to livestock or wild beasts (because they live in a mindless or wicked manner)."[32]

Beyond these explicit repudiations, Gregory's antagonism to animality also emerges in more subtle ways—through telling shifts in vocabulary and emphasis. Calling on a Johannine vocabulary, Gregory begins his oration by invoking Christ: "the true light which illumines every human being was coming into the world."[33] Throughout the discourse, Gregory employs John's pervasive light metaphors in order to describe baptism as illumination.[34]

Gregory's account of illumination does not echo John's exactly, but changes the substance of John's luminous metaphor. In John's prologue, the divine Logos illumines humanity with the light of life (*zōē*)[35] and throughout the gospel illumination names a process of enlivening what is dead, bringing to health that which is subject to death and decay.[36] Illumination is therefore animation. *Zōē*, after all, is the life of every animal (*zōon*). In contrast, within Gregory's oration light bears knowledge (*gnōsis*). Illumination becomes a metaphor for enlightenment rather than animation. The link between God and humanity does not reside in the vitality of the flesh (that is, in human animality) but in the highest reaches of the mind.[37] Insofar as "life" is shared by animals and humans in common, Gregory's displacement of life (*zōē*) with knowledge (*gnōsis*) functions as a subtle betrayal of human animality. On Gregory's reading of John, the divine Logos that illumines the world is contiguous with the logos of human thought and speech:

> The same Logos is both naturally fearsome for the unworthy and attainable out of benevolence for those who are well-prepared—that is, as many as have purged the impure and material spirit from their souls and swept clean and ordered their souls with knowledge. . . . Let us light within ourselves the light of knowledge. At that time we should speak of God's wisdom, which has been hidden in a mystery and we should shine out to others. But until then, we should purify and initiate ourselves in the Logos in order that we might do exceedingly good things for ourselves, working ourselves into godlikeness and welcoming the coming Logos—not only that, but seizing and showing forth [the Logos] to others.[38]

Gregory buries the connection between light and life in order to undergird the continuity of human and divine logos in knowledge (*gnōsis*).[39] The occlusion of *life* from Gregory's use of the Johannine vocabulary, then, marks a subtle erasure of animality, symptomatic of a broader disavowal of human animality within Gregory's anthropology. Replacing animation with enlightenment ensures that the illumination of the divine Logos further secures the categorical uniqueness of human beings over against other creatures.[40]

Purification prepares the human subject for the illumination of the mind by transforming the obscuring and encumbering weight of the impassioned flesh into something easily pushed aside in loftier contemplation. Flesh and human animality are obstacles and impurities that must be conquered through purification; they play (almost) no positive role in Gregory's account of human redemption. Contemplation of divine glory and expressions of praise entirely occupy redeemed humanity and the dense and darksome flesh no longer plays any significant role.[41] Gregory affirms the resurrection of the body, and it is clear that corporeality is not a provisional or temporal aspect of humanity, but this is more a doctrinal concession than a point of enthusiasm.[42] The transformed and redeemed body which has been rarified ("made light") through purification is significantly different from the burdensome, heavy body of present experience. Stripped of its irrationality, the flesh no longer weighs down or impedes the properly human activity of rational contemplation. It is not so much the flesh that is eliminated in the purified body of the resurrection, but the animality of the flesh. Gregory never writes of a redeemed affinity with animals because it is the animality of the flesh that is eradicated through purification and illumination.[43] The flesh itself is, at best, a theological stowaway on the journey of salvation, a residual reminder of the foreign land from which the redeemed human has been fortunate enough to escape.[44]

Despite the antagonism that Gregory's spirituality of purification harbors against animality, Gregory's theological anthropology holds hints of a night in which animals venture out by the light of the moon and make barely acknowledged contributions to Gregory's anthropology before retreating unthanked. In other words, Gregory's theological anthropology cannot afford the total success of its own purification regime because the final sacrifice of human animality would cut the human being off from salvation. Two examples follow.

First, even as Gregory's sacrificial spirituality disavows human animality, the flesh is not so superfluous to human communion with God as Gregory's most ethereally contemplative passages might suggest. Although its importance remains understated, the flesh is essential to humanity's collective creaturely vocation and likewise to the historical encounter between humanity and God in Jesus Christ. The fleshy commonality of human beings with other animals is the hidden scaffold that holds the logic of Gregory's theological anthropology together even though it never appears plainly.

Humanity is absolutely unique in the cosmos because no other creature is made of the same stuff—or rather, of the same combination of materials. Unlike either angels or animals, human beings alone are both mortal and imperishable, spirit and flesh, visible and intelligible, belonging to the earth and longing for heaven, connatural with both angels and the dust of the earth, an odd mixture of mud and soul.[45] While the angels and powers (whom Gregory refers to as the "intellectual creation") fill the heavens with God's praise, the material creation ought also to resound with worship. Yet only a material creature also endowed with an intellectual nature could perceive and praise God—Gregory assumes that animals universally lack religious subjectivity (more on that shortly)—and so, humanity's paradoxical composition reveals humanity's collective raison d'être: "Just so, it was necessary for the worship of this [divine] Three or One, not to be restricted only to creatures above, but rather for there to be some worshippers below as well, so that all things might be filled with the glory of God, since [all things are] also from God. For this reason, the human being was created and honored with God's hand and God's image."[46] Human commonality with nonhuman animals is essential to the human vocation for Gregory because it enables human beings to echo angelic praise in a material context. Even though Gregory's account of human materiality is, from the beginning, an account of categorical human uniqueness relative to other animals, humanity's fleshy nature is indispensable for its highest calling: "the seed of the spiritualization of the perceptible world."[47] The tragedy of the fall into sin for Gregory lies in humanity's neglect of its spiritual vocation for the sake of reveling in commonality with animals. Yet, God's redemption draws human beings back to their original purpose by "natures made new":

> What is the great mystery concerning us? Natures are made new! God became a human being; the one who has mounted upon the heaven of heavens through the sunrise of his brilliance is glorified in the dusky twilight of our cheapness and humiliation. The Son of God deigns to become a son of humanity as well, and to be called upon as such. He did not transform

> what he was (for he is unchangeable), but received what he was not (for he is a benefactor) in order to contain the uncontained and associate with us by means of flesh—like a veil—since something of an originate and corrupt nature could not bear the purity of his divinity. For this reason, unmixed realities were mixed: not only God with the originate, not only mind with flesh, not only the atemporal with time, not only the illimitable with measure, but also childbirth with virginity, and dishonor with the most highly honored of all, and the impassible with passion, and the deathless with corruption.[48]

By means of "mingling" the "unmingled," God incarnate in Christ illuminates darkened human minds so that once again, true worship and praise might ring out through the material realm.

It is worth noting that flesh plays a double role in the redemptive maneuver of the incarnation. On the one hand, flesh is one of the terms that is "mingled" with its opposite; on the other, it is the medium in which the coincidence of opposites takes place—the site in which the incorruptible Creator joins the corrupted human creature. Gregory wavers between thinking about the flesh as a "veil" that God wears in Christ (remaining unconfined, immaterial, and unchangeable) and the flesh as a substance that God redirects and redeems by joining it to the divine nature. The interval between the two views preserves the categorical difference between God as creator and human beings as creatures by leaving a "back door" in Christ's flesh that maintains conceptual space for the uncontained excess of divinity. Regardless, flesh is essential to the renewal of human nature through divine grace.

As much as Gregory might prefer to encounter God in a luminous blaze of intellectual glory, he is constrained to recognize that humanity and divinity meet—first and foremost—in flesh. While Gregory's spirituality of purification is a top-down discipline that the mind carries out upon the unruly flesh, his account of the transformation of human nature works in the opposite direction: "The condemnation of the flesh was dissolved in the putting-to-death of death by means of flesh."[49] The incarnation is a bottom-up transformation of human beings, a renewal of the flesh that frees human minds for angelic praise and contemplation. Were Gregory's spirituality of purification to succeed in cutting off entirely the influence of the flesh upon the mind, it would also cut off the avenue by which divine grace works its transformation upon human beings.

It is remarkable that associations between flesh and animality appear only when the flesh is the target of purification and not when God takes up the flesh in order to renew human beings in their cosmic purpose. Once again, although flesh itself plays a role in human redemption, Gregory's depiction of redeemed flesh is always flesh whose animality has been drained away. A limit to Gregory's appetite for paradox remains: the association of divinity and animality (the opposite horizons that define and differentiate humanity) remains a step too far.

A second example: With some ambivalence, Gregory does lay claim to his own animality at one key juncture in Oration 39: "I confess myself to be a human being, a correctable animal of a fluid nature. I readily accept this and worship the one who has given it. I share it with others, and from mercy I bestow mercy. I know myself to be 'robed in weakness,' and just as I measure, so will I be measured."[50] Why is it that when Gregory acknowledges that he is an animal—a rare admission in his corpus—he does so in the midst of confession? On the negative side, Gregory associates animality and sin so strongly that they enter his discourse hand in hand; Gregory is an animal because he is a sinner. On the positive side—and I want to develop this intuition further—Gregory embraces his animality because its mutability is an essential precondition for confession, forgiveness, and sanctification.

The "inner human being" of Gregory's theology would be irredeemable without the mutability, or "correctability" that he associates with animality. The final assimilation of the human mind into the pure light of God's radiant life remains dependent upon the dense and darksome flesh upon which Gregory heaps so much blame, because fleshly animality harbors the possibility of change while purely intellectual natures remain fixed and static.

The aspect of human beings most apt to approach God—the mind—is also most resistant to transformation. The hierarchy that places mind above flesh not only maps an order of moral and spiritual value, but also degrees of mutability. The material realm is most susceptible to flux, while intellectual natures (angels, for example) are most stable, least tractable to the vagaries of change and decay. Immateriality and immutability are linked.[51] In fact, Gregory must repeatedly correct himself after saying that intellectual natures are totally immutable, remembering aloud that the devil and the fallen angels have abandoned good and embraced evil.[52] Gregory conceives of a mutable intellectual nature only as an exception or anomaly; pure mind is nearly immutable. Inasmuch as human beings are flesh, they are subject to the change and flux that characterizes the whole material realm; inasmuch as human beings are also mind, they bear an identity that resists change. Human beings are mutable because they are composite—both intellectual and material. Thus within the topology of Gregory's anthropology, flesh and animality are aligned with capricious flux while mind and humanity are aligned with stability.

The solitary point at which Gregory identifies his subjectivity with flesh and animality is the point at which he takes refuge in their "fluid and correctable nature."[53] Gregory more often laments the union of mind and flesh because he sees the capricious flesh as a weight that burdens and blinds the mind, but this union turns out to be the fundamental precondition for human redemption. The human mind remains ontologically resistant to change, but full conformity to God requires that it undergo transformation. Being united to the pliability of the flesh is an asset for the human mind just to the degree that it requires transformation in its connatural contemplative ascent toward God.

The mind that completely sacrificed or sloughed off the "fluid and correctable nature" of the flesh would be hardened and incapable of repentance. While the mind must purify and tame the animality of the flesh in order to perceive God, it also depends upon the mercurial flesh as the point at which the transformative grace of God gains traction on human life. For the most part, Gregory strategically evades the necessity of animality and the flesh by binding ontology and epistemology together; he describes union with God as the luminous acquisition of intimate knowledge rather than as a vivifying transformation. Nevertheless, the structural necessity of fleshly animality becomes apparent where Gregory recognizes the human predicament as a problem deeper than ignorance. The spirituality of purification must stop short of a total sacrifice of human animality insofar as cutting off the influence of the flesh would leave the purified mind entirely static. Without the fluidity of animal flesh, the fallen mind is an isolated, frigid monad, imprisoned in its pretention to self-sufficiency.

The Intelligence of Unthinking Creatures

Oration 28 is the second of Gregory's five "Theological Orations" delivered in Constantinople in the summer of 380 prior to his elevation as bishop of the city. Gregory asserts a pro-Nicene, homoousian theology as the true understanding of God.[54] In Oration 28, Gregory leads his hearer toward genuine knowledge of God through two ascents into divine mystery, the first framed by the Sinai narrative of Exodus 19, the second by the hexaemeron creation account of Genesis 1. These two ascents are of particular interest here because the figuration of animals differs radically between them. In the span of the same homily Gregory figures animals both as enemies to the knowledge of God and as icons of divine mystery. Animals appear differently in the two biblical texts, to be sure, but Gregory's interpretive hand is fairly heavy, adding layers of meaning to the scriptural animals. The difference between the animals of the first and second ascents, then, cannot be attributed to scripture alone. The contradictory depiction of animals in Oration 28 exposes the unstable and contradictory treatment (or more accurately, treatments) of human animality within Gregory's anthropology.

In the first ascent, Gregory introduces himself as Moses, already having arrived on top of Mount Sinai through a life of philosophic restraint and contemplation. His discourse (*logos*) will show the way for others to reach his lofty height: "May this discourse become a shining ray from the divinity who is singly divided and divisibly united."[55] From his vaunted vantage point, this new Moses looks down the slope of Mount Sinai and declaims a descriptive taxonomy of other biblical characters at their various stages along the way. Implicitly, his performative articulation of these categories asks his audience to locate themselves somewhere on the slopes below: Near to Gregory, but slightly lower, Aaron waits to assist Gregory in the cloud of divine mystery. Next are Nadab and Abihu, the elders. Further down, crowds throng in anticipation of hearing the words of God at a safely mediated distance. Below the attentive crowd are the unhallowed and uninterested masses. Finally, Gregory spills an inordinate amount of ink describing the lawless and unholy animals at the mountain's base:

> But if someone is a wicked, savage beast, entirely spurning contemplative and theological discourses, let him not destructively and maliciously lurk in the forests to snatch up some

> belief or saying by leaping upon it all at a sudden, and to chew sound discourses (lógous) to shreds by abusive insults. Instead, let him remain still farther away; let him flee from the mountain or he will be stoned and pulverized—the wicked will be wickedly destroyed. For true and firm discourses (lógoi) are stones to the beastly. [He will be stoned] whether he be a leopard (let him die with his spots!); or a bellowing, thieving lion seeking to make meat of any one of our souls or speeches; or a swine trampling the beautiful, translucent pearls of truth; or an Arabian wolf, a foreigner, or one even keener in sophistry; or a fox, some duplicitous and faithless soul conforming at any given time to the moment's needs, and feeding upon the dead and reeking bodies, or upon "the little vineyards," having fled from "the great ones"; or any other creature feeding on raw flesh and cast aside by the law, impure for both meat and enjoyment.[56]

Gregory posits irreconcilable enmity between the discourse of truth and the wild, carnivorous beasts at the foot of the mountain. If someone is to climb up and glimpse God, the spirituality of purification demands that the animals be left for dead. Gregory's heretical, idolatrous wild beasts find the words of truthful discourse to be hurled stones; and conversely, whenever wholesome discourse walks unguarded through the woods, teeth and claws threaten to tear it apart. Wolves, leopards, lions, foxes—unclean and predatory animals outside the law—are forbidden on the slopes of the mountain and fit for nothing but brutal slaughter by stoning or crushing.

Gregory's exhortation sets animality under the sign of sacrifice even though he does not directly advocate killing particular foxes, wolves, or leopards. It is a worthwhile (even if impossible) task to trace out the complex multidimensional exchanges between symbolic animals, real animals, stereotypical animals, and the moral valence of animality. The text of Exodus (insofar as it purports to describe a historical encounter) describes the spatial restriction and slaughter of real animal bodies. Gregory takes up these animal deaths as powerful symbols for the purification of the church. He asserts that heretics are hardly human, worse than animals, in part because the assumed ferocity of carnivores provides a powerful rhetorical hook for his hearers' imaginations. But Gregory's metaphorical reference to killing turns one more time against real animal bodies insofar as it reinforces the shared supposition that carnivorous beasts (literary or real) are too disgusting to associate with God and must be killed in order to establish the purified tranquility that contemplation requires. Metaphors are never "just" metaphors. Connections formed in the realm of knowing derive from and return to the realm of acting. The material consequences of symbolic sacrifice reinforce patterns of stereotypical recognition in which animal bodies (and human animality) always appear as threatening, to be met with preemptive violence.[57]

Aside from the passage's symbolic and corporeal violence, the way of ascent into spiritual knowledge is barred for animals and animality. Genuine theological knowledge belongs to purified humanity alone. Animality that is not hostile to God is still assumed to be indifferent and insensitive to God's self-revelation at the summit of earthly experience. Divinity and animality lie at opposite horizons of the limits of human thought; and Gregory is able to suppose, therefore, that God is opposed to animals.[58] The purity required to ascend the mountain and encounter God requires that both animality and heresy be left behind—and Gregory does not wish to parse too finely the difference between the two.[59] Ascending the mountain visited by God, animality must flee forever or be slain by the stones of discourse.

Toward the end of Oration 28, Gregory maps a very different ascent into the knowledge of God. The second ascent works through the hexaemeron of Genesis 1. Although Gregory sometimes describes a direct illumination of the human mind by rays of divine light, it remains more common for human beings to approach God's mystery by means of material images and metaphors.[60] Accordingly, in Oration 28 Gregory reverse-engineers the six days of creation, tracing backward through God's works from the sixth day to the first to approach God's ungenerated and eternal light. Gregory begins with human beings at the end of the sixth day and then praises the divine wisdom manifest in all the elements of creation "between" humanity and the Creator, as if peering back through the warp and weft of creation's fabric allows for a clearer line of sight onto God's brilliant mystery. The days of creation become a ladder of ascent toward God; Gregory's audience contemplatively climbs through the mysteries of the natural order. Because Gregory seeks creation's divine origin by working backward through the creation narrative, humans begin from the bottom of this ladder and must look up to the animals created earlier to climb to God. In the structure of this second ascent, animal intelligence reflects the wisdom of God, serving as a guide for human thought and model for human subjectivity. Unlike the animals surrounding Sinai—impediments to ascent who must be abandoned or killed—the animals of the hexaemeron are iconic signs and traces of divine wisdom in creation, a ladder for human intimacy with God.

Referring to the creation of land animals on the sixth day, Gregory asks, "Do you also want [to know] the differences among all the animals, from us and from one another?"[61] But Gregory's account of species difference is lost in a flood of questions that outpaces even Gregory's energy to answer. Like the divine speech in Job, Gregory's river of rhetorical questions overwhelms his hearers with awe at the wisdom expressed in the natural world. Gregory wonders at the "orchestral" songs of birds and the "cosmetic" plumage of peacocks, and the sheer variety of specializations by which animals fit their own peculiar niches.[62] But Gregory has even higher praise for the geometry and architecture practiced by bees and spiders.[63]

> Where does the industry and artistry of bees and spiders come from? They fabricate and hold honeycombs together with hexagonal, alternating pipes, the stability of which is systematically worked out through partitioning walls and alternately interweaving the straight lines of the corners. And all of this in such dusky light that the formations of the beehive must be invisible! [Spiders] weave complex webs stretched in many shapes with threads so very fine and nearly aerial that these are invisible from the beginning. Of the same web they make worthy homes and hunting grounds where they enjoy weaker creatures as food. What Euclid could mimic these—contemplating lines without substance and struggling in their demonstration?[64]

Gregory is awash in wonder at the order and beauty manifest in his creaturely neighbors, regarding each as an icon of the divine intelligence.

Amidst this sea of animal questions, however, Gregory holds one assumption constant: only humans employ discursive thought (logos).[65] Gregory's inquisitive laud for the ordered habits of animals never calls the supposition of their irrationality into question. Gregory leads his audience to externalize the source of animal wisdom—to attribute the intelligence in animal behavior to a source beyond the animals themselves. The "Euclidian" wisdom of bees and spiders does not demonstrate that insects have surpassed Euclid as skilled geometers, only that they enjoy an unreflective participation in the creative Logos of God. Bees and spiders are better geometers than Euclid, working in solid form and without the need for proofs, only because their unthinking instincts are structured by divine wisdom. Paradoxically, elevating these animals as icons of divine mystery allows Gregory to rob them of subjective intelligence. Accordingly, without any apparent irony, Gregory exclaims to his listeners, "I beg you, admire the instinctive intelligence of unthinking beings and present your explanations!"[66] Only the marvelous Logos of God could account for the well-ordered wisdom of animal life.

Yet, Gregory's suggestion that manifestations of animal intelligence are, at bottom, signs of God's infinite wisdom at work in creation cannot be contained so easily. Gregory means to explain the rational behavior of irrational creatures, but he inadvertently describes ordinary animals as living in a mode of intimacy with divine intelligence that is indistinguishable from his account of the highest aims of human contemplation. Although Gregory could never say so explicitly, these "unthinking animals" are models of creaturely reverence, contemplative transparency, and perfectly ordered obedience. The immediate intimacy of animals with God forecloses the space of self-aware discursive thought, but it also forecloses the space of prevarication and disobedience. The bees reflect the Euclidian dimension of divine wisdom by participating in the creative Logos of God in every movement of their whole being, not by a cognitive recognition or laborious ascent. This immediate, obedient intimacy is the ultimate goal of human contemplation—and although Gregory will not acknowledge it—this intimacy is already manifest in animals' well-ordered behavior.

The "unthinking intelligence" of bees and spiders is inseparable from the intelligence of God—and that inseparability of divine and created intelligence is the goal of Gregory's contemplative discipline. It is exceedingly difficult to imagine relevant differences between Gregory's description of the engulfing, transformative "mingling" of a human mind with the light of divine intelligence and the mode of subjectivity that belongs to the Euclidian spider. Both conform to the wisdom of the divine Logos with their entire being, expressing the illuminating wisdom of God in their own peculiar creaturely forms. Contemplative practice cultivates a form of intelligence that is, in a sense, "unthinking" (*alogos*). Any proprietary human logos that seeks to comprehend God on its own terms, or any mind distracted by personal desires or self-aware pride requires further transformation to enter full communion with God.

Returning to the Johannine vocabulary illustrates the point further. Despite Gregory's claims, it would seem that the ideal contemplative philosopher is a spiritual animal, a creature whose knowledge of God has dissolved into a life *with* God. Knowledge measures a distance between knower and known—the interval of representation. Unthinking animals, in contrast, live directly from the life of God. This quieter mode of animal illumination (where light brings life) integrates flesh and mind; desire and knowledge; humanity and animality; Creator, creature, and creation. While Gregory shifts the substance of Johannine light away from life and toward knowledge—a maneuver that disavows any connection between divinity and animality—Oration 28 suggests that the person genuinely seeking God would do better to learn the steps of ascent through an apprenticeship in animality. The deepest and most immediate conformity to God's Logos, it seems, opens only from the subject position of the animal.

But such an apprenticeship is nearly impossible within the sacrificial logic and sacrificial spirituality that upholds Gregory's anthropological exceptionalism. Perhaps the contemplative approach to God—despite Gregory's cathartic statements to the contrary—is a process of becoming more and more animal, rather than an amplification of normative humanity at animality's expense. Despite Gregory's militant efforts to eradicate animality from human flesh, the completely purified mind only ends up replicating another version of animal subjectivity living in immediate and transparent intimacy with God. Wherever purification stabilizes the human mind in isolation from the influence of animality, it also walls off human subjectivity from the kind of immediate, instinctual conformity to divine wisdom that bees and spiders enact with their whole being. In other words, at its limit, Gregory's spirituality of purification nurses an antagonism toward animality that is itself an impediment to union with God.[67] Purification—especially that violent form of purification described in Gregory's first ascent—must stop short in order to achieve its own goal. The pure light of knowledge must leave room for the radiant life of God diversely manifest in creaturely forms.

Conclusion

Gregory's spirituality of purification is an operation of the mind worked out upon the flesh and structured by antagonism of humanity toward animality. That antagonism crosses boundaries between the inner and outer worlds of the human—readily apparent in Gregory's rhetoric regarding nonhuman animals, but equally present in Gregory's treatment of human animality. Nevertheless, despite Gregory's disavowals, human animality remains essential to Gregory's account of redemption. Unacknowledged as such, animality remains indispensable for the creaturely vocation of human beings, shelters the condition of possibility for human transformation, and presents a mode of subjectivity perfectly united with divine intelligence.

Gregory draws a categorical distinction between humanity and animality, but maintaining this distinction burdens his theology with two major tensions. First, with regard to animality, Gregory sacrifices conceptual stability and consistency for the sake of a fundamental difference. Within the same oration, animality figures as a violent morass of disgusting and ignorant urges and as the well-ordered manifestation of divine intelligence. Gregory suppresses and then romanticizes animality in turn, but its fundamental difference from humanity remains constant in both operations. Animality remains plastic enough to function as a multivalent foil for humanity, providing contrasts in a number of different registers. Because animals and animality are peripheral to Gregory's theology, he is never bothered with the (likely impossible) task of unifying these concepts across his writing. Second, Gregory must disavow any theologically positive role for animality within human redemption. To explicitly name animality in its positive roles would surrender theological validation for his categorical differentiation of humanity from animality. Redemption sets humanity and animality at opposite poles of a hierarchical trajectory. Animality is what the human being is redeemed from, even where animality itself plays an unnamed role in the process. Gregory's descriptions of the process of salvific transformation continue to rely on characteristics previously aligned with animality (mutability, corporeality, subjective transparency to God), but Gregory is at great pains not to directly name animality in its positive functions, because to do so would call anthropological exceptionalism into question. Essential bonds between humanity and animality can appear only as threatening within Gregory's theology.

Gregory's theological anthropology leaps over a number of constitutive contradictions surrounding animality. Animality is a stowaway aboard Gregory's anthropology, yet a stowaway who (alone and silently) keeps the engine running and the whole craft moving smoothly. Animality is the scapegoat whose life outside the community—forgotten and abandoned—knits the life of the community together. Animals must appear in many (contradictory) roles in order to shore up the consistency of Gregory's anthropological exceptionalism within the narrative of transformation and salvation as it plays out between the proper humanity of the mind and the threatening animality of the flesh. Animals appear at the bottom of God's holy mountain as the disgusting, dangerous, and uncontrollably consumptive horde that humanity must escape or slaughter. But they also appear above humanity as exemplary citizens within a well-ordered whole, indirectly directed by the divine Logos, corporeally alive in an intimacy with God from which humanity finds itself estranged. Just so, the density and opacity of the flesh functions as a scapegoat for the mind's shortcomings in approaching God, yet fleshly animality also remains the site where God's redemption gains traction upon the whole human person.

The spirituality of purification is Gregory's effort to resolve the problem of human animality. Through sacrifice and erasure, Gregory labors to strain out every impurity from the flesh in order to open the way for the mind's uninterrupted communion with God. Purification strips the flesh of its influence upon the mind and disciplines its uncontrolled animal inclinations. On the surface of Gregory's text, it is clear that the process of purification silences and thins the flesh by eradicating its animality, but does not destroy the flesh altogether. In the deeper structural logic of Gregory's theology, however, human animality cannot be so easily extricated from the operations of redemption. The problem of human animality is manifest in Gregory's theology in the tension built into the spirituality of purification. Where purification succeeds in the sacrificial eradication of human animality, it also cuts the human being off from the working of God's grace. If Gregory were to relax his commitment to a categorical human-animal distinction, the sacrificial impulse of his theology might lose much of its drive and space would open for an explicitly positive theorization of human animality's part in communion with God. Following up on this kind of counterfactual imagination remains the task for the constructive portion of the project, but it is well-worth noting that—precisely through his conflicted and contradictory treatment of animality—Gregory himself has provided ample material for a constructive theological account of human animality.

Returning to the image that opened the chapter: the daylight of Gregory's theological writings holds no haven for animality, but if one waits for sunset, Gregory's theology harbors an implicit ecology in which humanity cannot be so easily isolated. "The moon gives the beasts fearless speech [*parrhesia*]; the Sun rouses the human for work."[68] After the sun has set, in the fog of weariness, when the mind is nearly exhausted, the good bishop Gregory (perhaps unknowingly) becomes animal in confession, repentance, and transformation. The lessons learned from bees and spiders crawl into the heart of his discourse. Perhaps the daylight denunciations that drive animals away from theological matters have masked the ways in which Gregory's discourse already holds whispers of animal parrhesia.

2

Gregory of Nyssa: Reading Animality and Desire

> No one who has an animal head may accurately be called Christian . . . double natured, something like the Centaur—both discursive and non-discursive. . . . [They have] a costume-mask of Christianity joined in life to a beastly body.
>
> —*Gregory of Nyssa*[1]

Gregory of Nyssa opens his letter to Harmonius with an anecdote about an ape.[2] There was a man in Alexandria who trained an ape to dance. The ape danced so well that when it donned a mask and costume, many people mistook the ape for a human being. One day, however, there was a clever fellow present who was not taken in with the crowds. This fellow threw a handful of nuts on the stage, at which point the ape tore off his mask in order to gobble them up, revealing himself to be "hideous and laughable."[3] Gregory offers the story in order to warn his readers to become true Christians, and not just imitators, lest the deceitful nuts of the devil reveal them as greedy, vain imposters.

Gregory returns to the theme of imitation later in the same letter, but the second treatment carries a positive valence. Gregory writes: "If someone were to express a conceptual definition of Christianity, we would say this: Christianity is imitation of the divine nature."[4] To be a true Christian, one must devote one's life to the imitation of God. Given Gregory's framing of the letter, the obvious analogy is difficult to avoid: the Christian imitates God just as the ape imitated a human being (but *not* as the false Christian imitates the true). The (reputed) natural talent of the ape for imitation provides the illustration and the model for a human being to draw near to God. The true Christian is the ape who is not exposed by the devil's clever trickery; the false Christian fails in the task of imitation and shows that he is "impassioned and beastly, being transformed by one passion after another, playing in his disposition the part of many forms of beasts."[5] Gregory thus expounds Jesus's injunction to "be perfect, as your heavenly Father is perfect," as a command to ape God without exposing oneself as an ape. The strange logic of this exhortation replicates on a small scale the logic of Gregory's account of divine-human communion. Gregory holds up animality as ridiculous or disgusting, something to be mocked, yet for all the abuse, animality turns out to be the substance of the union itself.

This logic appears on a large scale in Gregory's *Homilies on the Song of Songs*—a text filled to overflowing with animals acting like humans, humans acting like animals, and (in Gregory's reading) Christians being drawn into divine perfection through imitation.[6] The Song of Songs, however, is not an easy text to interpret. As erotic poetry, the Song of Songs was a puzzle and perplexity for many Jewish and Christian thinkers. Because the book was secure within the scriptural canon, however, these interpreters could not dismiss the text as lewd and unspiritual; they had to devise interpretive strategies to incorporate the text into a broader understanding of God's relationship to creation. Gregory—among others—employed an elaborate theological exegesis to lay bare a narrative of love between God and God's creatures hidden in the erotic movements of the Song of Songs.

Gregory's effort to sublimate the Song of Songs into a narrative of human-divine communion is aided by the surplus of animal imagery employed within the descriptions of the bride and bridegroom. Across the span of cultural and historical difference, the literary animals of the Song fall flat as erotically alluring images—they fail for Gregory as much as for readers of the present. The days when romantic encounters could be sparked by comparing a partner's hair to goats and teeth to a flock of sheep were sadly few. For this reason, the pervasive animal metaphors open up a space in which the text can be (and for many interpreters, *must* be) about something other than its erotic themes. In this way, the animals of the Song facilitate the oblique, allegorical readings of the Song that dominate the Christian interpretive tradition. Gregory's unflagging homiletical efforts to provide masks, costumes, and clothing to all the lovely, loving, beloved, erotic creatures of the Song provide an excellent opportunity to examine the conceptual entanglement of divinity, humanity, and animality in Gregory's theology.

My analysis of Gregory's text will be bolstered by setting it in conversation with another text, Jacques Derrida's *The Animal That Therefore I Am,* which works through many of the same themes—textuality, metaphor, exposure, desire, humanity, and animality.[7] Derrida's text traces the trajectory of an "immense disavowal" of animals in Western philosophy running from Descartes to Levinas. Derrida names this disavowal as the performative production of humanity by means of a stark contrast with a concept, "the animal"—an enormous, falsely homogenous, bounded set, capturing millions of different species in a single term. The conceptual function of the term *animal* as the foundational contrast for ideas about humanity far outstrips its descriptive usefulness as a category that is supposed (somehow) to capture commonality between an echidna, an ostrich, and a tuna. For Derrida, the ability to name every other living creature under the category *animal* provides a kind of mask by which a human being is able to strategically conceal his own animality from himself while also carrying out acts of great violence upon animals. Yet, in addition to this critical project, Derrida also stretches out, with stumbling words, toward a mode of subjectivity not predicated on a disavowal of animality, a mode—in some sense no longer human—in which one might return the gaze of an animal without shame. Derrida's account of his naked confrontation with a little black cat provides a counterpoint to the erotic interactions of human and animal bodies in the Song.

This chapter ventures a reading of Gregory's *Homilies on the Song of Songs* alongside Derrida's *The Animal That Therefore I Am.* Gregory's discourse concerning human animality remains irresolvably conflicted in ways analogous to the philosophical texts under Derrida's scrutiny. Yet the trajectory of Gregory's own theological anthropology breaks out of the containment provided by his too narrow conception of humanity—toward something like the mode of subjectivity that Derrida seeks. The theological anthropology underlying Gregory's anagogical exegesis of the Song of Songs breaks open in a felicitous failure to contain creaturely life: human animality is necessary to reach the deepest meaning of scripture and the summits of spiritual ascent, despite Gregory's explicit claims that spiritual transformation entails the transcendence of humanity beyond animality. The operation of Gregory's anagogical reading of the Song depends absolutely (but disavowedly) upon the animality that he labors to excise from the text. In the end, Gregory's theology cannot abide the categorical distinction between humanity and animality that his exegesis presumes to cut.

Anagogical Exegesis

At the beginning of his series of homilies, Gregory explains his exegetical method in order to attune his hearers' ears to the deeper meaning of scripture and to counter anticipated antagonism from "certain Church leaders" who strongly disapprove of Gregory's mode of interpretation.[8] All things equal, Gregory would prefer to call his approach to scripture "anagogical interpretation" rather than "allegorical" or "typological," but he is more eager to defend his exegetical method than to quibble over its title.[9] Gregory's style of exegesis stands in a tradition traceable back to Philo and Origen, but he is uniquely interested in the ways in which an ascetically attuned reading of scripture "leads upward" (*anagein*) drawing the reader toward God.[10] Gregory conceives of proper biblical interpretation as an upward movement in which human understanding transcends animality, or put otherwise, excises the animal meaning from what is properly a spiritual (read "human") text.

Gregory argues that each book of scripture bears its own unique aim (*skopós*)—he uses Proverbs, Ecclesiastes and the Song of Songs for examples—and that each book accomplishes that aim through its own unique (and perceptible) logical sequence (*akolouthía*).[11] Each book of the bible accomplishes some particular purpose in the reader by leading the reader through a series of well-ordered steps laid out in the text. The purpose (*skopós*) and operational logic (*akolouthía*) of each book must be ascertained through careful, contemplative reading rather than assumed from the outset. Gregory follows Origen in reading scripture as a canonical whole, a practice that validates connections between far-flung passages on the basis of a shared word or image.[12] For example, Gregory makes sense of the bride's comparison to a dove by reference to the appearance of the Spirit as a dove at Christ's baptism.[13] Unlike Origen, however, for Gregory the meaning of a passage is first governed by the sequential logic in the book where it is found, rather than an overarching canonical theme.[14] Nevertheless, understanding the spiritual meaning of a text according to its *skopós* involves what Norris calls "transposing" the historical narrative and material imagery up into a spiritual register.[15] Gregory himself uses the image of *transfiguration*: as the dusty, tired body of Christ was found to be unbearably radiant upon a mountain, so also does the properly attuned reader find a deeper and mysterious light emerging from the plain page of scripture.[16]

The particular *skopós* of the Song of Songs, as Gregory conceives it, is to draw the soul into loving union with God.[17] He writes: "I bear solemn witness to these things because I am about to apprehend the mystical sense in the Song of Songs. For through what has been written there, the soul is led like a bride toward a spiritual, unstained, and bodiless union with God."[18] The *skopós* of the text is a function of divine authorial agency and not something thematized by the "Solomon of flesh and blood"; Gregory suggests that there is another "Son of David" speaking through Solomon, on whose account the text is replete with true Wisdom.[19] As Norris notes, anagogical exegesis is not merely a technical skill practiced upon an inert text.[20] Rather, it is an approach to a text which is embedded within a particular vision of the world—and specifically of the way that language, text, meaning, understanding, and spiritual progress operate across a boundary between the visible material creation and the invisible intelligible creation. The practice of anagogical exegesis mirrors Gregory's cosmology, in which a spiritual/intellectual layer of creation is always distinct and superior to, yet nevertheless inseparable from a material layer of creation.[21] The Song of Songs bridges these worlds: it (passively) contains a narrative of the union of a soul with God, but for Gregory it also (actively) hooks readers and draws them into a similar union. A proper understanding of the text, for Gregory, always includes progress in an immaterial journey.

The text's meaning works itself out in the reader as much as the reader works out the meaning in the text. Accordingly, the *skopós* of the text does not lie flat on the page, waiting to be grasped and articulated. Gregory attributes agency to the text itself, or finds a divine agency working through it:

> By means of the elaboration [of the Song] the things of a wedding are sketched out, though what is intuited is the mingling of the human soul with the divine. For this reason the "son" of Proverbs is named "bride" here and "Wisdom" passes over into "Bridegroom" so that the human being becoming a pure virgin (from a "bridegroom" [courting Wisdom]) may be betrothed to

> God and joined to the Lord, and may also be one Spirit through mingling with the impassible and uncontaminated, becoming pure thought as opposed to weighty flesh. The one speaking is Wisdom, so then, love as much as you can—with your whole heart and strength—and desire to your full capacity. I will audaciously add these words: May you be smitten-in-love [*eràstheti*], for this passion for the incorporeal is irreproachable and impassible, just as Wisdom speaks in Proverbs ordaining this kind of love for divine beauty.[22]

Gregory suggests that the Song's account of union between bride and bridegroom is an outline meant to be filled in by pupils (*hypographómenon*), just as a child learns to write her letters by copying over faint tracings.[23] In this case, the person who truly reads and understands the Song of Songs traces over its narrative sequence (*akolouthía*) not by repeating the same bodily motions, but by being carried through the same affective, intellectual, and spiritual transformations described by the text's "higher" meaning. Operating through this pedagogical exercise, the text (or God working through the text) lures interpreters toward God, sparking the same kind of desire that the text describes in order to affect a transformation upon the reader herself.[24] Within Gregory's anagogical framework, the text is not interpreted correctly until it is interpreted in a participatory manner.[25]

However, the upward movement in Gregory's anagogy is not entirely irenic. Any reading of the Song fixated upon the text's sexual interactions is vacuous and superficial. A focus on the material appearances of the text fails to engage the text's inner meaning, which for Gregory is immeasurably more valuable.[26] Inasmuch as Gregory associates sexual activity and sexual urges with animals, the transcendence of the Song's anagogical meaning over its material content corresponds to the transcendence of human understanding over human animality. Given humanity's precarious position straddling the boundary between the intelligible creation and the material creation, human animality always threatens to overcome human transcendence, swamping it with animal passions.[27] Accordingly, Gregory raises an exegetical hedge meant to keep animal associations out of any reading of the text: "Whoever introduces a passionate and fleshly line of thought, or lacks the garment of conscience fitting for the divine wedding—let them not be bound up by their own thoughts, dragging the uncontaminated speeches of the bride and bridegroom down into the passions of livestock and animals."[28] Here, human animality threatens to intrude and defile the purity of the scriptural text whereas proper anagogical exegesis would transcend the mire of human animality.[29]

Exegeting the Song, however, is all the more difficult because the text itself has a threatening animality. Gregory not only polices the desires that arise in readers, his exegesis must also police the text. Or, to use Gregory's own metaphor, his exegesis prepares a "raw" text for proper human consumption by refining and cooking rough words fit only to be gobbled up by animals:

> The necessity is evident for an interpretation of [scripture's] words according to their intent [as opposed to their material sense], even though it pleases some to reject it. It seems to me that to do so is as if someone set out uncooked crops on the table for human consumption without grinding the stalks, without separating the kernels from the husks by winnowing, without refining the wheat into flour, without providing bread in the proper manner of food-preparation. Just as uncooked produce is food for livestock and not humans, someone might say that without being prepared through a refining interpretation, the divinely inspired words [of scripture]—not only of the Old Testament, but most of the gospel teaching—are food for non-discursive animals more than for discursive creatures [i.e., humans and angels].[30]

Under the direction of the Spirit, anagogical exegesis mills and extracts (not to say "cooks up") the meaning that is truly human. Such exegesis is thoroughly implicated in the discernment, placement, and reinforcement of the boundary between humanity and animality. Gregory's reading seeks after a properly human meaning of the text, secured against the threats of animality that arise on all sides—in the inappropriate passions of the reader and in the raw sensuality of the text.[31] The operation of Gregory's exegesis moves to excise animality—whether in the text or in the reader—as an impurity or excess which would prevent human union with God. The following sections explore the ways in which Gregory's sharply cutting exegesis necessarily fails to parse humanity from animality, demonstrating that, in fact, animality remains central and indispensable to Gregory's exegesis in unacknowledged (and even disavowed) ways.

The Anagogical Garment and the Naked Song

Gregory's literary modesty around the Song's salacious details may be helpfully compared with other treatments of nudity and animality. In *The Animal That Therefore I Am*, Derrida introduces a common domestic scene. Stepping out of the shower one day he stood naked, face to face with a little black cat. The cat was, of course, also unclothed. The cat's eyes incited shame in Derrida; more particularly, an intense impulse to cover himself. Gregory of Nyssa, too, carries a strong sense of shame and much like Derrida, his modesty appears when he sees (and is seen by) animal eyes. Gregory squeamishly clothes the text of the Song of Songs by thickly cloaking the passages that erotically display the bride and bridegroom's bodies in layers of theological interpretation, thoroughly covering any merely carnal understanding of the text.

Many scholars have discussed the interaction between Derrida and the "*petit chat*" (little cat) whose gaze confronts him with his nudity, but fewer have taken Derrida at his word when he claims that his text is at heart a discourse about "the truth of modesty."[32] That is not to say that Derrida is primarily concerned with the complex of shame, nakedness, modesty, and clothing—although it has been one of the many ways in which humanity has set itself apart from animality. Rather, Derrida suggests that the Western philosophical tradition lavishes inordinate attention upon a constellation of attributes ("nonfinite" in quantity) by which humanity may be divided from all other animals precisely in order to compensate for, mask, or ornament a felt lack or deficiency—as clothing covers perceived nudity. The attributes of proper humanity which purportedly set humanity apart (for example, reason, speech, responsiveness, self-reflection, consciousness, laughter, deception, tools, culture, awareness of death, or excess labor) are a supplement for the perception of an original fault.[33] What sets humanity apart is the sense of a fault, or a lack (discovered against the foil of the animal), a haunting incompleteness that generates the myriad, somewhat frantic ways that humanity "announces itself to itself" as other-than-animal.[34] The topic of Derrida's discourse is the truth of modesty because it is incompleteness that drives the carnophallogocentric subject to make something of himself and cover (by displacement or repression) his nakedness and deficiency.[35] Within this picture, animality represents a kind of fullness or immediate self-presence that humanity lacks.[36]

Derrida's analysis of modesty helpfully illuminates the way that shame, nakedness, and animality intersect within Gregory's interpretation of the Song of Songs. The operation of Gregory's exegesis reinforces the division between humanity and animality through his interpretation of the textual animals of the Song of Songs, especially where they stand in as figures for human nudity. Given the sheer number of animals who represent humans in the Song, Gregory might be expected to configure the relationship between humanity and animality as something other than categorical difference. After all, the text's two most prominent human figures are persistently likened to animals and Gregory reads their union as a transparent account of divine-human communion. The bride appears as a lion or leopard, a horse, a turtledove, birds, goats, sheep, fawns, a bee, a gazelle, and a deer; the bridegroom appears as a gazelle, a fawn, a raven, a dove; and other characters in the narrative take on animal guises as well. Not only that, but the overwhelming majority of these animal associations are positive ones. That is to say, Gregory takes the animal metaphors as *praise* of the bride or bridegroom rather than censure.[37] Nevertheless, rather than using these textual human-animal assemblages to undercut the conceptual boundary between humanity and animality, Gregory uses them to further reinforce that boundary. Nudity and animality intersect in at least four ways within Gregory's homilies on the Song.

First, in some passages Gregory attempts to shame erotic nakedness as animal, pressing the assumption that nudity is less than human. Gregory strategically associates carnal sexuality with animality so that authentic humanity "naturally" transcends it. Such a maneuver relocates human sexuality to the other side of the human-animal distinction, so that it appears in human life as something to be controlled, tamed, and overcome, rather than as something that belongs to humanity as such. For Gregory, copulative genital intercourse is unnatural and improper to humanity in God's image.[38] The person who sees the nudity of the Song in a sensual manner "is passion-ridden and fleshly, still stinking with the stench of the dead, old man; [such a one] ought not pull the meaning of the divinely-inspired thoughts and words down to a sense fit for non-discursive livestock."[39] Thus, nakedness in any highly sexualized sense belongs properly to animals rather than to humans.[40]

Second, though rare, there are moments in Gregory's interpretation of the Song when the lovers are literally naked in their own bodies. This literal nakedness might be recognized as "animal" within the economy of Gregory's theology inasmuch as the physical interactions of the bride and bridegroom stand in the foreground while the subjective, conscious, and intellectual aspects of their interaction recede. "My beloved, she says, put his hand through the opening, and my inmost parts [*koilía*] cried out for him."[41] While Gregory continually warns against a sexual understanding of such passages from the Song, he must also allow glimpses of this sensuous content to appear (even if only by means of his enthusiastic protests) because they are indispensable to his anagogical project. So, Gregory quickly spiritualizes the Song's vulnerability and intimacy by sanitizing an erotic vocabulary: *koilía* (inmost parts, bodily cavity, womb, belly) is quickly replaced by the more symbolic, less carnal term *kardía* (heart) in Gregory's rendering.[42] Still, the sensuous image is the material anchor for the theological metaphor of human-divine communion. Without at least some hint of the corporeal interaction of the bride and bridegroom, Gregory's discovery of exalted spiritual descriptions of divine-human communion in the Song would be totally untethered. And furthermore it is the base, animal, erotic desire (in sublimated form) that drives the reader toward God; without the connection to the erotic beauty of the corporeal bride and bridegroom, the alluring anagogical attraction of the Song would fall flat. "The discourse now before us . . . sets forward an image of the pleasures of this life as a device for its teachings."[43] Inasmuch as corporeal procreation is, for Gregory, a vestige of animality in human life, Gregory must call at least minimal attention to the animal nakedness in the Song in order to ground his theological exegesis.

Third, the bride and bridegroom frequently appear naked under the guise of animal metaphors. The Song uses animal imagery to describe the bodies of bride and bridegroom and Gregory is more than content to take up the animal metaphors of the Song in his anagogical exegesis. In Gregory's homilies, the human nakedness which would appear too sexually charged—and therefore too animal—is tamed and muted precisely by means of the animal images, which partially veil and obscure the human bodies described, or at least distance them from a straightforwardly sexual legibility.[44]

> The soul purified through the virtues was likened [in Song 3:9] to *that* horse, but has not yet come under the hand of the Logos nor carried upon herself the one who rides such horses unto salvation. For it is first necessary that the horse be fully ornamented [i.e., Song 3:11] and then, so dressed, to receive

> the king to ride. It makes no difference to the meaning here whether the one who, according to the prophets, mounts upon us horses and rides upon us unto our salvation is fit from above or whether he comes to be in us, he who slips through into the deep parts of our souls, dwelling and walking about. For to whomever the one happens, the other comes along with it. The one who has God upon him also has God completely within himself, and the one who receives in himself is under the one who has come to be in him. Thus the king intends to rest upon this horse.[45]

The nonthreatening nudity of animals stands in for human nakedness when Gregory desires to make theological points that are thoroughly anchored in sexual metaphor. Because the unclothed bodies of animals do not appear immediately sexual, they provide some modest cover for the sexualized nakedness of the Song's human bodies.

Fourth, the *modality* of the bride and bridegroom's nudity in Gregory's homilies is the same sort of undecidable nudity that we perceive in animals. We perceive animals as clothed within their skin in a manner that our skin always fails to cloth us. The visible surfaces of animal bodies are ambiguous. If animals are naked, they do not reflect upon their nakedness, nor regard it as a problem. Neither is animal nudity ever, prima facie, a matter for human reflection or concern. In the same way, the bride's body appears all through the text, yet she never seems to be totally bare. She is naked in the way that animals are naked—unreflectively. The proper shame that accompanies human nakedness as its authenticating supplement remains notably absent, leaving the nudity in Gregory's text ambiguously human at most. There is a dark and violent scene in the Song where the bride wanders the streets of the city looking for the bridegroom. In her wanderings she is accosted and beaten by watchmen of the city who strip her of her veil. Gregory allegorically negates the violence and fear in this passage insofar as the bride's clothing has come to symbolize the bride's separation from her beloved, similarly transforming the violent watchmen into benevolent angels. Where the bride in the Song cries out in fear and shame, in Gregory's text she finds joy in her further unveiling.[46] Furthermore, seeing her stripped in this way, the flock of attendants marvel at her beauty and ask where they might also be similarly stripped of their veils.[47] The bride does not offer so much as a blush at her exposure before these friends in the Song, and perhaps more remarkably, Gregory hardly blushes at her exposure before his congregation. Under the aegis of this theological interpretation, human nakedness becomes a garment of glory; an animal freedom from shame at her nudity becomes here a sign of the bride's perfection.[48] Thus, not only does the bride appear under the guise of animal metaphors as she progresses spiritually, but inasmuch as her perfection is demonstrated by a certain shame-free and unreflective nudity, she enters into an animal mode of corporeal exposure.

None of these intersections of animality and nudity in the Song transgress Gregory's sense of an abyssal difference between humanity and animality. Paradoxically, Gregory preserves the humanity of the bride and bridegroom in categorical opposition to animality precisely by means of the text's animal imagery. The unity and integrity of Gregory's conception of humanity, however, depends on disparate, even contradictory, notions of animality. First, sexual impulses and actions are expropriated from humanity and rendered proper to animality so that they may register as something "other" to be excised, tamed, or slaughtered. Subsequently, however, animals stand in for humans in the text's references to "union" so that the nudity therein can be taken as shame-free, perfected nakedness-without-fault. In other words, Gregory doubles animal nakedness so that it appears both as hypersexual, shameful, degraded nakedness (so that the bride's humanity transcends it) and as the perfected, exalted nakedness which knows no reason for shame and no longer suffers from any fault (a nakedness to which humanity ought to aspire). In both ways Gregory uses the animals of the Song to transpose the bride and bridegroom's interactions from a sexual register to a spiritual register. Without the animal metaphors to distract, delight, and teach his audience, Gregory would be left with the shamelessly sexualized animal nakedness of the Song. With the cover of the animal metaphors, however, Gregory reads the Song as an account of perfected humanity, for whom nudity represents the absence of guile, impurity, and other barriers to communion with God.[49] Gregory's multiple, contradictory conceptions of animality serve his effort to stabilize a transcendent and normative notion of humanity.

Derrida's text helps us to see that Gregory employs an empty concept of animality—little more than a word, an *animot* (*animaux* + *mot*)—to flesh out his notion of human modesty.[50] The alterity of animals conveniently figures both as the shamelessness that is "beneath" humanity and the shame-free intimacy toward which humanity rightly aspires. Thus, Derrida might say, Gregory's concept of proper human modesty cannot stand on its own but always "follows" an animal in one way or another. Still, the animals of the Song have no theological weight of their own; they figure in Gregory's anagogical exegesis only as metaphorical tools, lending all their energy to the spiritual progress of the bride. While animality seems to play an indispensable role in what we have seen of Gregory's exegetical project, it does so in such a way that the categorical difference between humanity and animality is reinforced rather than questioned. In the end, however, Gregory's anthropology short-circuits so that spiritual ascent and anagogical interpretation turn out to rely on animality in even more structurally essential ways.

Following and Being Transformed

Throughout *L'animal que donc je suis*, Derrida plays upon the homonymy of the first-person present-tense forms of the French verbs "*être*" (to be) and "*suivre*" (to follow).[51] The English title, while naturally translated as *The Animal That Therefore I Am*, could equally be rendered *The Animal That Therefore I Follow*. The verbal pun bears a philosophical point about identity formation: humanity identity is discovered or constructed only through an encounter with animality or in relation to animals, even if such a relation or encounter is entirely conceptual.[52] Indeed, Derrida argues that in philosophical discourse the words *animal* and *animality* are abstract rhetorical tools—necessary for the formation of a human identity, but which function as a disavowal of real animals, a turning away from the eyes of fellow creatures.[53] Derrida acknowledges his own complicity as a subject formed in the tradition of Western anthropology running from Aristotle through Descartes to Lacan, confessing that he too follows "animality" in this abstract way,[54] but he also wonders if he might follow an animal, a cat in his case, into a different identity, a mode of subjectivity that sees and is seen by the eyes of other creatures.[55] Likewise, in Gregory's most treasured image for spiritual ascent, following an animal leads to the transformation of human subjectivity in conformity to Christ. The bridegroom appears repeatedly as a deer bounding across the hilltops, luring the bride—and simultaneously, the reader—into a chase: "She begins to see the one she yearns for. . . . He leaps upon the mountains, springing from the ridges to the prominent hills."[56] The spiritual transformation of bride and reader take place by following this divine animal; and as it turns out, animality is not superfluous in the process. Derrida's corporeal encounter and Gregory's figurative encounters may prove to be mutually illuminating, as both promise transformation for those willing to follow without reserve.

For Gregory, the image of the deer leaping away from hill to hill describes the anagogical function of the *text* of the Song as it incites desire within its readers for God's elusive mystery.[57] The bridegroom's animal appearance as a deer signifies God's inscrutability in such a way that the reader is drawn into pursuit. Through a logic known as the "mirror of the soul," the Song transforms the reader by setting out visions of God that lead to a life of desire, the life of a faithful lack, a stretching out toward the inscrutable beloved:[58] "Humanity is transformed in accordance with the appearances it chooses, and so, truly seems like a mirror. For if someone looks upon gold she appears as gold, and by way of its appearance she manifests the shining of that material. And if someone reflects some fetid thing, he imitates its shame by way of a resemblance, acting into its natural appearance—be it a frog, toad, millipede, or some other unpleasant sight, whichever he is found to be facing."[59] Gregory argues that whatever object a human soul fixes its gaze upon, the soul begins to assimilate to that object. The Song works by transfixing a person's gaze upon God's beauty, a gaze that is held firm by the ever-increasing desire fueled by the Song's sensual language, so that the reader is caught up in an infinite pursuit of God that increasingly conforms the reader to God. Here, at least, the reader is conformed to divinity by gazing more deeply upon animality. And in doggedly following the bridegroom as a divine animal, the bride/reader becomes animal, being found in the form of a deer or gazelle, like her beloved.

Beyond the transformations that take place through fixing one's eyes on animals, animality is integral to the process of the Song's spiritual transformation at yet another level. For Gregory, desire (*epithumia*) is a function of the appetites and impulses that humanity shares with other animals. The text of the Song functions anagogically not primarily because it *teaches* a person about the nature of God or the path toward God, rather, the text functions because it *incites* desire within the reader by presenting God's beauty; it leads the properly attuned reader up into love.[60] The orientation and increase of the reader's desire is a central concern of Gregory's exegesis; Gregory's fundamental commitment to the incomprehensibility of God means that the soul's gaze is a gaze of loving desire, and not the gaze of knowledge:[61] "The desire of the one ascending never settles on what has been known, but instead, by one desire after another, each greater again than the last, excels on to the next in line. The ascending soul makes its way toward the infinite, always by higher things."[62] The priority of love and desire over knowledge entails that human animality takes the lead in spiritual ascent rather than docilely following after humanity's distinct and exclusive traits.[63] Ultimately for Gregory, God's transformative grace does not utilize the faculties that set humanity apart from other animals (discursiveness, being *logikos*), but draws humanity forward through a faculty that all animals hold in common—namely, desire (*epithumia*).[64] Derrida articulates the dynamics of Gregory's approach flawlessly, "[There is] One who says: I am He who is, who follows you and whom you are (following), who is (following) after you with a view to seducing you and to have it be that, coming after, you become one who follows me."[65] Unsurprisingly, in the contexts where Gregory centers spiritual transformation on desire, he no longer recognizes desire as a function of animality—to do so would undermine the anthropological exceptionalism that he has labored to establish. Nevertheless, it is clear enough that desire is proper to that part of the soul which a human being shares with the animals and Gregory offers no argument to suggest that desire focused upon God derives from a separate desiring faculty.[66]

Scholarship on Gregory commonly considers the centrality of desire within Gregory's depiction of the soul's approach to God, but most scholars follow Gregory in eliding desire's "animal" provenance when it has a positive spiritual or theological function, skipping over the short-circuit in Gregory's categorical distinction between humanity and animality.[67] An incautious reader might easily conclude that desire is a function of animality when it leads to dangerous distraction and promiscuity, but not when it is directed toward God; yet Gregory provides no basis for such a distinction.[68] Clearly, the anagogical meaning of the Song of Songs relies upon the sexual desire that Gregory associates with animality to "hook" the reader and lead her forward. But recognizing animality in the transformative desire through which scripture operates on its readers would call into question humanity's supposed transcendence over other animals. As it stands, Gregory's short circuit amounts to an ideological device safeguarding anthropological exceptionalism: the authentic human being transcends animal desires because she is uniquely discursive and spiritual, yet as she progresses (under the tutelage of the Song of Songs) to the highest reaches of spiritual transformation, desire returns as the engine of spiritual progress—but a mode of desire no longer named as animal. Animality suffuses human desire at one moment, then vanishes the next.

Gregory did not avail himself of an alternate path through the short circuit: to acknowledge the continuity of animal and spiritual desire. To recognize intimacy with God as a function of animality (rather than of human exceptionalism) would be to doubly emphasize the importance of the animal metaphors of the Song as they illustrate the spiritual pursuit of the elusive God. In pursuit of the divine-deer-bridegroom bounding over the hills, the bride's becoming animal would be a truly anagogical metaphor. According to the logic of the "mirror of the soul" and the roots of desire in animality, the bride might become a spiritual animal through her unbroken gaze, a creature whose desires orient her instincts, impulses, and attentions and drive her on after God's mystery. For Gregory to think in this manner, however, would require a fundamental reconfiguration of the categories "human" and "animal" wherever they are taken to signify an absolute contrast or metaphysical difference.

Confronted with very different gaze—that of his little cat—Derrida opens up a line of thought that converges with Gregory's. In the eyes of animals, Derrida suggests that we confront an abyssal surplus of inaccessible meaning—a whole world which is not open to us (from the standpoint of understanding), yet a world in which we are cohabitants. With his "*je suis*," Derrida recognizes that his identity "follows" animals in two ways: he finds that he is made subject in the eyes of his cat, and that his standing as a human-subject-traditionally-conceived follows on a certain conception of animality, employed as a point of contrast from which enough leverage might be gained to construct a human subjectivity. The bulk of *The Animal That Therefore I Am* exposes this latter following as a project of Western philosophy—contingent, flawed, and arbitrary. But the more imaginative sections of his text construe the former following as an entryway into a mode of subjectivity that is something other than, something more than being human in the traditionally constrained sense. "*L'animal que donc je suis*," means *following* an animal and becoming animal, openly and reverently relating to entirely mundane creatures who nevertheless transcend the limits of human comprehension and control.[69] Derrida radically reconfigures the frontier between humanity and animality, working to transform a single boundary which outlines humanity's dominion and control over all the "lower" creatures into multiplied limits of mutual regard, reverence, and respectful withdrawal. Living within a more complex set of human and other-than-human relations entails acknowledging that encountered creatures are irresolvably and inscrutably mysterious, even in relations as seemingly tame as that between the "man of the house" and a domesticated cat. To return to Gregory of Nyssa's exegetical register, locking eyes with the divine stag draws a person into transformations of character that cannot be expected to conform to narrow philosophical boundaries drawn around parochial notions of human propriety. To follow God, then, is to take up an identity, a subjectivity, that disregards humanity's proper boundaries as one is thrown ever deeper into profound and *personal* relations to beings inhuman, a-human, nonhuman. Only a misplaced expectation could ever presume that God should end up on our side of the lines drawn neatly between humanity and animality.

Conclusion

The pervasive presence of animals in the text of the Song launches Gregory's theological interpretation. The literal zoological excess of the text renders the Song strange in the genre of erotic writing, and since Gregory remains anxious to displace such "base" erotic meaning in any case, the animal imagery provides an ideal pretext for an interpretation that maintains the elevated dignity of holy scripture above raw animal passions. Animals force the literal meaning of the Song into the mill of theological interpretation so that it can be refined into something capable of nourishing its readers. Paradoxically, the prominence of animals in the text presents an excess that allows for the erasure of animality. The Song can be sublimated because its animals almost demand an allegorical (or anagogical) reading. And yet, for all the rhetorical bluster with which Gregory divides humanity from animality, traits and features associated with animality turn out to be constitutive of human perfection. Gregory marvels that the Song storms the castle of sensuousness in order to turn its power to good use: "What could possibly be more paradoxical than to make [human] nature purify itself of its own passions by legislating and teaching impassibility in customarily passion-ridden speech? [Solomon] does not say that it is necessary to be beyond the movements of the flesh, and to 'mortify one's members upon the earth,' and to purify the mouth from the speech of passion. Rather, he manages the soul so that it looks toward purity through things that seem incongruous [with purity], translating undefiled thought by passion-ridden speech."[70] The power of desire constitutes the hook in the lives of readers for the anagogical function of the text. While Gregory constantly warns about the dangers of allowing desire to slide toward the passions shared with animals, the total eradication of the animal aspects of desire would leave a human desiccated and unresponsive to divine allure.[71] Thus, the obverse of the paradox in which the Song teaches *apátheia* by means of passion-ridden language is that, once purified, human animality must take the lead in the journey of salvation. As Smith notes, Gregory's narrative of salvation is "in essence a narrative of the transformation of the bestial passions into holy desires."[72] The entailment that always remains unspoken, however, is that the beast remains in the soul made passionately holy.

Gregory's theological exegesis breaks down around the problem of human animality: On the one hand, human animality must be denied and staved off in order to prevent a misleading and carnal understanding of the text. On the other hand, human animality seems to be a hidden supposition without which a properly spiritual reading of the text would fall flat, being received by lifeless and phlegmatic ears. Gregory of Nyssa's Homilies on the Song of Songs contains a failure analogous to the failures that Derrida uncovers in the anthropological projects of Descartes, Kant, Levinas, Heidegger, and Lacan. While Gregory does in fact labor toward a categorical distinction in which humanity (the subject of a spiritual reading) altogether transcends animality (the subject of a material reading), his project necessarily fails inasmuch as he can never completely harden the boundary he seeks to draw. The problem of human animality quietly persists in Gregory's erasure of the animal origin and substance of desire.

Gregory upholds difference in the attributes proper to humanity and animality—the human is still discursive, still the subject of modesty, an animal is still characterized by its passionate desire. Yet over the course of the transformations narrated in Gregory's theological interpretation of the Song, the desires proper to animality become indispensable to human perfection in an unacknowledged way. The breakdown in Gregory's anthropology inadvertently opens possibilities for thinking differently about the relation of humanity and animality in a theological register—trajectories which are to be fleshed out in the constructive portion of this project. The transcendence of the human over the animal, turns out to include a return of humanity to its animality—only now in a perfected state. The perfected human-animal has utterly focused desires, and is revealed (exposed, laid bare) for all the world to see without the (human) supplement of shame, without the second-guessing and inward turns of self-reflection. Cut off from animality, humanity becomes aesthetically out of tune, insular, ashamed, and unresponsive to the anagogical grace of divine beauty, which leads the spiritual creature along the journey toward God.

3

The Problem of Human Animality in Contemporary Theological Anthropology

> It is as if alongside and external to lions, tigers, rabbits, and all other actual animals, which form when grouped together the various kinds, species, subspecies, families etc. of the animal kingdom, there existed in addition the animal, the individual incarnation of the entire animal kingdom.
>
> —*Karl Marx*[1]

> The great transcendent horror is loneliness, excluded encagement in the self.
>
> —*David Foster Wallace*[2]

Wherever Christian theology approaches human animality, the discourse seems compelled to speak in several directions all at once. Competing constellations of conviction produce logical knots and internal tensions. On the one hand, a commonality between human and nonhuman animals arises from affirmations of the goodness of creation, the blessing of embodied life, bodily resurrection, the comprehensive scope of redemption, and virtues such as humility and gratitude. On the other hand, categorical human uniqueness comes to the fore in the image of God, the divine election of humanity, human sin and responsibility, the incarnation of God as a human being, and the priority of enduring spiritual realities over fleeting material goods. A number of rhetorical strategies have allowed theologians—past and present—to avoid getting stuck in these logical tangles. Some, such as Gregory of Nazianzus, revel in paradox, celebrating tensions without any compulsion to resolve resulting conceptual problems; others, such as Gregory of Nyssa, emphasize commonality where it aids their argument and then—often within a few pages—quietly shift to an emphasis on disjunction where it is more germane to the theological matter at hand.

Human animality operates as an essential pivot or hinge hidden deep within the machinery of any Christian theology built on anthropological exceptionalism. The function of the machine depends on flipping this mechanism between affirmation and disavowal; human animality can neither be removed nor fixed in place (that is, rendered stable) without shutting down the operation of the whole. The problem of human animality names this constitutive ambiguity and the strategies that are used to preserve and conceal it.

The preceding chapters sought to illustrate this ambiguous function of human animality within the anthropology of two late ancient theologians. Both Gregory of Nyssa and Gregory of Nazianzus disavow human animality and yet also depend upon it within their accounts of human redemption. In part, it is possible to regard these tensions as the result of a late antique philosophical/scientific framework. Someone might imagine that the problem of human animality dissolves with the abandonment of the substance metaphysics behind talk of "essences" and "natures," for example, or the rigid distinction between the body and the mind/soul. This chapter argues that such historical compartmentalization is mistaken. The problem of human animality is not endemic to late antiquity and its philosophical assumptions. Rather, contemporary theologians continue to disavow human animality in order to shore up human uniqueness, while nevertheless relying upon human animality within their accounts of human transformation.

Contemporary works of theological anthropology approach a consensus on the idea that human beings may be categorically differentiated from nonhuman animals on the basis of a constitutive "openness to God." I use the term *consensus* advisedly, since such openness goes by a variety of names: availability to transcendence, fundamental eccentricity (that is, being "centered" outside one's own being), or basic orientation toward the horizon of the infinite. So long as "openness to God" is interpreted broadly enough to include such variations on the theme, I do not think that *consensus* is a misleading term for the state of contemporary theological anthropology on questions of human uniqueness.[3] This form of the human-animal distinction, I contend, produces anthropological tensions and contradictions around human animality that differ in specific content, but are structurally analogous to the tensions and contradictions examined in the ancient figures above. The aim of this chapter is not to trace a line of historical influence or continuity between the ancient and contemporary figures, but instead, to demonstrate that the problem of human animality pervades the discourse of Christian theological anthropology—showing as prominently in contemporary thought as in the thought of late antiquity.

The chapter is divided into two parts: First, in order to support my claim of a consensus around "openness to God" as the site of human exceptionalism, I provide very short descriptions of the way that the human-animal distinction operates in a selection of influential theological anthropologies. Second, I examine the anthropologies of Karl Rahner and Wolfhart Pannenberg in greater detail, arguing that human animality remains ambiguous for both in ways that are analogous to the tensions encountered in Gregory of Nazianzus and Gregory of Nyssa. I did not choose Rahner and Pannenberg because they are adamant about the human-animal distinction—if anything, they are particularly concerned to reframe theological anthropology in terms amenable to the evolutionary continuity of human beings with other animals. Rather, I have selected these theologians because each presents a particularly clear and well-argued form of the claim that fundamental openness to God constitutes human uniqueness. In principle, similar analysis could be carried out on other theological projects. In addition to demonstrating a pattern of thought spanning millennia of Christian theology, exploring the particular contours of the problem of human animality within contemporary theological anthropology will also set up the constructive interventions of the chapters that follow this one.

Consensus: Openness to God

Theologians employ a wide variety of technical terms to describe what I call "openness to God." A sampling: openness to the world, awareness of a transcendental horizon, orientation toward the true infinite, availability for covenant, participation in an ontology of personhood, constitutive relationality, attunement to divine address, genuine freedom with genuine responsibility, and fundamental eccentricity. The argument here for a consensus appeals to family resemblance among these concepts rather than terminological uniformity. These characteristics have three things in common in their deployment as marks of authentic humanity in contemporary theological anthropology. First, they are given as the *sine qua non* of authentic humanity. The humanity of the human being derives from the possession of this characteristic (or from the potential to develop it). Second, they are marked as the condition for the possibility of authentic fellowship between humanity and God. Third, they also function as the line that cuts a categorical distinction between human beings and other animals. Humanity is differentiated from all the other animals by some form of openness to God, which is often supposed to underlie "more obvious" differences ranging from rational self-consciousness, to technological mastery, to clothing and bodily shame.

To be sure, few theologians explicitly deny nonhuman animals basic, or even intimate, connections to God. Nevertheless, most assert that animal relationships to God are of a fundamentally different kind than human relationships. Or, often, humans and animals are said to share a foundational creaturely dependence upon God, while human beings are subsequently differentiated by the capacity for an additional layer of relationship—more personal, more mutual, more communicative—from which animals are categorically excluded. These conceptual cuts between human and nonhuman animals inevitably leave their mark within the structure of theological anthropology as well.

In the effort to demonstrate this consensus, I am not evaluating the relative adequacy or inadequacy of "openness to God" as a template for theological anthropology. I mean only to draw attention to the presumed connection between this constitutive openness to God and a categorical distinction that separates humanity from animality. It is this connection that knits the problem of human animality into the fabric of contemporary theological anthropology.

Robert Jenson

The denial of a fundamental difference between human beings and all other animals results in what Robert Jenson regards as a slippery slope of "anthropological nihilism."[4] Theatrically, Jenson claims that activism for animal rights is a project morally aligned with Nazism.[5] In a more serious vein, Jenson argues that God personally addresses only human beings, and so, only human beings respond to God as personal subjects in prayer and aesthetic delight.[6] God's species-targeted personal address forges an original difference in humanity that blossoms into an array of other categorical differences. Since God does not speak directly to any of the other animals in address, they are not individual personal subjects, nor do they join together in bonded community, nor do they exercise moral agency or bear responsibility for their actions.[7] Within Jenson's theology, then, proper humanity appears as receptivity and responsiveness to divine address; human animality appears as the threat of uniformity with the inarticulate and impersonal material of the nonhuman world.[8]

John Zizioulas

John Zizioulas insists upon an ontological distinction between the category *person* and the category *nature*, and uses trinitarian theology to warrant the claim that personhood is ontologically prior to nature such that authentic persons always have freedom relative to their nature.[9] Human beings are persons; other animals, categorically, are not. Personhood is ontologically "ek-static," fundamentally oriented to interrelation with God (primarily) and other persons (secondarily).[10] Humans alone ask the question "Who am I?,"[11] alone are given the freedom and desire to become creative "world builders,"[12] and alone serve as the link between God and material creation.[13] Animality, then, for Zizioulas is a living bondage to one's particular created nature, existence in mere "thing-hood,"[14] an unreflective immediate self-presence that forecloses any freedom to transform the self or the world.

Karl Barth

Karl Barth articulates human uniqueness as a function of the covenant established through divine election.[15] Human beings are distinct from all other creatures because God has ontologically determined humanity as God's created counterpart through God's own self-revelation in Jesus Christ.[16] God's human self-revelation is not based upon any quality or capacity within humanity which "attracts" God. Only God's election of human beings to covenant in Jesus Christ sets humanity off from other animals.[17] That said, Barth subsequently acknowledges that humanity's "being-in-covenant" requires a set of capabilities that enable human beings to be responsive covenant partners (he names rational thought, speech, and moral responsibility) and these too differentiate human beings from animals.[18] He clearly avers, however, that humanity's unique covenant-openness is the result of God's election of humanity to covenant, rather than its cause or source.[19] Humanity proper, for

Barth, appears in "being covenanted" and the particular openness to God and God's self-revelation which is the corollary of that covenant; animality is the merely natural course-of-life upon which God intervenes to covenant and reveal, a backdrop to the drama of election.[20]

Hans Urs von Balthasar

Hans Urs von Balthasar regards the human being as categorically different from all other creatures because of an "ex-centric" reflexivity, a freedom to take one's own self as the object of thought. This reflexivity is humanity's "spirit and person[hood]" and it generates the "reason and freedom (which are two aspects of the same thing)" that enable human beings to shape their own lives even in ways that oppose "the laws of self-preservation," leading to humanity's "dominance" and "transcendence" of the world around them.[21] Humanity's categorical difference from other animals derives from humanity's role in a grand drama much bigger than creation. Even though humanity shares worldly life with other creatures, animals are fixed within their environs, while there is "something a-cosmic" about humanity.[22] Animality for von Balthasar appears as an enclosed and "centric" form of life which is completely embedded in its ecological relationships, formed by them, and unable to perceive a larger transcosmic history.[23]

Paul Tillich

For Paul Tillich, humanity alone has the freedom, the courage, true vitality, and the awareness to be a transcendent "world-building" creature.[24] Humanity is comprised of individuated rational creatures, in whom the whole cosmos is represented in consciousness.[25] Furthermore, it is precisely this conscious awareness of the totality of the finite world as such that opens humanity to fundamental questions of Being itself and of the existence of God.[26] In contrast, animals ("even the most highly developed animals") are dominated by conformity to their species;[27] they are "ontologically incomplete" and rightly called "subhuman."[28] Because they lack reason and the self-reflective freedom that accompanies reason, they are "poor in world" embedded within their environments.[29] While animals possess a kind of "natural perfection," humanity's rational perfection is of a completely different ontological order, transcending the determinate necessity of a specific natural context.[30] Human animality, then, is the pole of human life that is embedded in material and ecological necessity, determined by species identity rather than personal decision.

José Comblin

José Comblin distinguishes between the external, objective body available for scientific observation and "my body" as the site of my own unique self expression. This latter aspect of human life is traditionally named "soul" or "spirit" and marks the point of receptivity to God as divine Spirit.[31] In Comblin's account, other animals possess only the former, objective dimension and thus are "programmed," controlled by instinct such that "life is not a problem for them."[32] They die but do not relate to death as a frightful tragedy.[33] Each animal is only numerically unique and "can simply be replaced by another just like it, and it will occupy the same place in history and do the same things."[34] In contrast, human beings are the "end and purpose" of the created universe" and "obviously, the liberation of humanity must include the conquest and domination of nature."[35] For Comblin, proper humanity is a quasi-sovereign self-mastery while animality is an instinctually driven, subconscious, and impersonal mode of life.

Arthur Peacocke

Although Arthur Peacocke attends to the evolutionary continuity between human beings and all other living creatures, he uses the concept of emergence to categorically differentiate human beings from other animals in an effort to avoid the charge of reductionism. Human self-consciousness, linguistic communication, and perception of "meaning" emerge as a distinct level of complexity so that "everything in the animal world is also in the human," while the human level genuinely transcends the lower levels and cannot be reduced to them. "The human is . . . biological, but what is distinctively human transcends that out of which and in which it has emerged."[36] Peacocke's employment of the metaphor of "levels," transmutes formal species-difference into a hierarchy and a teleology. Human consciousness, personhood, and communication represents the "ultimate purpose" for the creation of the universe. The emergent level at which human beings categorically transcend animal life is also the level at which human beings become "persons" and the level at which God communicates.[37] Humanity uniquely has a sense of being "mis-fit" within mundane surroundings and by virtue of this estrangement stands open to God as an ultimate context for human life, while animals, insofar as they have not developed "personhood" remain categorically closed off to divine communication and communion, satisfied within their material environs.[38] Human animality, then, is the "lower level" of human life which remains embedded within impersonal ecological contexts insensitive to divine communication.

Kathryn Tanner

Kathryn Tanner argues that all creatures, animate and inanimate, image God by way of basic participation in the goodness of existence, goodness which ultimately derives from God.[39] Nevertheless, human beings image God in several "higher" senses that set them apart from all other creatures. Humanity is the only species to lack a self-contained "nature" of its own, and is only completed by being conformed to the Word and Spirit.[40] Whereas the lives of other animals are "highly canalized"—that is, tightly restricted by the specificity of their natures—human beings have a highly plastic and mutable existence characterized by a constitutive openness to the Word and Spirit, in whose presence humanity takes shape.[41] Human animality, then, is that pole of human life which is fixed in mundane patterns of behavior that resist change or are relatively immutable; humanity proper is the fluid pole of human life that stands open to God as its completion and embraces the transformation required to conform to the divine image.

Stanley Grenz

While Stanley Grenz explicitly follows Pannenberg's notion of a uniquely human "openness to the world" and (more cautiously) Zizioulas's distinction between personhood and nature, his most intriguing claim is that the *imago dei* (which categorically differentiates humanity from other animals) should be understood as sexuality.[42] While human beings do reproduce like other animals, romantic attraction and "genital sexual expression" are only incipient and incomplete forms of "sexuality."[43] The highest form of human sexuality is a drive toward interdependent community. In distinction from animal reproduction, human sexuality thus finds provisional fulfillment in the church community and ultimate fulfillment in eschatological community with God. "Viewed in this light, sexuality, understood as the sense of incompleteness and the corresponding drive for wholeness, forms the dynamic that not only seeks human relationships but also motivates the quest for God."[44] Thus, for Grenz, proper humanity emerges in the orientation of basic biological processes toward a spiritual sociality that transcends copulation; in contrast, animality is entirely "at home" within the limits of ecosystemic and physiological processes.[45]

Rosemary Radford Ruether

Rosemary Radford Ruether takes care not to divide human beings from other creatures. She regards human consciousness and intelligence as the extension of the "radial energy" present in all creatures and matter itself.[46] She explicitly repudiates the effort to set humanity above nonhuman nature in a hierarchy, because humans are only one "inextricable part" of the "living system" that makes up the earth.[47] Nevertheless, her theology follows the contours the contemporary consensus in two ways: First, human beings are the only creatures in which the developing cosmos becomes conscious of its own development.[48] Humanity is thus open to the whole, or self-reflective in a way that other creatures are not. Second, human beings alone possess the capability to sin, and as a corollary Ruether implies that humanity has a unique moral or prudential responsibility before God. Humanity alone "disrupts and distorts the balances of nature" and therefore, humans must "convert [their] minds to nature's logic" in order to be reconciled to the cosmos and abandon ecologically destructive estrangement.[49] Thus Ruether marks proper humanity as the exercise of a responsible moral or prudential agency, while animality figures as an amoral enmeshment within the balance of natural order.[50]

David Kelsey

David Kelsey refrains from drawing the human-animal distinction in explicitly contrastive terms.[51] Nevertheless, the contours of an implicit contrast between humanity and animality are readily apparent where he attributes to human beings a unique capacity for free, personal response to divine calling. Kelsey reserves the use of the adjective *personal* for human beings alone and claims that human beings are personal only because they are personalized by hearing and responding to the divine address as it is mediated through concrete sociocultural interactions with other human beings.[52] Kelsey defines personhood by three criteria—complex, reciprocated emotional sensitivity; moral responsibility; and rationality. These characteristics also set human beings off from other animals.[53] Kelsey never resolves the tension between these claims. On the one hand, he defines personal life by capacities that (supposedly) distinguish humanity from other animals. On the other hand, he claims that human beings are only personal because God addresses them and holds them accountable for a response.

As it stands, however, what emerges from Kelsey's scheme are two distinct levels at which God relates to creatures. Humans and animals share a basic immediate intimacy and dependence upon God ("basic identity"), but humanity is uniquely rendered personal—that is, free and responsible both to God and to other human beings—through divine address ("unsubstitutable personal identity").[54] Despite his sustained effort to avoid any contrastive identification of humanity, his anthropology remains remarkably similar to accounts that explicitly differentiate humanity from other animals (Jenson's, Barth's, and Pannenberg's, especially).[55] While Kelsey insists that describing humanity alone as "personal" does not set up any hierarchy of human beings over other creatures because "personhood" is not grounded in human dominion over other creatures or any unique capacity by which human beings relate to God, the tight connection between the personalizing divine address and the capacities that correspond to personal life set up clear lines of contrast. His account of human uniqueness based on divine address looks so substantially similar to other, explicitly hierarchical accounts, that his self-differentiation sounds like special pleading. After all, in Kelsey's picture of creation, human beings alone receive God's call in ways that they can be held accountable for their responses. The animal has *only* an immediate relation to God, the animal lacks language and lacks the mediated, proximal responsible relation to God that results from God's address to humanity. The use and possession of language does not personalize human beings *per se*. But God's address through human language generates categorical difference by constituting human beings as persons—a very thin difference. In Kelsey's scheme, proper humanity bears the burden of accountability for response to God's creative, reconciling, and consummating relations to creation, whereas animality represents the passive position in which each creature is created, is reconciled, and is brought into consummate fellowship with God.[56]

Despite many differences, the theologians mentioned so far are united in a broad consensus that distinguishes humanity from animality at the specific point of humanity's openness to God. The alignment of human difference with receptivity to God makes it strikingly easy to describe any human closure to God in the terms also used to characterize animality—and, in fact, these descriptions appear quite often. Even where animality is not explicitly linked to closure, human animality remains basically irrelevant within theological narratives that focus on the development of the capacities of proper humanity through the work of divine grace. God's grace works in human life at the point of human uniqueness, rather than at the points of creaturely commonality with nonhuman animals. Humanity's continuity with other animals appears as a vestigial connection to a common origin in creation, but plays little role in teachings about human redemption and eschatological consummation. The next section traces the problem of human animality through the anthropology of two contemporary theologians whose work should also be included within this consensus—Karl Rahner and Wolfhart Pannenberg.

Rahner, Pannenberg, and the Problem of Human Animality

The difference between ancient theological anthropologies like those considered in previous chapters and contemporary accounts is often attributed to a modern "turn to the subject" in which notions of human nature centered upon some combination of substances (body, mind, soul, spirit) give way to accounts focused on consciousness, subjectivity, experience, and ongoing projects of self-realization or collective flourishing.[57] Yet functional commonality persists across these different frameworks. Both ancient and contemporary anthropologies work to categorically distinguish humanity (and human self-understanding) from animality. A strong account of human uniqueness remains one of the most consistent products of Christian theological anthropology across the entire history of the tradition. Attention to the problem of human animality in the anthropologies of Gregory of Nazianzus and Gregory of Nyssa revealed the incoherence of attempts to construct a clean conception of humanity's transcendence over animality. Similar failings emerge in the work of Karl Rahner and Wolfhart Pannenberg.

Karl Rahner

Rahner describes humanity as "the event of God's absolute self-communication."[58] God's self-communication ontologically constitutes humanity by opening human consciousness to an awareness of the finite world as a totality, and thus to a dialectic intuition of (and desire for) the infinite.[59] God's self-communication is a "supernatural existential," which is to say that in creating human beings God has freely attuned the parameters of human consciousness to the knowledge of divine love.[60] In this way, Rahner asserts that God's self-communication to humanity is entirely a function of God's gracious freedom (not human merit), but also that God's self-communication is not alien or extrinsic to the constitution of human thought—human nature is grounded in divine address freely given. This supernatural attunement is the key to human knowledge of God, such that Rahner can claim, "dogmatic theology today must be theological anthropology."[61] The supernatural existential endows every human life with the transcendental freedom to affirm or resist God's loving self-communication, even if such resistance contradicts the very conditions of one's own subjectivity.[62] Although such a transcendental affirmation or denial is inseparable from the particular events of each life, no particular historical act (or set of acts) perfectly corresponds to either affirmation or denial. Transcendental experience inheres within categorical/historical experience without ever being reducible to the categorical/historical level.

The constitutive "openness" of finite human beings toward the infinite endows human subjectivity with unique freedom. The recognition of the finitude of one's self and one's surroundings pushes human consciousness toward an infinite horizon, setting in motion self-reflective questions about personal connections to the infinite.[63] So God's self-communication not only grounds transcendental consciousness, it also establishes humanity's categorical difference from other animals: "It can be said absolutely that the established world finds itself in man, and that in man it makes itself its own object. . . . We are after all beings who, even in that consciousness with which we engage in our physic-biological fight for existence and for our earthly dignity, live and act (in distinction to the brutes) out of a formal anticipation of the whole."[64] Animals are psychically enmeshed within their surroundings in such a way that they are unable to comprehend themselves and their contexts as finite. For Rahner, to lack awareness of finitude-as-such is also to lack self-consciousness altogether, because it is the finite/infinite dialectic that sparks self-consciousness and self-reflexivity.

By themselves, human corporeal and intellectual capacities are always comparable to those of other animals and are, for that reason, an insufficient basis for assertions of human uniqueness. Nevertheless, Rahner argues that humanity's unique transcendental consciousness is manifest in secondary characteristics, that is, achievements in social collaboration and technological mastery.

> In our context the main point in such a determination of human beings is to distinguish them as clearly as possible from animals without at the same time obscuring their bodily and sensory characteristics, which, while not simply identical to those of the animals, nonetheless are comparable to them. . . . But at the same time one cannot grant natural science the right to reduce humankind to the level of the animals, thereby overlooking the fact that human beings are creatures with a language proper to themselves, creatures of culture and of history. . . . Theologians need only be able to affirm that human consciousness possesses that unlimited transcendentality in which there is present an openness, capable of legitimizing itself, to the absolute reality of God. If this transcendentality is peculiar to human beings, if there is present in it the possibility of a confrontation in freedom with themselves, if they can rethink their own thinking (as the modern expression goes) and if this transcendentality is not present in the animals (has anyone ever tried to demonstrate this in animals?), then theologians have what is required for human beings and their essential difference from animals.[65]

Rahner distinguishes humanity from animality on the basis of transcendentality—an orientation toward the infinite that keeps the human being "open" to more than finitude, a unique "unlimiting of the limited."[66] Proper human transcendentality establishes a categorical difference manifest in other secondary differences: language, history, and culture.[67]

For Rahner, humanity is the unique point at which creation communicates with the creator—the apex of creation. While human beings share many characteristics with other animals, humanity is the "being in whom the basic tendency of matter to find itself in the spirit by self-transcendence arrives at the point where it definitely breaks through."[68] Humanity's transcendental consciousness and commerce with God's loving self-communication establishes humanity as a mediator within creation. Rahner links Christology and anthropology, arguing that the human species represents a fitting vessel for God's redemption of creation through divine incarnation.[69] Human exceptionalism facilitates God's exceptional act of self-communication in Christ. Just so, Rahner's Christology reflects back upon his anthropology, reconfirming humanity's theological prominence within creation.[70]

Rahner's distinction between human beings and other animals also structures an intra-anthropological distinction between proper humanity and human animality. Unlike the authors of late antiquity, Rahner does not associate animality with materiality or the body, but rather with a lack or deficiency of transcendental consciousness. Because transcendental consciousness is a basic structural element of human nature, it is impossible for any human person to actually "escape" the transcendental; even the utter rejection of God is a function of a freedom that results from divine self-communication: "[Human] freedom, however, is freedom vis-à-vis its all-supporting ground itself . . . it can culpably deny the very condition of its own possibility in an act which necessarily reaffirms this condition."[71] However, even if it is only counterfactual speculation, Rahner can imagine forms of "human" life that have negated proper humanity and become entirely animal. Because the word *God* names the transcendental horizon that marks the threshold of anthropogenesis, Rahner claims that a human society that allowed the word *God* (or its equivalents) to fall entirely out of use would cease to be human: "[Were he to forget the word 'God'] Man would have forgotten the totality and its ground, and at the same time, if we can put it this way, would have forgotten that he had forgotten. What would it be like? We can only say: he would have ceased being a man. He would have regressed to the level of a clever animal."[72] For Rahner, proper humanity does not inhere in rational thought, language, or even culture, but in the transcendentality in which thought, language, and culture open toward the infinite. Human animality, then, appears where transcendentality is negated, ignored, or methodologically resisted.

The developmental distinction between human animality and proper transcendentality also emerges in the relationship between theological anthropology and the natural sciences. Rahner cedes the study of human beings to the natural sciences—to biology, neuroscience, psychology—on the condition that they acknowledge another register of knowledge derived from the study of proper human transcendentality. Human beings are susceptible to objectification—but only under the aspect of their animality: "The only condition for this abstention on the part of theology is that in this stage of human evolution it is conceded that a level has been reached different from the previous stage, on which level the human being is essentially distinct from the animal, and that natural science does not lay sole claim to the description of the nature of the human being as long as natural science and metaphysical anthropology have to be differentiated (and rightly so)."[73] Human transcendentality and animality are correlated but irreducibly distinct because they belong to different "stages" or "levels" of human development, as do the discourses that study them.[74] The natural sciences approach human beings as complex organisms whose physiology, social patterns, and evolutionary history may be observed and measured analogously with other animals. In contrast, theological anthropology studies human transcendentality and approaches human beings as fundamentally mysterious, self-aware agents.[75]

The same intra-anthropological distinction operates in the structure of self-reflection: The knowing self is the properly human subject-agent of transcendental consciousness whose inward gaze takes in the passive animal-object-self as the content of knowledge. Rahner writes, "Being situated in this way between the finite and the infinite is what constitutes man, and it is shown by the fact that it is in his infinite transcendence and in his freedom that man experiences himself as dependent and historically conditioned."[76] Human animality is the pole of human experience marked by embeddedness and enclosure in historical situations; proper humanity is the pole of human experience which recognizes embeddedness and enclosure as such—and dialectically, through such acts of recognition humanity opens to what transcends historical conditioning.

While transcendentality marks the threshold of proper humanity, it also provides access to the true significance of God's gracious acts in history. Transcendental experience correlates to categorical/

historical events, but stands out as a layer of significance not apparent within the events themselves. Similarly for Rahner, authentic spirituality emerges only within transcendental consciousness as a higher level of meaning. Without transcendental analysis, theology risks becoming mythology or epic saga: "Without an ontology of the transcendental subject a theology of grace (and hence all theology whatsoever) remains fixed in a pre-theological picture-language and cannot give evidence of a starting-point for transcendental experience. This transcendental experience is indispensable today if theology is to do justice to modern man's questions as to whether all the talk of 'Divinization', 'Sonship', 'God's indwelling' etc. is not merely poetic concepts and indemonstrable mythology."[77] The life of Jesus of Nazareth—in full historical specificity—can be understood as universally salvific only within a transcendental frame, in which Jesus appears as an "absolute saviour."[78] As the Christ, Jesus mediates the beatific vision of God to humanity—the full flourishing of transcendental consciousness united with the divine condition of its own possibility.[79] Accordingly, Rahner writes of Christ as the "concrete historical mediation of our immediate relationship to the mystery of the God who communicates himself."[80] The "historical mediation" of Jesus remains absolutely indispensable, but the "immediate" transcendental relation remains the ultimate purpose of any historical interaction. Elsewhere, Rahner claims: "Salvation does not mean a reified and objective state of affairs, but rather a personal and ontological reality. Hence salvation and fulfillment take place in the objectively most real reality of the most radical subjectivity."[81] Salvation is ultimately a matter of a human being's relation to the transcendental horizon of her existence and can be reflected only fragmentarily and imperfectly in categorical experience. As the pole of historical self-enclosure within human life, human animality participates in divine grace only in a secondary way since transcendental mediation is always required for full significance of grace's operations.

There is something like a tectonic pressure that builds at the fault line between the categorical and transcendental in Rahner's work. The categorical and transcendental layers of human experience are inseparably nonidentical, they mutually condition one another, but are mutually irreducible.[82] Rahner's readers have struggled over this interface and Rahner himself noted that it raises thorny questions, "I would say that there are few philosophical, anthropological, and theological problems that are more difficult to answer, when correctly weighed, than that of the relation of transcendentality and history."[83] Jean Porter, for example, worries that Rahner's correlation of transcendental and categorical experience remains insufficiently concrete. If a person's immediate relation to God or final rejection of God is actualized through course of a whole life, it need not ever touch down in a specific historical experience.[84] Since one's transcendental disposition toward acceptance or refusal of God's self-communication inheres in (and is expressed by) every categorical act, it is impossible to know what would constitute a specific categorical acceptance or refusal.[85]

Johann Baptist Metz, raises similar concerns that Rahner's transcendental method subordinates historical/categorical relations (especially political antagonisms concerning matters of justice) to an ultimate transcendental resolution.[86] Metz's criticism is not that Rahner's theology is a-political or overly individualistic. It is rather that Rahner's universalizing descriptions of subjective experience presume an irenic plane of existence in which social, political, and economic antagonisms are already overcome within a single transcendent horizon. Such an account struggles to account for the *religious* significance of conflictual confrontation, negotiation, reconciliation, and liberation wherever socio-political antagonisms radically condition people's experiences of God.[87]

Notably, the indeterminate relation between categorical and transcendental experience also functionally subordinates human animality insofar as the ultimate meaning of properly human life is expressed at the level of transcendental freedom and transcendental consciousness. Rahner asserts the *meaningfulness* of the contextually embedded life of human animality, but any actual *meaning* arises only at the transcendental layer of experience.[88] Rahner claims: "[The transcendental method] does not entail a rationalistic and unhistorical reduction of man to the status of an abstract transcendental being in his merely formal structure as such, as if what is historical and not deducible and what is experienced concretely a posteriori had no significance for salvation. It means that *everything of significance for salvation is to be illuminated by referring it back to this transcendental being.*"[89] At the level of transcendental experience, the beatific vision provides a fixed goal for human freedom, but the greater significance of historical/categorical actions and interactions can never be known without a transcendental determination that alters historical experience by reconstituting its horizon. While human animality is always a necessary substratum of transcendental experience, human animality is not sufficient for proper religious subjectivity without transcendental conditioning.

Karen Kilby points out that Rahner's use of the term *transcendental* draws together the more esoteric, Kantian sense of the term as the conditions for the possibility of knowledge with the more commonsense, non-Kantian notion of the "beyond."[90] Human animality becomes insufficient for proper subjectivity and authentic religious experience precisely where these two meanings converge. This convergence is evident in claims such as, "Transcendental experience is the experience of transcendence."[91] Because God's self-communication is the transcendental condition for proper humanity's differentiation from animality (in the Kantian sense), animality is also incapable of self-transcendence and personal communion with God across the horizon of the infinite (in the non-Kantian sense). Insofar as the highest goods of human life are realized in transcendentally conditioned relations to God and neighbor, Rahner functionally subordinates human animality to proper humanity.

One form of the problem of human animality in Rahner's theology, then, is that human animality—in the form of enmeshment within concrete historical contexts—remains essential to the human union with God, but only in a way that can never be specified or described. Human animality is formally presupposed in Rahner's account of salvation, but is ultimately stage dressing for a more ethereal drama.

Additionally, the problem of human animality arises in Rahner's theology in the clear parallels between his descriptions of sin and animality. On the one hand, Rahner unambiguously affirms the goodness of the entire material creation, including animals and animality, according to the multitude of good purposes for which God created it.[92] Nonhuman animals are incapable of sin, because sin requires the transcendental freedom that belongs only to human beings.[93] On the other hand, Rahner's account of human sin as the negation of transcendentality unmistakably echoes his description of animality. The fundamental form of human sinfulness is a resistance or refusal of God's self-communication that results in self-enclosure within the categorical realm. Rahner writes, "Wherever there is freedom in and before the reality of the cosmos as a whole, and in a transcendence towards God, there can also be a guilt and freedom which closes itself against God, there can also be sin and the possibility of perdition."[94] Such resistance is not only a refusal of divine self-communication, but also resistance to anthropogenesis—the transcendental conditions of one's own personalization. For Rahner, the total refusal of divine self-communication is a form of self-contradiction that is ultimately impossible for human beings, yet it is worth noting that such a self-contradiction—even the in the case of a nascent and partial refusal—strikes against the supernatural existential that differentiates humanity from animality.[95] Thus, the basic tendency of sin in Rahner's account pushes toward the negation of the proper transcendental difference between humanity and animality, even if, by divine grace, such negation never succeeds. Lacking transcendentality, animals are entirely bound within their categorical/historical/ecological contexts, they have no transcendental consciousness. Were sin's refusal of divine self-communication to reach its impossible limit, the result would be a similar self-negating self-enclosure within the categorical—in other words, animality.

To be clear, Rahner never marks finitude or animality as sinful. However, the parallel between sin as the negation of transcendentality and the absence of transcendentality in animality generates unmistakeable tensions around human animality. While human animality in itself must be affirmed as good, any hypothetical failure to affirm and embody the difference in kind between humanity and animality through transcendental consciousness would be sinful insofar as it would also be a negation of the possibility of self-transcendence into God. Human animality must always be covered or conditioned by proper human transcendentality. Avoiding sinfulness means reinforcing anthropological exceptionalism.

Rahner might have resolved the conceptual tension around human animality in his anthropology in one of two ways. First, Rahner could have abandoned a categorical differentiation between humanity and animality, allowing for nonhuman forms of transcendental consciousness (each differentiated in its own way). Such a shift would destabilize the hierarchy in which human beings are clearly at the spiritual apex of God's creation. Abandoning a unified concept of animality as life that lacks transcendentality would break down the conceptual parallel between human sin as *resistance* to divine self-communication and animal consciousness as closed to it. Alternately, Rahner might have identified particular mental or relational capacities as the aperture through which human beings attain transcendental awareness (in rationality, love, or hopeful expectation, for example). This link would more rigorously determine the interface between the transcendental and categorical realms, moving Rahner's anthropology toward a theological actualism. Such a connection would have two other consequences: It would specify the kinds of historical-categorical events in which divine self-communication particularly presses on human life. It would also open the possibility that at least some animals, through the exercise of analogous capacities, might have access to transcendental experience and transcendental meaning. In such a creaturely redeployment of the transcendental method, the question of the infinite might no longer be framed as a recognition of the totality of finitude and its limits—that is, from the objectification of one's context as "Other" through reflexive self-awareness—but rather as a pervasive and mysterious depth present within the finite itself recognized through reflexive awareness of the multiplied alterity of creaturely "others."

Rahner's transcendental account of "spirit" already does much of the work necessary for either of these resolutions. Spirit inheres within all matter, drawing it toward the transcendent horizon. Once a statement such as the following is no longer restricted to human beings alone, Rahner's theology provides a potent resource for a creaturely theology: "the spirituality of the creature always remains spirituality in materiality right up to its absolute perfection."[96] On such an account, a full enmeshment in a concrete politico-ecological context need not be regarded as a neglect or negation of transcendental experience.

As it stands, however, despite innumerable differences with the late ancient authors considered earlier, Rahner's transcendental anthropology inherits and reinscribes the problem of human animality. Rahner's commitment to a distinction between proper humanity and animality ambiguously frames human animality both as blessed participation in the goodness of finite categorical creation and as a form of enclosure that must be conditioned by properly human transcendentality to rise above sin.

Wolfhart Pannenberg

For Wolfhart Pannenberg, all of humanity's unique characteristics—and he names many—derive from one fundamental difference between human beings and nonhuman animals: "exocentricity" or "openness to the world" (*Weltoffenheit*):[97]

> Only human beings, it seems, know themselves to be selves; only they know that they are given to themselves as both gift and task. . . . The structure of the ego is determined by

> exocentricity, insofar as human beings can be present to themselves only by being present to what is other than themselves. But to the extent that even when present to others the ego is, in the final analysis, present only to itself and not truly present to others, it shuts itself up in a quasi-animal centrality. . . . Animal centrality, which lacks self-consciousness, is spared subjection to this kind of dialectic. The animal lives in its environment [*Umwelt*] without any interior break. Despite its centralized organization, or rather in virtue of it, it is open to its environment. It is self-consciousness that makes possible an ambiguous presence to the other and therefore also a closing off of the self to the otherness of the other in consequence of the self-constituting of the ego. For when human beings experience self-consciousness as immediate identity with themselves and therefore as constitutive of the self, they close themselves against the divine power that establishes their existence and, in consequence, against the otherness of others within the world.[98]

For Pannenberg (as for Rahner), nonhuman animals are cognitively enmeshed with their surroundings, while human beings are endowed with a basic religious impulse that looks beyond what is immediately perceptible, and ultimately toward God. While humanity's "self-centeredness" or "egocentricity" looks similar to the "centrality" that characterizes animal life, this analogy conceals a deeper dissimilarity. Human egocentricity differs in kind from animal centrality because it carries an inward division that every animal lacks; one's self is both an object of reflection and also the most-intimate site of one's own experiential perspective.[99] A human being can regard herself, simultaneously "seeing" as a conscious subject and "being seen" as an object of her own interest.

Being cognitively enmeshed within their phenomenological context ("*Umwelt*"), nonhuman animals lack the inner division that gives rise to self-consciousness. *Umwelt*—a term that Pannenberg appropriates from biologist Jakob von Uexküll—does not name an objective view of a creature's surroundings (as the usual translation "environment" might suggest), but rather the world as it appears from the perspective of each animal's sense organs and material interests.[100] Famously, a tick's *Umwelt* is built around the warmth of sunlight high on a blade of grass, the smell of mammalian sweat, and the temperature of blood. Pannenberg argues that nonhuman animals are entirely embedded within their phenomenological worlds, while human beings "have" a world, an abstract and objective self-distancing from one's own experience, akin to the phenomenological reduction.[101] Humanity's liberation from the animal *Umwelt* entails that human consciousness stands open to the distinction between the finite and the infinite, and this openness to the infinite represents the necessary created condition for the possibility for interaction with God: "It is of the nature of our human form of life to be 'eccentric' relative to other things and beings, in awareness of a horizon that transcends their finitude, and hence to be able to move on constantly to new experiences. An expression for this is 'openness to the world.' More precisely we should speak of an openness beyond everything finite that itself also transcends the horizon of the world because only in awareness of the infinite can we think the thought of the world as the epitome of everything finite."[102] Humanity is constituted, then, by a role within a broader theological narrative.[103] Within Pannenberg's future-oriented theology, human life has a teleological structure in which the eschaton shapes the present. Proper human life is a future-oriented project, a self lived forward toward an eschatological identity.[104] Lacking a fixed nature and a determined relation to the world, every human being must make herself, but does so most authentically only in relation to God who has given the makings of a self to each and every human being.[105] Nonhuman animals, in contrast, have no inherent theological narrativity. They are fixed within the present, identified entirely with the *Umwelten* in which they are enmeshed.[106] Even if nonhuman animals enjoy life in the eschaton, the lives of animals are not structurally oriented toward an eschatological future. Thus in an early text, Pannenberg claims: "What the environment is for animals, God is for man. God is the goal in which alone his striving can find rest and his destiny be fulfilled."[107]

Exocentricity's inner break between the seeing-self and the seen-self also forms the boundary between human animality and humanity proper in Pannenberg's anthropology. The "centric" aspect of the self which is objectified and looked upon from the surveilling perspective of self-consciousness represents human animality, while the active self as surveilling subject represents humanity proper. Self-assessment is a central human capacity in Pannenberg's account, because human nature is a developing project rather than a fixed essence. Human beings receive their essence as an "ought" rather than an "is," an exocentric imperative to self-transcendence rather than the unfolding of an indicative origin: "It is precisely the natural conditions of their existence, and therefore that which they are by nature that human beings must overcome and cancel out if they are to live their lives in a way befitting their 'nature' as human beings."[108] Oriented toward a future of perfect communion with God, proper humanity transcends its finite, natural conditions and renders plastic the natural constraints of humanity's common evolutionary heritage with other animals.[109] One finds proper humanity at the subjective pole of human existence as it tends toward fluidity, change, futurity, and transcendence; human animality is found at the objective pole of human existence grounded in finite context and routine, resistant to change.[110]

Any disorder or regression in the movement from centricity toward self-transcendence appears as sin for Pannenberg, and this movement is tightly linked to his hierarchical arrangement of humanity over animality.[111] Sin is a self-centered resistance to one's exocentric destiny/identity in God, or else a self-abandonment that inhibits the realization of such a destiny/identity.[112] In both cases, a human being negates proper exocentricity and gives himself over to his "animal centrality" in such a way that he becomes enmeshed within his environment.[113] Nonhuman animals are incapable of sin because only human beings are constituted by an essential orientation toward the fulfillment of their identity in the future.[114] The immediate "centrality" of animals is not sinful because their creaturely identity is bound up with their *Umwelt.* But the human being who, in resistance to his exocentric future destiny, fails to transcend an analogous egocentricity remains mired in sin because humanity is uniquely defined by a calling to self-transcendence.[115] Pannenberg writes, "Only because the destination of human beings is exocentric and finds fulfillment solely in the radical exocentricity proper to them as religious beings can the egocentricity that is analogous in them to animal centrality turn into a failure of their existence, their destination as human beings."[116] While transcending animality and evading sin are not identical projects, their trajectories are closely aligned. Humanity's evolutionary continuity with nonhuman animals is not the source of human sinfulness, but self-enclosure nevertheless remains the basic form of insensitivity to God in both animality and human sinfulness.[117] Unreflective enmeshment—whether animal or sinful—must be overcome through proper self-transcendence. Perhaps even more than for Rahner, Pannenberg's human animality remains ambiguously stuck between blameless animal finitude and culpable human sinfulness.

Beyond the parallel between animality and sin that Pannenberg's theology shares with Rahner's, the problem of human animality leaves at least two additional conceptual tangles in Pannenberg's anthropology, one in the logic of redemption and the other in the definition of proper humanity in explicitly Christian terms.

First, the logic of sin and redemption in Christian theology—and Pannenberg is no exception—relies on some notion of species solidarity whereby the action of a single person at a critical juncture (e.g., Adam and Jesus) can affect every other human being.[118] Pannenberg's account of redemption stumbles over the ambiguity of human animality within his anthropology insofar as self-transcendence and exocentricity explicitly aspire to move the human being beyond species solidarity.[119] The eschatological destiny that lures proper humanity toward its completion in communion with God functions to individuate and personalize human beings beyond their background in species conformity. The vector of eschatological fulfillment runs away from animality. Christ establishes a mode of being human that no longer resists the lure-from-the-future of God's transformative reign.[120] Tension arises because the trajectory of redemption (that is, human transcendence of finite natural conditions in an open orientation toward futurity and the true infinite) would seem to be at odds with the ontological *mechanism* of redemption (that is, the enmeshment of each human being within a species solidarity whereby the acts of God in Jesus Christ affect the whole). The crux of the problem is that the very species solidarity (always associated with animality) that proper humanity is meant to transcend through self-reflective orientation to eschatological communion is also the means by which God's incarnation redeems particular human beings from their subjection to sin and death. Species solidarity both provides the medium of redemption's transmission and marks the limitations that are to be transcended and overcome in the life of the redeemed. As with the ancient authors, human animality simultaneously figures as part of the ontological mechanism of redemption and as that which redemption leaves behind. The fate of human animality within the trajectory of salvation remains enigmatically doubled.

Second, Pannenberg's conception of proper humanity not only offers a taxonomic criterion dividing humans from animals, but does so through a developmental logic that potentially divides into full humans, not quite humans, and less than humans. The ongoing colonial and white supremacist history of such arrangements is readily accessible.[121] The fundamental difference between human and nonhuman animals lies in humanity's exocentric openness to God. But Pannenberg presents a graduated account of openness and closure—not a strict binary, but a matter of degrees. It is the variability of human openness to God that makes human life a teleologically oriented project. However, because exocentricity operates both as an evaluative measure of progress toward an eschatological destiny and as the watershed criterion within a taxonomic system dividing human beings from animals, there is a strong sense in which the person actively anticipating her perfect communion with God is more authentically human than the person transfixed by the aesthetic immediacy of his context. Within the logic of progress, some projects inevitably move ahead more quickly than others. To the extent that Pannenberg eventually defines human openness and exocentricity in explicitly Christian, Trinitarian terms, the logic of his text opens the possibility that the adjective *non-Christian* might be aligned with the adjective *subhuman*. To be clear, Pannenberg advocates no such scheme. Even if it remains unspoken, however, the logic of racism, sexism, and colonial repression is latently available. The plasticity available within a future-oriented account of human nature offers a genuine theological breakthrough; the darker political potential of developmental criteria for genuine humanity, however, must not be ignored, and Pannenberg does not adequately attend to them.[122] The problem of human animality in Pannenberg's theology potentially generates schemes of dehumanization where humanity's transcendence of animality maps onto the political domination of some human beings by others.

In these conceptual problems, as elsewhere, the problem of human animality derives from the subordination of animality to authentic humanity. Hypothetically, Pannenberg's exocentric anthropology could stand without such a subordination and distinction. Pannenberg's claim that animals live *in* the world (enmeshed within their particular *Umwelten*) while human beings *have* worlds is closely aligned with a distinction between nature and culture.[123] The nature-culture distinction validates a mistaken notion that "cultural" human activity is free, creative, and constructed while "natural" animal activity is entirely constrained by innate instinct. Drawn in this way, however, the distinction is a false one. Human cultures constrain human behavior by engaging physiological impulses, psychological tendencies, and instinctual desires.[124] Likewise, instinct does not determine nonhuman animal behavior in the way that a computer operating system rigidly determines a processor's actions; animals respond creatively to their contexts on the basis of their perceptions, impulses, and practical judgment—even as those responses follow predictable patterns.

Pannenberg claims that there is a categorical difference between the natural enmeshment of animals within the finite context of their *Umwelt* and humanity's openness to the world—or to a variety of culturally configured worlds.[125] However, if one considers the human capacities and drives which structure language use, subjective experience, self-reflective consciousness, and the desire for God as creaturely attunement to a particularly broad and adaptable *Umwelt,* then this distinction melts away. The human *Umwelt* could be recognized as a natural-cultural reality in which the constructed, cultural world that human beings "have" corresponds to the interests, drives, and capacities with which human beings are "naturally" endowed.[126] From our perspective, the human *Umwelt* appears much richer, more varied, more expansive than those of animals; but we often fail to recognize the limits of our ability to understand another creature's own rich internal experience of his or her "world." Our world may very well appear flat and uninspired from other species' perspectives.

As soon as one expands the notion of an *Umwelt* beyond an inaccurately flattened stimulus-response scheme in order to include subjectivity, cultural formation, social pressure, and the desire for the transcendent, human beings are no less enmeshed within *Umwelten* than animal neighbors are. To situate human life within an *Umwelt* would be to insist that self-transcendence is not the transcendence of the authentic human beyond the constraints of animality, but rather a particular, transcendent configuration of animality itself. Exocentricity and orientation toward God are not necessarily at cross-purposes with the ontological species solidarity presumed in Pannenberg's account of redemption, so long as that redemption is not moving away from animality. Likewise, if coming into one's true identity in God is no longer a matter of becoming more human and less animal, then the pattern of logic capable of dehumanizing those who have made "less progress" breaks apart.

The problem of human animality generates conceptual problems in Pannenberg's anthropology analogous to the tensions analyzed in

Gregory of Nyssa and Gregory of Nazianzus insofar as Pannenberg's account of salvation simultaneously presupposes animality and repudiates it as beneath proper human transcendence.

Conclusion

The problem of human animality is not essential to Christian theology—Christian theology can think otherwise—and yet, the heritage of this problem has persistently shaped Christian thought for millennia. Gregory of Nyssa and Gregory of Nazianzus distinguished humanity from animality by the possession of a rational, responsible mind; contemporary theologians turn this mind inward on its own constitutive experience and distinguish humanity from animality on the basis of self-consciousness, which also functions as a spiritual availability to divine communication. Regardless, human animality still bends around the heart of persistent conceptual knots in which divergent theological commitments strain against one another.

While the contemporary version of the human-animal distinction encourages reflection on constitutive social relationships rather than the possession of rationality, the end result hardly differs. Where humanity is set off categorically from all other animals—by a single capacity or basic structural orientation—one finds a correlative distinction operating between human animality and humanity proper, whether or not it is named. Accounts of human sin often contain significant conceptual and terminological overlap with characterizations of animality. Whatever characteristic is assumed to be common to all animals emerges under the label of *sin* where it appears in human life. Whether animality's specific content appears as irrationality, sensuality, untamed desire, unrestrained impulse, lack of self-awareness/self-reflection/consciousness, closure to transcendence, lack of moral/spiritual accountability, or lack of freedom, proper humanity must rise above such traits. The pattern implies that participation in the life of God necessitates becoming less and less animal—even as God's loving intentions for all animals may be explicitly affirmed. To say the same thing within an evolutionary framework—animality lies in humanity's past, communion with God lies in humanity's future, and therefore, any assimilation of human beings to the current state of other animals represents a regression in a process which is ultimately meant to run the other way.[127]

The project's conclusion argues that this persistent disavowal of human animality represents a cornerstone of the pervasive ideology that allows human beings to knowingly drive so many animal species into extinction and even to undercut the long-term viability of human life. The conceptual disavowal of human animality bears cruel material consequences. Where human animality is finally and conclusively mastered, proper humanity may find that its natural habitat is a smoldering, lifeless world, stripped bare.

While the project to this point has been working in a critical mode, demonstrating the incoherences and tensions that arise out of the theological problem of human animality, the structure of the problem also opens the possibility for theological alternatives. Where theologians have almost universally resolved tensions around human animality by subordinating, sublimating, or sacrificing animality in service to anthropological exceptionalism, these tensions offer starting points to begin again in another direction. A theological anthropology that discovered divine grace at work in human animality—accentuating human commonalities with fellow creatures rather than attenuating them—would yield very different results. The moment that theologians disavow animality is also an opportunity to press the logic of Christian thought toward its submerged and undiscovered alternatives. The following chapters offer just such a counterproposal, an outline in three chapters of a theological anthropology centered upon human animality. Chapters 4, 5, and 6 involve a rereading and rethinking of traditional anthropological themes—human nature and the image of God, human sin and redemption, and eschatological transformation—arguing that the theological narrative might revolve around human commonality with other animals rather than the point at which humanity purportedly differs from them.

PART II

Constructive Animalities

4

Animality and Identity: Human Nature and the Image of God

Drawing on the works of several philosophers, I would like to begin the constructive portion of the project by marking the limits of human thought at the boundary between humanity and animality. Each of these philosophers turns toward theological language just as they peer beyond the limits of humanity. Agamben, Derrida, Deleuze, and Guattari stop short of crossing over—for reasons of modesty or prudence—into what each describes as an impossible (or perhaps eschatological) terrain—a kind of promised land. Nevertheless, these thresholds are remarkable points at which skeptical and spare thinkers venture a hint of hope, a gesture or attitude that could easily be mistaken for a theological impulse—and may provide a theological opening.[1] Explicitly situated in a discipline (constructive theology) whose academic propriety remains perennially suspect, the chapters that follow imaginatively venture across the well-established boundary between humanity and animality, transgressing and complicating its assumed integrity. That each of these philosophers restrains himself at the threshold of the theological offers a warrant for theologians to press on a few steps further.

The Threshold of a Different World

Giorgio Agamben approaches the threshold of theological discourse not only when he claims that the "most luminous sphere of our relations with the divine depends in some way, on that darker one which separates us from the animal,"[2] but also when he describes the "jamming" of the "anthropological machine":

> It is not here a question of trying to trace the no longer human or animal contours of a new creation that would run the risk of being equally as mythological as the other. . . . In our culture man has always been the result of a simultaneous division and articulation of the animal and the human, in which one of the two terms of the operation was also what was at stake in it. To render inoperative the machine that governs our conception of man will therefore mean no longer to seek new—more effective or more authentic—articulations, but rather to show the central emptiness, the hiatus that—within man—separates man and animal, and *to risk ourselves in this emptiness: the suspension of the suspension, Shabbat of both animal and man.*[3]

Agamben recognizes that exploring the "central emptiness" of the boundary between animality and humanity carries a risk—we might lose ourselves or our self-hood—but in this suspension we might also share divine repose with fellow creatures in our common creatureliness.

Derrida searches for a mode of living as a creature, or a mode of subjectivity not constructed through the disavowal of animality—without the maneuver that sets "them" on the far side of a categorical difference. What would it mean, he asks, to conceive of the alterity of other creatures in such a way that we recognize ourselves within a web of differentiation and commonality, rather than in hermetic isolation from animals? He takes up a prophetic perspective, claiming to speak, "As if I were the secret elect of what they call animals. I shall speak from this island of exception, from its infinite coastline, starting from it and speaking through it."[4] Derrida complicates the contrast maneuvers through which the concept "humanity" is constructed, suggesting that attention to all the dimensions of difference would lead to an acknowledgment that the excluded otherness constitutive of humanity is shared by gods, angels, and animals alike—a kind of divinanimality.[5] I have no intention here of evading Derrida's critique of a "Judeo-Christiano-Islamic tradition of a war against the animal, of a sacrificial war that is as old as Genesis."[6] Nevertheless, in his meticulously apophatic descriptions of a mode of subjectivity accountable to the gaze of animals, it is not difficult to perceive tones of an impossible hope or expectation, a cousin of the quasi-theological messianicity to which he occasionally refers.[7] For example:

> As with every bottomless gaze, as with the eyes of the other, the gaze called "animal" offers to my sight the abyssal limit of the human: the inhuman or the ahuman, the ends of man, that is to say, the bordercrossing from which vantage man dares to announce himself to himself, thereby calling himself by the name that he believes he gives himself. And in these moments of nakedness, as regards the animal, everything can happen to me, I am like a child ready for the apocalypse, *I am (following) the apocalypse itself*, that is to say, the ultimate and first event of the end, the unveiling and the verdict.[8]

Were these moments of nakedness sustained, what sort of human being might emerge at this crossroads, the crosshairs of some other creature's gaze? Derrida describes a moment of great possibility and great risk, a moment in which worlds are brought to their ends.

Gilles Deleuze and Felix Guattari are adamantly antitheological in their text *A Thousand Plateaus*, refusing orders, foundations, taxonomies, and stasis.[9] Nevertheless, "becoming animal" approaches the threshold of theological discourse as the apocalyptic undoing of humanity.[10] There is a kind of immanent apocalypticism within becoming animal, an undoing that casts judgments (though certainly not a unified divine Judgment) upon the present order of the humanized world.[11] The "reality" of becoming animal cannot be reduced to imitation (acting like an animal) nor to "being" animal (placing oneself elsewhere within the *taxis* of a system of species, genera, phyla, and kingdoms). Instead, it is a different configuration of living, a matter of "alliance" and the formation (or "involution") of unheard-of "packs," "bands," and "multiplicities."[12] These formations are the site, for Deleuze and Guattari, of resistance to the pervasive logic of Western capitalism and the "world" that it creates and sustains. Becoming animal has a positive valence within Deleuze and Guattari's text precisely because it signifies—if only in localized, immanent, and highly particular ways—an end to current political, economic, and cultural orders. Such apocalyptic philosophy reaches toward the advent of worlds unimaginable from any subject position within humanity.

Perhaps Deleuze and Guattari's "becoming animal," the strange self-recognition that Derrida searches for in another creature's gaze, and Agamben's "Shabbat" can be momentarily aligned in order to indicate a line of thought for what follows. For all of these thinkers, the suspension of humanity invokes very different worlds, worlds that can scarcely be described in the language that we possess (and which possesses us). The suspension of humanity requires the restructuring of language, or a new language, whose political functions, connotations, and formative influence differ radically from present possibilities for thought and speech. I would like to linger at this threshold for the next three chapters, sketching the kind of living (beings) that might await on the other side.

The preceding chapters put a spotlight on the irresolvable tensions and breakdowns of theological discourse around the problem of human animality. Chapters 4, 5, and 6 take these tensions as starting points, approaching these fractures in theological logic as an opportunity to craft alternatives to theology's fundamental hostility toward animality. The moments of disavowal, sublimation, and subordination that I have traced are forks in the path that have brought the Christian theological tradition to its current state. These decisions cannot be ignored or undone. But embedded within the texts of the theological tradition (and perhaps embedded within theological discourse itself) are memories or memorials of these decisions. Although no one can return *historically* to the moments where animality was laid low within theological anthropology in order to reshape a different Christian tradition, one might return *imaginatively* to these points in theological discourse to see what might have been down the paths not taken. Perhaps a cloud of such interconnected moments of theological imagination can raise a well-matched resistance—and this is the wager of the constructive work that follows—to counteract the ongoing subordination, sublimation, and disavowal of animality in prevalent conceptions of humanity along the very contours where these patterns were established.

This chapter works toward a theological ecology of human nature/identity. I focus on questions of human nature/identity, extending theology's social-relational turn by treating interspecies interactions as constitutive of the personal and political dimensions of human existence (rather than peripheral to them). Where this chapter takes up the identity/nature of the human being as a creature among so many others, chapters 5 and 6 work with other themes within the narrative range of theological anthropology: sin and redemption in the next chapter, and then eschatological transformation in the following.

Although theologians frequently acknowledge that human beings are, in some fashion, animals who share life in common with other creatures, this acknowledgment is generally a preliminary step or caveat on the way toward developing an account of humanity's categorical uniqueness. On such schemes, animality (however conceived) remains the uninteresting, uninspired, and theologically neglected aspect of human life. The thread of argument running across this chapter links moments of possibility for a theological account of human life in which animality moves to the forefront of identity, sociality, and politics. Along that thread, the chapter cycles through new beginnings, working to think humanity differently out of junctures at which human animality has traditionally been subordinated and scorned. At each point, temporarily suspending the longstanding habit of subordinating animality beneath proper humanity opens room for a theological resistance, the recovery or imagination of a way of being human in which the approach to God takes place alongside nonhuman creatures and in relations of interdependence with them.

Specifically, this chapter begins by claiming that the turn in twentieth-century theology toward relational accounts of human nature/identity remains incomplete wherever theological anthropology neglects nonhuman neighbors. Second, since theological forms of anthropological exceptionalism are sustained through the alignment of the *imago dei* (in Genesis 1) with claims to sovereignty (dominion), the chapter offers a theological-biblical counterpoint from the book of Daniel. Third, I argue that Jesus's messianic proclamation of the "realm of God" raises questions of sociopolitical belonging that ultimately decenter proper humanity for the sake of the livelihood and wellbeing of fellow creatures. Fourth, I offer a theological account of human identity focused on the material interactions of human beings with our creaturely neighbors and argue that this approach offers both a critique of the current structures of human identity formation and possibilities for as-yet unimagined ways-of-living among our fellow creatures. Connecting each of these discussions, the broad arc of the chapter's argument is the claim that human beings enjoy the greatest proximity to God in moments of commonality and connection with nonhuman creatures, rather than in moments of categorical uniqueness and separation.

The constructive work here concentrates on fragments of the theological tradition that generate friction for the tradition's mainstream anthropological exceptionalism. Necessarily, then, the method is not the standard, straightforward exposition of scripture and reputable authorities of Christian history that culminates in a refinement or adjustment of theological categories. Even the constructive work here may strike some readers as being quite critical. Yet, the depth and breadth of the Christian tradition's theological revulsion to animality requires working through a series of pointed interventions (connected by an overall thread of argument), rather than a more irenically subtle shift in theological emphasis and priority. Put otherwise, I am working out of an agreement with Agamben, Derrida, Deleuze, and Guattari that the fabric of Christian theology—its language, its structure, its world—is woven through and through with the distinction and separation of humanity from animality. There is no whole cloth from which one might fashion an alternative theological discourse; the best course of action takes mismatched seams apart in order to reassemble animality and humanity in a different arrangement in the hopes that such a reconfiguration makes space for modes of creaturely life that ultimately escape the hold of these binary categories in ways that are, at present, impossible.

Turning to the (Animal) Subject

Christian theological anthropology has assimilated the Enlightenment "turn to the subject" by shifting emphasis from the substance of human composition to the formation, vocation, and identity of human subjects. Expositions of Genesis's laconic phrase "the image of God," for example, have broadly shifted from "substantial" accounts emphasizing the possession of soul, mind, reason, or language toward "relational" or "functional" accounts.[13] More recently still, many theological anthropologies have replaced early modernity's individualistic, self-contained, and inscrutable accounts of human subjectivity with accounts of the sociopolitical formation of human subjects. In Christian theology, this criticism of the individualistic paradigm has come primarily from two trajectories of thought: feminist theology and the revival of trinitarian theology.

Catherine Keller offers a particularly vibrant example of the feminist critique, arguing that androcentric culture valorizes one isolated pattern of masculine experience—an individualistic, aspirationally sovereign, "separative" self—while devaluing formative social relations by coding them as "feminine."[14] The separative self (the subject position marked masculine and typically embodied by men) makes a show of separation from every relation of dependence—paradigmatically from his mother, from whom he must establish sexual and personal difference. Where the self-contained, sovereign individual is held up as the universal ideal of human subjectivity, patriarchal culture tends toward matriphobia and generalized misogyny.[15] The separative self feverishly maintains the illusion of being a "self-made man," shunting away the idea that his personhood, rationality, and free decisions depend on networks of formative relations. In contrast, "soluble" selves (the subject position marked feminine and typically embodied by women) tend to absorb or be absorbed into the identity, thinking, and decisions of others. Keller argues that the path out of patriarchy for soluble selves is not the disavowal of formative relationships in an effort to stake a claim on autochthonous separative sovereignty, but to recognize *over*-identification and resist it with a healthier interdependence.[16] In answer to current, oppressive patterns of gendered subject formation, Keller argues for the empowerment of women and a period of "compensatory gynocentricity," an apprenticeship in subjectivity through which men may learn authentically masculine modes of interdependence.[17]

Second, the twentieth century saw a revival in the doctrine of the Trinity, particularly emphasizing the mutuality and eternal co-inherence of the three persons. A number of theologians argued that the mutual constitution of the three trinitarian persons is a foundational analogue for relationally constituted accounts of human personhood—and even for a relational ontology as the core of a doctrine of creation.[18] The details of these particular proposals are of less concern here than their common repudiation of the monadic rational subject valorized in early modern conceptions of ideal humanity and divine sovereignty. These theologians claim that the early modern understanding of human personhood functionally denies each person's basic dependence upon God and obscures the social or relational constitution of all identity. Human persons, just like the persons of the Trinity, are who they are through ongoing relationships to one another; to deny this fundamental social matrix is to distort one's view of the origin and purpose of personhood in the direction of self-sufficiency.

These paradigm shifts have changed the landscape of theological anthropology so that even lofty theological affirmations about humanity—the divine image or basic openness to God, for example—are explained as the product of (grace-infused) social formation rather than as a *deus ex machina* interjection into an abstract and ahistorical human nature. In these accounts, caring familial interaction, language acquisition, and sociopolitical formation establish the capacities through which human beings receive divine communication and personally relate to God.[19] Human relationships to God are explicitly embedded within the matrix of social and cultural relationships. God's transcendence of the limits of human speech and thought no longer translates, in these accounts, into an assumption that human relations to God somehow transcend the formative relational network of human communities. The human being is relationally constituted all the way down—and all the way up, too.

However, theological reflection upon the relational constitution of the human being has been almost entirely limited to interhuman relations. Theological accounts of human subjectivity tend to negate or occlude interactions with nonhuman creatures by contrasting human personhood with supposedly impersonal animal life. David Clough identifies these patterns of negation and occlusion as two modes of what he calls "not-animal" anthropology: the first actively separates humanity from all other animals through the contrast maneuver that defines "human" over against the category "animal" on the basis of some pseudoempirical criteria; the second separates humanity from animality by omission, describing human relations in isolation from the context of other creaturely interactions.[20] Despite a theological turn toward social and political formation of human subjects, there has yet to be an *ecological* turn that would treat material interspecies interactions as constitutive of human subjectivity before God.

It is true, of course, that contemporary theological anthropology attends to the evolutionary past as a point of deep connection between human beings and other creatures, and even as ground for creaturely solidarity.[21] Is this emphasis not an interspecies account of human subject formation? I am persuaded that accounts of the evolutionary origins of humanity function differently in theological anthropology than accounts of the social and political formation of human subjects. In fact, the difference highlights the persistent conceptual division between human animality and humanity proper. Social and political formation generates human subjectivity, structures the psyche, determines moral sensibilities, and inculcates spiritual desire, but affirmations of humanity's evolutionary origins connect human beings to other animals at the level of embodiment, ecological interdependence, and finitude. Very little conceptual traffic occurs between the registers of subjectivity and corporeality. Accordingly, recourse to evolutionary narratives often functions to reinforce the ascendance of proper humanity over human animality by offering one (ecologically inclusive) narrative for the origins of the human being qua organism and another (narrowly human) narrative for the origins of the human being qua subject.[22] Insulating accounts of human subjectivity from constitutive relations with nonhuman animals (falsely, in my view) lowers the stakes on ecological, political, and ethical questions about human-nonhuman interactions because such questions never impinge upon self-understanding as matters of primary importance. Rarely, if ever, do we think that human identity, subjectivity, agency, and morality arise through interactions with nonhuman animals (although just about any selection of children's books fatally exposes this assumption). Where a person's "truest" self emerges in a discursive field that contains only relations to other human beings and an anthropomorphized God, ecological concerns and myriad creaturely lives are, by default, secondary matters.

A more adequate account of relational subject formation would begin from the full range of our creaturely relations and not just intrahuman interactions. Restricting one's anthropological account of subjectivity and identity to the human community provides for methodological parsimony and clarity that is muddied if the social matrix includes nonhuman creatures. But insofar as humanity and animality are always mutually constituted categories, such parsimony produces distortions. As Aaron Gross notes, we cannot help but think with animals:

> We can, at least, acknowledge that because of the unique way in which "animals"—the biological beings "out there"—are always already implicated in our self-conception, we have no way of completing the critical task of thinking in genuinely new ways about animals [or human beings]. Perhaps the best we can do is follow the lead of thinkers like Derrida by remaining vigilant on both fronts—problematizing the very categories we use to conduct our analyses and responding to the pragmatic reality of animal suffering.[23]

Animals and, perhaps even more, *conceptions* of animals are inextricably bound up with our self-understanding, not least where animality offers a point of contrast for proper human identity. If individualistic and monadic accounts of human identity traffic in misogynistic, alienating distortions, what kind of distortions arise when we presume to treat human identity and personhood in isolation from everyday relations and interactions with other creatures? Carrying the relational turn forward requires thinking human identity in the context of material interactions with creaturely neighbors. In the following section, I take up the story of one human subject transformed and drawn into communion with God through animal relations.

The Animality of the Sovereign: Nebuchadnezzar and the Image of God

God's creation of humanity in the divine image, recorded in Genesis 1, looms large for any theology that attempts to connect humanity to God via animality. The *imago dei* has been a central theme—perhaps *the* central theme—within Christian theological anthropology even though the concept is only a minor concern in the Hebrew scriptures.[24] The outsized influence of the *imago dei* has certainly not been hampered by the fact that the notion remains thoroughly underdetermined in Genesis, offering a semantic vehicle ready to be loaded with meaning by whatever hermeneutical framework is brought to bear on the text.[25] While the *content* of the *imago dei* has varied wildly within the history of Christian theological reflection, the two basic functions of the concept have remained remarkably stable: the *imago dei* warrants the claim that human beings are distinguished from all other creatures by a special relationship to God and authorizes a deputized and derivative sovereignty (but a sovereignty nonetheless) for human beings in creation.[26]

Yet Genesis 1:26 is hardly the final word in the scriptures on the themes of sovereign responsibility and creaturely difference. In large part because of its function as a cornerstone of anthropological exceptionalism, a number of theologians and biblical scholars have drawn on other texts and other concepts to displace the *imago dei* of Genesis 1:26 from theological anthropology's center. Catherine Keller turns to the divine speech in Job (as does Richard Bauckham); David Kelsey turns to Wisdom literature; David Cunningham turns to common creaturely constitution as "all flesh"; Jürgen Moltmann counters the *imago dei* with humanity as the *imago mundi*; David

Clough works toward the *imago dei* from a Christology of creatureliness.[27] Adding to these efforts, I suggest that the story of Nebuchadnezzar from the book of Daniel offers another scriptural counterpoint to the function of the *imago dei* as the theological lynchpin of anthropological exceptionalism.

At first glance, the book of Daniel and Genesis 1 have very little in common, but important connections lie just beneath the surface. Both texts grapple with the preservation of cultural identity in the context of exile: Genesis 1 subversively echoes a Babylonian creation myth while Daniel provides examples of transformative perseverance under cultural pressure toward assimilation. What is more, both texts take up the themes of sovereignty in the context of human-animal differentiation.

The personal transformation of the Babylonian tyrant Nebuchadnezzar provides a thread of coherence across the apparently episodic narratives of the first four chapters of Daniel. While Nebuchadnezzar figures as the capricious, megalomaniacal despot in each of the first three chapters, there are hints of change as Nebuchadnezzar's attitude toward the God of Israel incrementally changes from ignorance (chapter 1), to a general recognition (2:47), to a fearful reverence (3:28–29). In the fourth chapter, the text suddenly allows Nebuchadnezzar to step into the role of the narrator. Nebuchadnezzar tells a story that ends with expressions of worship and personal devotion reminiscent of the Psalms (4:2–3, 34–45, 37).[28] The fourth chapter, then, is the culmination of a trajectory, Nebuchadnezzar's gradual recognition of the God of Israel as the Most High God.[29]

The chapter is framed as a letter addressed to all the people of the earth.[30] Nebuchadnezzar tells the reader about a dream which remained inscrutable to him and to his most trusted advisors. Nebuchadnezzar then relates the dream to Daniel, who warns the king that the dream's dire predictions will be visited upon him:

> Let him be bathed with the dew of heaven,
> and let his lot be with the animals of the field
> in the grass of the earth.
> Let his mind be changed from that of a human,
> and let the mind of an animal be given to him.
> And let seven times pass over him . . .
> The sentence is rendered by decree of the watchers,

the decision is given by order of the holy ones,
in order that all who live may know
that the Most High is sovereign over the kingdom of mortals;
he gives it to whom he will and sets over it the lowliest of
human beings.

(4:15–17 NRSV)

Nearly a year later, Nebuchadnezzar stands on the roof of his palace and proudly surveys the kingdom under his sway, crediting himself with prudence, power, and magisterial importance. Immediately, his mind leaves him and he lives among the animals, eating grass "like an ox," and being drenched by the dew until "his hair grew like feathers . . . and his nails like the claws of a bird" (4:33). The text itself signals Nebuchadnezzar's loss of human language and cognition as the first-person narration shifts into the third person.[31]

Surprisingly, becoming animal has a salutary effect on Nebuchadnezzar's character. Not only does he begin to offer praises and prayers to God—and commend this worship to all the people of earth through his letter—but the story contains hints that Nebuchadnezzar's attention turns toward justice for those he has oppressed (4:27, 37). Earlier, when God rescued three young Israelites from his fiery furnace (ch. 3), Nebuchadnezzar fearfully proclaimed that anyone who uttered anything to anger such a powerful God would be "torn limb from limb and their houses laid in ruins" (3:29). In contrast, becoming animal seems to have given Nebuchadnezzar a deeper wisdom, a sense of social responsibility, and a personal reverence for God.

Almost universally, commentaries describe Nebuchadnezzar's temporary transformation as a period of "insanity"—taking license beyond the text in order to mark Nebuchadnezzar's animality as a kind of mental illness. Yet, Nebuchadnezzar's transformative experience also presents a glimpse of what Deleuze and Guattari describe as "becoming animal":

> Becomings-animal are neither dreams nor phantasies. They are perfectly real. But which reality is at issue here? For if becoming animal does not consist in playing animal or imitating an animal, it is clear that the human being does not "really" become an animal any more than the animal "really" becomes something else. Becoming produces nothing other than itself. We fall into a false alternative if we say that you either imitate

> or you are. What is real is the becoming itself, the block of becoming, not the supposedly fixed terms through which that which becomes passes. Becoming can and should be qualified as becoming-animal even in the absence of a term that would be the animal become. The becoming animal of the human being is real, even if the animal the human being becomes is not; and the becoming-other of the animal is real, even if that something other it becomes is not. This is the point to clarify: that a becoming lacks a subject distinct from itself; but also that it has no term, since its term in turn exists only as taken up in another becoming of which it is the subject, and which coexists, forms a block, with the first. . . . Becoming produces nothing by filiation; all filiation is imaginary. Becoming is always of a different order than filiation. It concerns alliance.[32]

Nebuchadnezzar does not merely "play at" being an animal by imitation, nor does he "imagine" himself to be an animal—his becoming is deeper and more transformative than that. At the same time, while he eats grass "like an ox" and appears in certain ways like a bird, it does not seem that he is actually transformed into any particular nonhuman animal. The animal whom Nebuchadnezzar becomes is only ever "himself"; it is an unfolding or reconfiguration of the creature he always was. The "becoming" is real inasmuch as Nebuchadnezzar's allegiance, his block, his place in the world is among animals—and he even forfeits something like proper human selfhood (although another self remains). As an animal, "he is not himself." He disowns his human filiation and is disowned by humanity so that Nebuchadnezzar is both a human being and also inhuman or ahuman. Nebuchadnezzar becomes a human being separated from humanity—a bodily form that leads one to expect humanity, but in which one encounters the "mind of an animal."

Yet, I imagine that the horror he imposed upon his neighbors as an animal was greatly preferable to the terror that he imposed upon them as a tyrant. Remarkably, by the end of his narrative arc within the book of Daniel, he appears as an exemplary "good king" in comparison to the account of Belshazzar that follows (and also to Antiochus IV, the tyrant with whom Daniel's original audience had to deal). And even though Nebuchadnezzar's transformation can be recognized as salutary only because it was temporary, the restoration of Nebuchadnezzar's humanity should not allow readers to skip too quickly over the animality through which Nebuchadnezzar's character was so greatly improved. Commentaries on Daniel tend to assume that this story both presumes and reinforces the human-animal hierarchy, so that becoming animal is a kind of punitive measure against Nebuchadnezzar, a humiliation that stands as fitting punishment for his pride.[33] I am not convinced that this is a necessary reading insofar as Nebuchadnezzar's animal sojourn seems to function rehabilitatively. To see the transformation as punitive is to instrumentalize the animality through which Nebuchadnezzar passes. It is also to divorce the mystic vision of God that transforms Nebuchadnezzar from the animal mind that received it, instead moralizing the whole encounter as a lesson about the dangers of hubris. Nebuchadnezzar's pride may have been healed through humiliation, but it was an *animal* humiliation and he turned to the God of Israel as an animal—details that do not seem altogether incidental. The melting away of Nebuchadnezzar's sovereign difference—his autocratic rule over Babylon and his anthropological exceptionalism—opened the space in which he encountered God.

Since Daniel 4 does not make claims about the human condition generally, it may seem an odd theological counterpoint to Genesis 1:26, which at least stands within an origin narrative. Nevertheless, Nebuchadnezzar's story does divulge an instance in which the sovereign differentiation associated with the *imago dei* actively prevents reverence for God and respect for his neighbors' concerns. He only learns to see God—and his neighbors' claims on justice—through animal eyes. If Nebuchadnezzar's becoming animal is rehabilitative pedagogy rather than divine shaming, then at least *sometimes* divine grace leads human beings to God by overcoming the *imago dei* as a bulwark of anthropological exceptionalism. Nebuchadnezzar came to know God through the alliances formed in becoming animal. A common defense of the *imago dei* in the face of ecological criticism is that sovereign difference is not the problem as such, but only misguided and perverted forms of sovereignty. But what is required to draw Nebuchadnezzar into worship and concern with justice is much more than a corrective retooling of his efforts at stewardship; his life only changes where his entire perspective comes unhinged and he sees the city that he has built from outside its walls and outside the human community. Nebuchadnezzar's story enacts in dramatic fashion a marginal and eccentric spiritual theme, in which alliance with one's creaturely neighbors is also the path of spiritual ascent.

Minimally, then, Nebuchadnezzar's story limits the universal function of claims about categorical human difference as the root of connection to God. More importantly, it demonstrates a mode of being human that finds God through animal alliance and creaturely kinship rather than the rights and responsibilities of the sovereign steward.[34] Human animality can, in other words, accommodate the transformative personal intimacy with God usually associated with the subject who transcends animality via the *imago dei*. In cases such as Nebuchadnezzar's, the pervasive theological subordination of animality beneath humanity distorts God's work in creation rather than revealing it.

Daniel's account of Nebuchadnezzar's transformation calls to mind Agamben's description of a manuscript illumination in a thirteenth-century copy of the book of Ezekiel.[35] The illumination depicts the messianic banquet on the "day of the Lord" when the righteous of Israel are admitted to perfect communion with God. A great feast is set at a large table and the righteous are seated around the table wearing the crowns that they have been given. This illumination's depiction of the messianic banquet is most noteworthy, however, because all the righteous seated at the table bear the heads of animals on their shoulders—an ox, an ass, a leopard, a lion, an eagle, a monkey. Perhaps, with a squint, one can even see Nebuchadnezzar among those at the table, feasting with God as the animal who had always been hiding under the pretense of sovereignty.

The Place of Animality in the Realm of God

My argument is that creaturely proximity to God can and should be regarded as a function of animality rather than as corollary of anthropological exceptionalism. The first two pieces of that argument have shown that accounts of relational subject formation and theologies of the divine image require greater attention to animality. As a third piece, I want to take up the life and teaching of Jesus of Nazareth, particularly insofar as Jesus's humanity frequently functions as theological validation for anthropological exceptionalism: a human savior working out human salvation places humanity at the center of the theological frame. My approach to Jesus here will be more messianic/apocalyptic than Christological—a distinction of emphasis rather than opposition (especially since the following chapter takes up Christological questions).[36] Jesus's apocalyptic preaching and ministry, as recorded in the synoptic gospels, refuses any privileged ordering of subjects in creation by upending and overturning worldly hierarchies. Therefore, I argue, the trajectory of Jesus's work finally repudiates any mode of subject formation that subordinates animality beneath humanity.

A messianic/apocalyptic approach to Jesus begins from his announcement of the coming of a *basileia theou* (realm of God), of which he is the vanguard and figurehead.[37] In synoptic memory, Jesus initiates his followers into the new life of the realm of God. His preaching describes the approaching realm while his healings and exorcisms are signs of its coming. Jesus's ministry, from start to finish, enacts startling upheavals of social, economic, and religious hierarchies.[38] In the realm of God, "the last will be first, and the first will be last"; likewise, "whoever wants to become great among you must be your servant" (Matthew 20:16, 26). In overturning entrenched patterns of oppression, the realm of God does not set the oppressed at the head of a new hierarchical regime, nor does it glorify "lastness" and "subservience" as such. The realm of God maintains perspectival solidarity with the "last" and the "servants" for the sake of an order in which "lastness" and "subservience" are eradicated.[39]

For example, while the narrative structure of the parable of the sheep and the goats in Matthew 25 hinges upon identifying some people as goats and some as sheep, the truly counterintuitive aspect of the parable is the perspective from which this determination of identity comes. One learns about one's subject position in the realm of God by asking, "Who am I in the eyes of the hungry, the thirsty, the foreigner, the naked, the sick, and the imprisoned?" Those who appear calloused from the perspective of the dispossessed are identified as goats; those who appear sympathetic and generous are identified as sheep.[40] The parable encapsulates Jesus's own practice: as he announces the realm of God and enacts its signs, Jesus not only identifies people differently than does the surrounding society, he also allows himself to be identified with excluded persons through conversation, physical contact, and the sharing of meals.[41] More subtly, however, Jesus's perspectival solidarity with the dispossessed entails that in the realm of God *everyone* is identified by those who society disfavors.

Apocalypticism is a mode of imaginative speech that belongs particularly to the dispossessed.[42] Apocalyptic literature depicts seemingly intractable empires—corrupt and senselessly destructive powers—as pliable and fleeting, opening space to imagine another way of life, another politics. Insofar as apocalyptic thought does not mask sociopolitical antagonisms but amplifies them, apocalyptic discourse locates hope in drastic discontinuity between the present world order and the realm of God, a realm where present structures of oppression have been entirely dismantled.[43] Thus, apocalyptic discourse offers tools for imagining the uprooting of an ideological pattern as widely pervasive as the hierarchical opposition between humanity and animality. Everything can change; everything can appear differently.[44]

Apocalyptic and messianic discourses are vulnerable to criticism for failing to recognize goodness within the present order as a gift of divine grace, for an antiecological disregard for the integrity of the natural world, and for a violent conception of transformation in which the transcendent imposes itself upon the immanent. In the typical spatial logic of transcendence, the realm of God is located "outside" or "above" the present world and must "break in." This spatial logic preserves a hierarchy in which the realm of God descends upon corrupt human political systems, which are themselves above the natural world. This picture reduces nonhuman creation to a stage and backdrop.

By highlighting an alliance between the realm of God and animality, I mean to employ apocalyptic thought in a way that answers these objections, breaking connections between transcendence and otherworldliness. The apocalypse of the divine realm throws off the corruption of humanity (and all humanity's corruptions) in order to expose a transcendent gift within an immanent ecology long bent under false conceptions and alien demands. The transcendent realm of God threatens to irrupt from within as the long-suppressed, disavowed, and negated core of immanence.[45] The apocalypse, the unveiling of God's realm, then, may be imagined as the end of humanity for the sake of all God's creatures in their common animality, human beings liberated no less than all the others.

In his messianicity, Jesus announces and inaugurates the realm of God as the habitat of redemption, an ecosystem that radically transforms creatures' ways of life. A messianic/apocalyptic focus on animality turns the politics of redemption into a political ecology of redemption, a description of the diverse interrelations of redeemed creatures who are formed and reformed within the realm of God.

What does it mean to be a creature in the proximity of the realm of God? What happens to human nature and human identity from the perspective of God's realm? Two points: First, one's identity in the realm of God is not a static personal possession but determined in interactions and relations with one's neighbors. Second, one's identity in the realm of God is especially determined from the perspective of the dispossessed among one's neighbors. Human subject formation in the realm of God, then, begins from the vantage point of animality—our common interdependence and vulnerability, for example—rather than from assumptions of anthropological exceptionalism.[46] As Peter Scott notes, "the sociality of nonhuman nature is a condition for the sociality of humanity."[47] If the realm of God locates and describes human subjects from the perspective of "the sociality of nonhuman nature," it unveils, apocalyptically, a very different account of human nature and identity. The particular nonhuman neighbors among whom we live, breath, eat, sleep, and die have knowledge of who we are, and though we might be inclined to resist such a connection for both trivial and momentous reasons, the logic of Jesus's proclamation presses the unsettling conclusion that these animals know, better than we do, who we are in God's eyes and God's realm.

The claim that creaturely neighbors "do not speak" is no reason to abandon the "listening" by which human beings might hear themselves identified from another perspective.[48] Derrida's line of questioning in *The Animal That Therefore I Am* presents a helpful guide to this task and its dangers: "Who am I, therefore? Who is it that I am (following)? Whom should this be asked of if not of the other? And perhaps of the cat itself?"[49] Caught in the eyes of his cat, he refuses to domesticate the cat's gaze (and by extension, the multiplicity of animals in whose eyes he might be caught) into a collapsed and fungible meaning—either as an anthropomorphized utterance in which he might "speak for" his cat or as a disavowal of the possibility that the cat's perception might have a claim on him.[50] He presumes neither to know already what the cat thinks nor that the cat is a dumb, thoughtless animal, but preserves an uncertain middle space in which the cat has something to say to identify him, but something which necessarily remains largely inscrutable. From within this middle space where we, in Val Plumwood's words, "allow the concept of mind to take radically different forms,"[51] human beings can "listen" by empathetically analyzing patterns of interaction with fellow creatures. However inadequately, one may venture to think human identity "from below"; one may attempt to "be seen" by animal neighbors and to think theologically about human identity while caught within their gazes.

The account of human identity that follows, then, makes itself accountable to the eyes of the animals among whom we live—even and especially when we deny them the chance to meet us face to face. A theological anthropology bound to the perspectives of creaturely neighbors refuses to regard relations of material interdependence, conceptual codetermination, and ecopolitical negotiation as secondary or irrelevant conditions of human identity before God.[52] Given the current patterns of human interaction with nonhuman creatures, this account of human identity is bound to be sharply critical, yet setting imagination off in this direction also opens up space to think "impossible" modes of cohabitation, creaturely interrelation, and theological illumination.[53]

Humanity from the Perspective of Animality

> The pensivity of animals, or at least what I am trying to designate and grasp with this term, is neither a diversion nor a curiosity; what it establishes is that the world in which we live is gazed upon by other beings, that the visible is shared among creatures and that a politics could be invented on this basis, if it is not too late.
>
> Jean-Christophe Bailly[54]

As the next step in the effort to open space for a theological anthropology that places animality at the center of human nature and human identity, I want to mitigate the oddness of thinking about relational identity vis-a-vis animality with an instructive parable. If the subject formation of the realm of God begins and ends in perspectival solidarity with the dispossessed and if, as I have argued above, the "dispossessed" of our world must necessarily include nonhuman animals and animality, then one of the urgent tasks before us will be to force open the structures of our empathy so that we can understand ourselves as seen by the creatures among which we live.

In 1917, Wolfgang Köhler published *The Mentality of Apes* based on a series of "problem-solving" experiments on chimpanzees captured from African forests—the chimps used sticks and crates to reach bananas placed out of reach. In John Coetzee's text, *The Lives of Animals*, the character Elizabeth Costello gives voice to Sultan—one of Köhler's subjects—to speculate about what he might have learned through the study.[55] Coetzee/Costello's account is remarkable because it dramatically expands the frame through which the reader sees such experiments; from Sultan's imagined perspective, the "problem" is not only the technical matter of reaching food but the social problem of a sudden change in relationship:

> Sultan is alone in his pen, He is hungry: the food that used to arrive regularly has unaccountably ceased coming. The man who used to feed him and has now stopped feeding him stretches a wire over the pen three meters above ground level, and hangs a bunch of bananas from it. Into the pen he drags three wooden crates. Then he disappears, closing the gate behind him, though he is still somewhere in the vicinity, since one can smell him. Sultan knows: Now one is supposed to think. That is what the bananas up there are about. The bananas are there to make one think, to spur one to the limits of one's thinking. But what must one think? One thinks: Why is he starving me? One thinks; What have I done? Why has he stopped liking me? One thinks: Why does he not want these crates anymore? But none of these is the right thought. Even a more complicated thought—for instance: What is wrong with him, what misconception does he have of me, that leads him to believe it is easier for me to reach a banana hanging from a wire than to pick up a banana from the floor?—is wrong. The right thought to think is: How does one use the crates to reach the bananas? Sultan drags the crates under the bananas, piles them one on top of the other, climbs the tower he has built, and pulls down the bananas. He thinks: Now will he stop punishing me? The answer is: No. The next day the man hangs a fresh bunch of bananas from the wire but also fills the crates with stones so that they are too heavy to be dragged. . . . One is beginning to see how the man's mind works.[56]

The gap in Sultan's narrative between "the right thought" (what the researchers presume Sultan to think) and what "one thinks" opens up the unsettling purpose of the parable. Even if the specific content of Sultan's thoughts here can undoubtedly be dismissed as anthropomorphic fiction, the account nevertheless functions to preserve the space of Sultan's thought from an all-too-common reductive collapse. The assumption that Sultan's thoughts are rigidly instrumental, focused narrowly on feeding himself, is no less an anthropomorphic projection than the social awareness that Coetzee attributes to him.[57] We cannot know what Sultan sees nor how he thinks about it, but Coetzee's narrative—qualified with such an apophatic reserve—rightly insists that Sultan perceives the world in a manner all his own.

While Sultan's researchers imagine that they have erased themselves from the situation in order to see what Sultan will "naturally" do, Sultan still thinks of his captors and keepers. The production of proper human knowledge involves the disavowal of a relationship. Sultan regards his handlers as generous, capricious, narrow-minded, manipulative, aloof, and coy; his handlers undoubtedly do not see themselves this way, but are these observations any less relevant? Any less true?

Allowing for the same sort of apophatic reserve, I want to speculatively offer fictional descriptions of human beings as seen from the perspective of our creaturely neighbors. Indulging the limits of empathetic imagination can produce only anthropomorphic projections, but we may safely assume that our animal neighbors identify us *somehow*—however inaccessibly—and that their perspectives hold accurate descriptions of human nature and identity. Further, in the relational ecology of the realm of God, whose perspectival solidarity always begins from among the dispossessed, such descriptions may carry the weight of divine approbation and divine judgment. That is to say, we cannot be sure that God does not see us through animal eyes.

What is the human being in the eyes of an animal confined within a factory farm? The average American consumes upwards of twenty-eight nonhuman animals per year, not counting fish.[58] By the time their muscles end up on dinner plates, the particular human beings into whose flesh these animals will be incorporated will be total strangers. Human figures more generally, however, will have been only slightly more familiar. In the dark and crowded shed where this animal's life was spent, human figures will always have been terrifyingly announced by sudden bright lights and the crashing open of doors—the only interruption from the usual din and darkness. These figures—vaguely recognizable as predators from vestigial instinctual memory—pass by quickly to check that food and water are passing by in the troughs and to clear the dead from cages. In this very cramped world, humans appear as the only creatures who move freely; they alone seem to be in control; they alone open and close doors at will. One imagines that confusion and fear predominate in the experience of creatures whose every bodily impulse to clean, nurture offspring, and interact socially with neighbors is frustrated by a cramped world in which none of these acts are possible. It is impossible to say how much of this fear and confusion is identified with the human beings who maintain its conditions. Looking into the eyes of a chicken in a battery cage, a sow in a breeding stall, a calf taken from its mother at four weeks, it is not hard to imagine that humans appear as calloused torturers, unresponsive, and without compassion.

What is the human being in the eyes of the few animals fortunate to live on a more conventional farm? For the comparatively few livestock who live in more conventional farming operations, the appearance of human figures presages excitement for the day's provision. Younger cows, pigs, or chickens will have understood from the responses of the older animals that the human figure can be cautiously trusted. This trust must be wary insofar as the human figure periodically appears with a betrayal rather than a gift—the shearing clippers, branding iron, or castrating band that forebode a final truck, knife, or shotgun—as some of the older animals know too well. The human figure bears an indecipherable ambiguity absent from other creatures whose posture, movements, and anatomy communicate either a threatening carnivorous or benign grazing demeanor. Looking into the eyes of a cow in a corral, a pig in a pen, or sheep in the pasture, it is not hard to imagine that humans appear as generous providers and masterful deceivers.

What kind of animal is the human being in the eyes of an urban animal? The mice, rats, squirrels, roaches, raccoons, and pigeons who occupy close quarters with human beings wait for fallen crumbs and opportune silences. They attend to the waste bins that miraculously fill with new rinds, spoils, and remnants soon after they are emptied. They have claimed the dirty, hidden cracks and corners of human constructions for their own and proceed with a caution ingrained through generations whose deaths have come in traps, poisons, and tramplings from the very creatures on whose excess they feed. While human profligacy provides daily bread, these animals know enough to assiduously avoid face-to-face encounters. Looking into the eyes of a park squirrel, a subway rat, or an apartment mouse it is not hard to imagine that human beings appear as loud, careless, and dangerous benefactors.

What kind of animal is the human being in the eyes of a laboratory animal? While the creatures in lab coats may offer tokens of warmth and concern for the caged inhabitants of their labs, ultimately they must turn on the animals in order to extract knowledge from their bodies. A creature on the receiving end of invasive surgery, behavioral experimentation, poisons, skin irritants, or electric shocks must fear the creatures with whom these processes come to be associated. The human figure must be identified with exhausted irritation for the creatures whose deaths are neatly tucked into the flow of a health and wellness news story: "Laboratory animals die when they are deprived of delta-sleep."[59] The gaze of the observer who collects knowledge must be indistinguishable from sadism for creatures to whom such knowledge means only subjection to pain. Looking into the eyes of a caged rat, rabbit, or monkey slated for experimentation it is not hard to imagine that humans appear as the agents of an instrumentalizing, dispassionate, and morbid curiosity.

What kind of animal is the human being in the eyes of a "wild" animal? Even if a creature never comes face to face with a human being, the smells of the human world are uniquely identifiable and difficult to avoid—exhaust, oil, pavement, fertilizers, pesticides. In the ever-expanding territory marked by these smells, creatures find monocultures of corn, soy, wheat, or mown grass; they find forests cleared, wetlands drained, grasslands plowed; they find migration routes cut by dangerous and bewildering freeways. While the "claim" of humanity's smell upon the land does not quite betoken a wasteland, the transformative use of those lands is so heavy that they hold a fraction of the life they might otherwise sustain. Where there is not active deterrent from entering human territory, there is often little incentive. In the transition from rural to suburban to urban, the constructed human world becomes an impenetrable wild of noise, movement, and danger. As humanity's claim upon the land expands, many creatures find it safest to crowd deeper into what wilderness remains. In the eyes of a wild creature it is not hard to imagine that humans appear as interlopers and tyrants, whose heavy toll on the land precludes overlapping cohabitation.

What kind of animal is the human being in the eyes of a pet? After whatever trauma lies in separation from parents and siblings, some human being (or group of them) becomes the pack, the family. Most pets soon learn what mode of interaction (or avoidance) is most appropriate to subtle differences in tone of voice, posture, and demeanor. Mundane routines become the content of a shared life. They rely on familiar human beings to guide them through unfamiliar situations. In the eyes of dogs, cats, and horses, it is not hard to imagine that humans appear as protectors and guides in a strangely constructed world and as counterparts within complex relations of emotional interdependence.

While these thought experiments could be expanded and multiplied, the point is simply to think human identity and creaturely relations from perspectives other than our own. Human cultures, economies, and political systems are always also ecological realities. However seldom we recognize it, we are subjects formed by our relationships with nonhuman animals just as much as by our position in the structures of human society. Ecology and enculturation are only separable as abstract concepts. Tarrying in humanity's material interactions with other creatures makes these connections clear.

Yet these political, economic, and cultural regimes that treat other creatures so poorly are predicated on a self-understanding that disavows human animality. The regimes of production, militarization, and capitalization that entrap nonhuman animals in systems indifferent to their suffering also poison our own water, devastate our own land, impoverish our seas, and destabilize the climate upon which we as animals (along with all our living neighbors) depend absolutely. Humanity's ideological disavowal of its own animality produces callously murderous forms of sovereignty and delusionally self-destructive ways of life. As Mary Midgley notes: "If we do not feel perfectly at home here, that may after all have something to do with the way in which we have treated the place. Any home can be made uninhabitable. Our culture has too often talked in terms of *conquering* nature. This is about as sensible as for a caddis worm to talk of conquering the pond that supports it, or a drunk to start fighting the bed his is lying on. Our dignity arises *within* nature, not against it."[60] Tragically, humanity's self-serving embrace of technocratic culture—like an alcoholic binge—impedes human survival in the long term for the sake of a relatively lavish way of life in the short term. More accurately, the prosperity of the few rides on the backs of the poor, who face the consequences of ecological degradation first and most devastatingly.[61] Western ideological socialization as the sovereign stewards of creation provides for a self-understanding structured by anthropological exceptionalism, but this exceptionalism necessarily falters upon common animality, and appears particularly obscene from the perspective of animal neighbors as we undercut the ecological integrity that sustains our common life. For this reason, Žižek extends Derrida's claim that "humanity" is the self-given name by which the human animal disavows its own animality by claiming that the human is the animal who adheres scrupulously to its own fictions—to the point of death.[62]

Thinking about human identity within the frame of common animality presses an indictment against humanity's presumptuous sovereign management of creation and—more importantly—reveals that our self-understanding is malleable because it is formed in relation to nonhuman neighbors. Working to see ourselves as seen by fellow creatures undermines our persistent ideological disavowal of animality. This work inculcates an empathetic mode of perception, that, if widely adopted, would quickly abolish the most restrictive and exploitative patterns of human interaction with nonhuman animals.[63]

To this point, the chapter has expanded upon several moments where theological discourse can begin again from traditional disavowals of human animality, choosing instead to focus an account of human nature and human identity on common animality. As a final moment, I want to return constructively to the thought of Gregory of Nazianzus, sketching an anthropology centered in animality from its latent and neglected possibility in Gregory's thought. This constructive work will also provide an opportunity to highlight the thread of argument running through the various moments of the chapter.

Animality and Being Created Human

Perhaps despite himself, Gregory of Nazianzus has already provided a theological framework for thinking about animality at the heart of identity and the significance of human embeddedness within the creaturely community. Although Gregory depicts the approach to God as a disciplined negation of animality (which is, he supposes, beneath the dignity of spiritual union), his text nevertheless leaves open another pathway of interpretation. Within his second contemplative "ascent" in Oration 28, a human being comes to know God by approaching God through the creatures made prior to the human being. While humanity's proprietary logos stands in tension with the life (*zōē*) that is the substance of divine light (*phōs*), the bare life of bees and spiders reflects the logic of the divine Logos. Gregory's mystic philosophy strains toward the immediate subjective transparency to the divine Logos that he attributes to bees, spiders, and other "irrational animals" (*alogoi*). Of course, having disavowed animality, Gregory cannot explicitly recognize this transparently spiritual subjectivity as animal, but nothing prevents us from doing so. On such a vision, it is in and through networks of creaturely relations—the stuff of instinct, embodiment, and interdependence—that creaturely subjects find themselves before God. Human logos may be too cramped, too limited, too enclosed within its own world, to inhabit such a subjectivity.

Barbara Smuts's experience studying baboons in Kenya provides a poignant example. As a scientist she took responsibility for objective observation of baboon behavior. Simultaneously (and not without relevance for the scientific observations she was making), she became acutely aware of her dependence upon the baboons as a participant in a larger biotic community:

> While one component of my being was engaged in rational inquiry, another part of me, by necessity, was absorbed in the physical challenge of functioning in an unfamiliar landscape devoid of other humans or any human-created objects save what I carried on my back. When I first began working with baboons, my main problem was learning to keep up with them while remaining alert to poisonous snakes, irascible buffalo, aggressive bees, and leg-breaking pig-holes. Fortunately, these challenges eased over time, mainly because I was traveling in the company of expert guides—baboons who could spot a predator a mile away and seemed to possess a sixth sense for the proximity of snakes. Abandoning myself to their far superior knowledge, I moved as a humble disciple, learning from masters about being an African anthropoid.[64]

Smuts's description breaks down her experience into "components" and "parts," exemplifying an ideologically generated split between proper humanity (the subject/agent of scientific knowledge) and human animality. Living well among the baboons required that she identify more deeply with her human animality than most people ever do. Smuts drew a lesson about identity from her experience,

"While we normally think of personhood as an essential quality that we can 'discover' or 'fail to find' in another, in the view espoused here personhood connotes a way of being *in relation to others*, and thus no one other than the subject can give it or take it away."[65]

Carrying the trajectory of this thought in a theological direction, the orientation of a human being to God is a function of common animality. Spirituality is not a supplement to animality but its substance. Our common kinship with other creatures—even when it takes antagonistic forms—is not a peripheral and secondary aspect of our identity before God but its primary context and content. Put otherwise, human identity in the realm of God is found only in material, ecological interactions with creaturely neighbors. We hardly recognize predation, parasitism, opportunism, scavenging, territory marking, and competition for prey as political interactions—deployments of power that shift patterns of cohabitation—and therefore hardly recognize that human beings participate in all of them. That is to say, we fail to recognize the politics of human animality. As discussed earlier, situating human beings in an ecopolitical field reframes human identity rather unfavorably, casting us in the role of despots, despoilers, tyrants, and terrorists. Yet, placing human identity in the context of political interactions with other creatures allows for more thoughtful reflection about how human power is being deployed. Understanding ourselves within this more expansive framework encourages reflection on how to inhabit networks of creaturely relationships differently, seeking less destructive modes of interdependence.

The ecosystems in which we live, massive and dispersed as they may be within globalized, urban, capitalist patterns of life, are nevertheless a kind of catechumenate or novitiate—a spiritual training ground where learning to live with (and from) other creatures may also draw one into virtuous communion with God. Different creaturely communities (both specific and interspecific) are bound by differing sets of norms and patterns for behavior, variously nuanced and partially overlapping.[66] Those who, like Barbara Smuts, inhabit the margins of "proper" human living, catch glimpses of an ecologically constituted identity, a self-understanding settled into animality. Alongside Smuts, one might look to Nebuchadnezzar among the beasts of the field, Annie Dillard among moths, muskrats, weasels, and frogs, Francis of Assisi among the birds and wolves, David Abram among the ravens, or Edward Abbey among mice and gopher snakes.[67]

To set the connection between animality and identity into Gregory's spatial logic, we rise toward God as we live prayerfully and attentively among the neighbors on whom we depend, turning our animality toward God rather than placing ourselves above the politics of creaturely life. I have argued that the preferential option of the realm of God signifies perspectival solidarity with animality. Of course, we think, pray, and communicate differently than our creaturely neighbors, but to make thought, prayer, and communication the difference that cuts between humanity and animality disavows the creaturely wisdom embodied in animal neighbors and preemptively negates whatever new form of being human before God might arise from attentive cohabitation. Where the creative capacity of human empathy opens up forms of self-understanding cognizant of a multiplicity of creaturely relations, human identity turns toward a long-disavowed becoming animal.

Conclusion

Georges Bataille attempts to articulate the perspective shift that accompanies empathetic "thinking with" animals:

> The only way to describe the world of the animal is through poetry. Poetry is the grasping at the unknowable most suited to thinking about the lives of animals. . . . Not being simply a thing, the animal is not closed and inscrutable to us. The animal opens before me a depth that attracts me and is familiar to me. In a sense, I know this depth: it is my own. It is also that which is farthest removed from me, that which deserves the name depth, which means precisely *that which is unfathomable to me*. But this too is poetry.[68]

The inscrutable depth that one finds in the eyes of animals is a mirror of the depth of animality within human beings. They uncannily confront us with our inability to know how we are known from their strange perspectives. In this strangeness, our own strangeness becomes visible to us in ways that are generally occluded by our more familiar habits of self-reflection. Here and there, where humanity's disavowal of its own animality can be momentarily suspended, we glimpse another way of inhabiting the world. The mode of seeing and thinking that we call poetry is capable of setting language on the threshold of other forms of life. It is a fragile way of seeing, a fragile way of thinking, and one risks one's own identity (allowing one's very self to become unsettled) to inhabit strange intimacies. But for all its fragility and elusiveness, poetic seeing is not daintily squeamish around torn flesh, blood, hatred, fear, longing, and attachment. Cutting through conceptual fog with the crystalline edges of carefully honed images is poetry's raison d'être. Battaille (and Derrida after him) mark poetry as the mode of human discourse most able to "see and be seen" by animals in ways that reframe human identity.[69] This chapter offers theological—if not quite poetic—reasons for the desirability of such a reframing; the next chapter continues by venturing an account of sin and repentance that reconfigures the usual role of animality.

An account of human identity grounded in animality is theologically viable and preferable in many regards to an account rooted in anthropological exceptionalism. The *imago dei* bears a theological, rhetorical, and political legacy that renders it deeply problematic in the context of concern for ecological integrity and the well-being of living creatures. For that reason, it is worth attending to the ways in which the themes traditionally attached to the *imago dei*—sovereignty and human difference—are called into question by other scriptural texts. Nebuchadnezzar's salutary sojourn among the beasts of the field is one good example. "Who we are" as creatures before God emerges from (political) relations and interactions with other creatures. As we think about human identity in the context of interspecies interactions, we may find ourselves seen, named, identified in a range of unsavory ways—as tyrants, interlopers, spendthrifts, and hoarders. If we are willing to face these relations squarely, however, they hold out the possibility of resisting the destructive elements of our formation, reshaping our interactions, and becoming animal in alliances unimaginable within the present economic, political, cultural, and ecological order. The shift wrought by such changes would mark the emergence of a different realm—not a world breaking in from beyond, but the dismantling of our well-ordered perception of this world—the unveiling of an ecological apocalypse.

5

Animality in Sin and Redemption

> When the reasoning and human and ruling power is asleep, then the wild beast within us, gorged with meat or drink, starts up and having shaken off sleep, goes forth to satisfy his desires; and there is no conceivable folly or crime—not excepting incest or any other unnatural union, or parricide, or the eating of forbidden food—which at such a time, when he has parted company with all shame and sense, a man may not be ready to commit.
>
> —*Plato*[1]

As a theological metaphor, "the fall" places human sin into a vertical spatial logic, a movement from high to low. Not infrequently, this descending movement maps onto the vertical logic of a hierarchy of creatures. Even when they are not explicitly identified, animality and sin have a conceptual affinity throughout the Western theological imagination. The fall of human beings figures as a downward plunge from the heights of angelic beatitude—some original heavenly perfection—into the mire of animal encumberment and struggle. Although theologians obligate one another to affirm actual animals (and the state of human animality) as basically good, they are nevertheless apt to describe sinful behaviors, desires, and values as "beastly," "wild," "ravenous," "ferocious," in need of "taming," or "reining in." No one blinks as James Baldwin writes, "He hated his sins—even as he ran toward sin, even as he sinned. He hated the evil that lived in his body, and he feared it, as he feared and hated the lions of lust and longing that prowled the defenseless city of his mind."[2] The conceptual bonds between animality and sinfulness are so thick that they cannot be cut. The metaphorical traffic between animality and sinfulness runs on so many different pathways that it cannot be exhaustively traced out, much less contained through any determined act of the will or a vigilant linguistic discipline. Striving to live a good life remains synonymous with becoming not-animal or less-animal—a tacit conviction impressed upon every human through subtle and not-so-subtle articulations of mutual recognition, approbation, and reproach. Even if the association between sinfulness and animality cannot yet be broken, it can be resisted through the development of alternative configurations of thought.

In service of such resistance, this chapter offers an imaginative reversal in the theological polarity of the pervasive value hierarchy in which true humanity rises above animality. As the previous chapter took up human nature/identity and the following chapter takes up eschatological transformation, this chapter works in the middle of theological anthropology's narrative—sin and redemption. Instead of placing sinfulness *beneath* true humanity as an expression of our lower nature, this chapter's account of sin focuses upon metaphors of false transcendence and presumptive isolation. I suggest that our entrenchment within *proper humanity*—a concept in which we are all caught by virtue of our very subjectivity—is the substance of sinfulness. Fallenness, then, is participation in a pervasive ideological construction; it is the unavoidable performance of humanity in sovereign differentiation from animality. Redemption requires the undoing of this sovereign differentiation (or at least of its sovereign prerogative). More often than not, theological accounts of sin and redemption have provided a mechanism for the disavowal of human animality. By intervening at key moments in the anthropological narrative of sin and redemption, this chapter demonstrates the hidden possibility that, in the habitual division between humanity and animality, the work of God stands in alliance with animality against an increasingly lifeless and alienated humanity.

First, I draw on Giorgio Agamben, Louis Althusser, and Judith Butler to explain the operation of proper humanity as an ideological apparatus or anthropological machine, which not only produces a concept of humanity by means of contrast with animals but—more importantly—is the matrix of interpellation for human subjectivity. "Humanity" as described here, is not an essential condition shared by all human beings, but the contingent and malleable product of a historical process. Second, I offer a rereading of Genesis 2–3 as the narrative of sin's origin, suggesting that these chapters preserve a mythic countertestimony, a critical lament that contravenes the claims on human uniqueness for which these chapters are often marshaled. Finally, I will turn to the gap between human logos and divine Logos in the first chapter of John in order to suggest that redemption from sin—as made possible through the grace of God's incarnation—does not emancipate humanity into the realm of pure Reason, but enmeshes human beings more deeply within the politics of animal interdependence.

Sin: Humanity as an Ideological Apparatus

This chapter concludes by discussing the prologue to John's gospel, so it is fitting to begin by returning to Gregory of Nazianzus's erasure of animality from the Johannine text. Gregory takes the vivifying light of John (*phōs*)—the light whose substance is life (*zōē*)—and sets in its place the light of enlightenment. In chapter 1, I argue that life/animality is displaced for the sake of a divine-human bond found in discursive thought and speech (logos). Attention to *zōē* and the *zōon* in Gregory's texts reveals that animality is more central to Gregory's account of salvation than he acknowledges explicitly.

Giorgio Agamben's 1995 text *Homo Sacer* also tracks *zōē*, laboring to provide a conceptual genealogy of biopolitics in Western thought and practice.[3] Agamben begins with the distinction in Aristotle's *Metaphysics* between bare life (*zōē* or *zēn*) and the good life (*bios* or eu *zēn*).[4] The good life emerges through the political arrangement of prepolitical life, directing it toward higher goods like justice and friendship.[5] The goal of political life (*bios*) in the city is to provide a setting where the bare life (*zōē*) of eating, sleeping, breathing, and procreation may be arranged for deeper flourishing. By itself, bare life (*zōē*) is dissolute, concerned only with basic material urges; in order to become truly good, life must be structured according to the higher values of a life pattern (*bios*).

Politics does not originate, however, in the moment that a community organizes bare life (*zōē*) in order to found a city. Agamben inverts this commonsense myth of political origins, arguing that the production of bare life (*zōē*) as a category is the basic task of political order. "The fundamental activity of sovereign power is the production of bare life as originary political element and as threshold of articulation between nature and culture, *zōē* and *bios*."[6] For Agamben, life is always already political; for this reason, appeals to prepolitical bare life are necessarily ideological. Bare life functions as both an abyss and a foundation, the threat of political order's dissolution as well as its mythic origin. Western political discourse suspends political order over fear of the prepolitical and the extrapolitical—the chaotic, dangerous life outside the present order. Politics operates as a superstructure that claims to be making the life of citizenship (*bios*) better than bare life, *zōē*, but actually consolidates power precisely by perpetuating the distinction between the two. Suspending *bios* over *zōē* in this way generates an actual bodily threat: If one is excluded from the city, from the law, from the protection of the political arrangement, one, in fact, "returns" to a state of bare life.

Political life produces bare life, then, in two ways: As a foundation, bare life functions as a mythical ur-concept which marks political life as "better than" the brute life that "preceded" it, even if no concrete memory of such a life exists. As an abyss, political life produces bare life by exclusion, occasionally denuding someone of the protection of the law and exposing him to whatever death or misfortune might befall him. Political life actualizes bare life by "baring" lives and exposing them to harm, an operation that also reinforces the legitimating effect of the founding myth. The fundamental political relation, then, is the "ban" in which someone faces exile from the subjecthood, subjection, and subjectivity offered by citizenship under the law. Whether this exilic reduction to bare life is actually enacted or only threatened, it remains the basic structuring relation of political order.[7]

Both bare life and political life, then, are contingent productions of an overarching (ideological) scheme that captures human life through a series of divisions. A residual contradiction remains, however. Conceptually, *zōē* is both excluded from the city (because city life is not uncivilized brute life) and incorporated into the city as the "raw stuff" that is felicitously arranged. This productive "zone of indistinction"—where bare life is both excluded from the city and presumed as its foundation—represents a constitutive ambiguity that holds the city together.[8] Both the fragile precarity of political life and the supposition of bare life as a natural condition outside politics are useful fictions within a larger ideological mechanism.

Homo Sacer has been criticized on a number of points.[9] Most saliently for my purposes, Matthew Calarco questions how Agamben can locate the origin of Western politics in a distinction between bare life and political life, yet fail to analyze the ways that this distinction is conceptually bound up with human relations to animals.[10] The ban of animals from human societies (and the reduction of animal life to property within them) is almost certainly a more original political relation than Agamben's originary intrahuman ban—and a model for it. Before *zōē* can be named as bare (human) life, it must be named animality; *zōē* is first of all the life of the *zōon*—the animal. Animality has always been the substance of the threat of the ban: the person exiled from the city must contend with the animals who have already been excluded, be devoured by them or live like them.

While *Homo Sacer* does not consider the origin of biopolitics in relation to the human-animal distinction, Agamben's later text, *The Open,* provides for just such a connection. Agamben's analysis in *The Open* repeats the analytical maneuvers of *Homo Sacer,* but does so with regard to the conceptual difference between humanity and animality. *The Open* argues that humanity is not a stable entity with a readily discoverable "nature," but is instead the ongoing operation of what Agamben calls an "anthropological machine."[11] Mirroring political life's inclusive exclusion of bare life—through the operation of what could be called a "biopolitical machine"—the anthropological machine establishes a "zone of indistinction" between human and animal, in which animality is both included as the "raw stuff" of humanity, and excluded inasmuch as humanity is supposed to rise above "the brutes."[12] The machine safeguards the conceptual integrity of the category "humanity" by discerning and disavowing an inner animality. Distinguishing an internal animal part (mute desire, passion, irrationality, bodily functions, etc.) from a kernel of true humanity (rationality, language, self-awareness, openness to a transcendent horizon, etc.) stabilizes the identity of humanity by offering a normative ideal, but it does so at the cost of setting animals under the mark of categorical alterity. In the same way that both bare life and political life are ideological productions of a biopolitical order, both animality and humanity are ideological productions of the anthropological machine.

The tight structural parallel in the arguments of *Homo Sacer* and *The Open* justifies reading the two texts together. Doing so makes it clear that bare life (*zōē*) and animality occupy the same structural position within Agamben's analysis, as do political life and humanity. Both the biopolitical machine and the anthropological machine operate by way of a discourse (logos) that safeguards the exceptional status of the higher terms (*bios,* proper humanity, human beings) by constructing something lower (*zōē,* human animality, "the animals") from which authentic humanity arises. *Humanity* is produced as a pure category through the discernment/construction of a second category *animality,* which lies at the foundation of human life but must be controlled or excluded in order to live an authentically human life. The human is the animal who purports to have overcome its animality.[13]

Animality is thus both the bare life of the human being as a living organism and that which is excluded and controlled under the norms, expectations, boundaries and threats of properly human life. Just as "life" is political through and through, every human being is always already enmeshed within humanity insofar as the discursive superstructure of civilization is inseparable from language acquisition, enculturation, and subject formation.[14] Nevertheless, closely examining the conceptual interval between human beings and humanity reveals that humanity's enfolding of human beings is never entirely smooth, never completely successful, and never equally distributed.[15] As Judith Butler notes:

> I propose that we consider the way "the human" works as a differential norm: let us think of the human as a value and a morphology that may be allocated and retracted, aggrandized, personified, degraded and disavowed, elevated and affirmed. The norm continues to produce the nearly impossible paradox of a human who is no human, or of the human who effaces the human as it is otherwise known. Wherever there is the human, there is the inhuman. . . . Some humans take their humanness for granted, while others struggle to gain access to it. The term 'human' is constantly doubled, exposing the ideality and coercive character of the norm: some humans qualify as human; some humans do not.[16]

Thus, this convergence of the anthropological machine with the biopolitical machine means that sovereign power retains the capacity to strip a human being of his or her place in humanity (or simply disregard it) so that someone is perceived formally as human, but treated morally and politically "like an animal."[17]

In summary, this exposition of Agamben contributes five points to this chapter's upending of the polarity of animality and humanity around sin: First, that "humanity" operates as an ideological category (ideological because it purports to reveal a common essence or nature, but in fact operates as a regulatory political norm); second, that every ideological notion of humanity remains dependent upon equally ideological conceptions of animals and animality; third, that the ideological correlation of humanity and animality lies at the root of politics generally; fourth, that politics and biopolitics always shape ecopolitics and humanity's concrete relations with other creatures; and fifth, that the ideological division of humanity from animality is always partial and conflicted, since it operates through the creation of a zone of indistinction that simultaneously includes and excludes animality in humanity.[18] Those points of conflict and contradiction, I am persuaded, are the points at which the anthropological machine might be jammed and and inverted.

From this general account of humanity and animality as ideological categories, it is worthwhile to think further about the way these categories operate in subject formation. In this regard, Agamben himself turns to Louis Althusser's concept of the ideological apparatus: "[Ideological] apparatuses are not a mere accident in which humans are caught by chance, but rather are rooted in the very process of 'humanization' that made 'humans' out of the animals we classify under the rubric *Homo sapiens*. In fact, the event that has produced the human constitutes, for the living being, something like a division, which reproduces in some way the division that the *oikonomia* introduced in God between being and action."[19] For Althusser, the concept of an ideological apparatus played a role in explaining the conditions of economic production. Specifically, he became interested in the conditions that provide for the reproduction of the subjects of economic labor—the workers, managers, and clerks who, generation after generation, "take their places" in an economic system. Thus, Althusser articulates how a pervasive and pluriform ideological regime might be internalized and iterated in the lives of its subjects.

Althusser became convinced that no social institution (school, church, business, or neighborhood association) was innocent of a role in the ideological formation of subjects for the continuation of the economic order of capitalism.[20] Ideological apparatuses operate when basic norms and patterns of subjectivity get communicated, imposed, and enforced through everyday interactions. The ways in which we greet, praise, scold, include, exclude, entertain, and describe one another communicate what we perceive in one another and what we expect of one another. These perceptions and expectations come to structure material and economic relations through soft but inescapably persistent forms of compulsion.[21] The common terms for this process are subjectivization and interpellation. As the last of a series of six theses, Althusser explains the subject formation of an individual as a process analogous to Agamben's inclusive exclusion of animality within humanity: "Thus ideology hails or interpellates individuals as subjects. . . . Individuals are always-already interpellated by ideology as subjects, which necessarily leads us to one last proposition: individuals are always-already subjects. Hence individuals are 'abstract' with respect to the subjects which they always already are. This proposition might seem paradoxical."[22] Interpellation does not take place in a particular moment when ideology subsumes a previously innocent individual; rather, ideology pervades the entire process of subject formation. To rephrase Althusser's sixth thesis according to the form of Agamben's arguments in *Homo Sacer* and *The Open*, we can assert that ideology forms subjects by suspending particular norms of subjectivity over the abstract and formal idea (always a fiction) of an individual human being who is unrestrained by such norms. Althusser (with deference to Jacques Lacan) sees the interpellating operation of ideology as bound up with language and language acquisition.[23] As students learn to write and speak effectively and beautifully, Althusser suggests that their schools are teaching them a "know-how (*savoir-faire*), but in terms which ensure *subjection to the ruling ideology* or the mastery of its practice."[24] Judith Butler pays special attention to this disjunctive "or," suggesting that subjection and mastery here amount to the same thing. To "master" a way of speaking is also to become subject to the constraints upon intelligibility borne by the semiotic range and gaps of that discourse. Becoming a subject through subjection to ideology is not to *lose* one's agency, but to gain it; as Butler notes, "submission . . . is paradoxically marked by mastery itself. . . . The lived simultaneity of submission as mastery and mastery as submission is the condition of possibility for the emergence of the subject itself."[25] Analogously, to master and perform the set of skills required to participate in human society is also to become subject to some particular, contingent (if nevertheless pervasive) framing of humanity. Humanity is performed and reiterated in every expression of human subjectivity, and to speak and act in ways that do not fit neatly within standard frames of humanity (to fail in one's mastery) is to risk exclusion from the human community (the stripping of subjectivity and agency).

The ideological regimes that enable us to recognize one another as intelligibly human offer great comfort. These regimes are nevertheless powerful constraints on human life insofar as the boundaries of recognizability are regulated with violence.[26] "Humanity" as an ideological apparatus of subject formation is bound up with the distinction between humanity and animality and a concomitant subordination and disavowal of the latter. Failing to perform "humanity" according to entrenched norms of recognition bears significant social, economic, and political repercussions.[27] Animals and animality are bound up with the very structure of human subjectivity and agency, even if only as the abjected and disavowed point of contrast.[28] Butler's concern for the differential application of norms of subjectivity in her investigation into why some lives are "grievable" while others are treated as hardly even statistically significant, then, turns out to be integrally connected to the suspension of humanity over animality. Butler herself acknowledges that animal life—with rare exceptions—is paradigmatically not grievable.[29]

The mechanistic metaphors employed here—the "matrices," "machines," and "apparatuses"—bear several claims. First, they express our lack of control over the formative conditions that determine the shape of our subjectivity and agency.[30] We are, even before our births, caught up in cultural patterns far larger than ourselves. We cannot radically alter the conditions in which we and others (including the children we raise) are formed as subjects and agents—which means that we can only describe this formation from within its aftereffects.[31] Simultaneously, however, these mechanistic metaphors also seek to convey that these formative operations are neither necessary nor inevitable in their specific details. We can certainly imagine that we could have been formed otherwise; the particular configuration of human subjectivity as it is leveraged over animality is neither "natural" nor "essential." *Some* formation is inevitable, but not *this* formation. Butler writes: "If a life is produced according to the norms by which life is recognized, this implies neither that everything about a life is produced according to such norms nor that we must reject the idea that there is a remainder of 'life'—suspended and spectral—that limns and haunts every normative instance of life."[32] Thinking with mechanistic metaphors denaturalizes the process of subject formation and names it as an operation. Attention to the gaps and remainders at the edges of the operation of interpellation can empower resistance to its most dominant and destructive forms. For human subjects, there is no "outside" to humanity, no access to animality that is not already constructed as a point of contrast for human agency and subjectivity. Yet, to perceive that humanity is a set of overlapping ideological norms which imperfectly and incompletely form our subjectivity in relation to animals and animality is to see that these norms are perpetuated through repetition or reiteration. The iterability of humanity as a norm means that while we may be bound to repeat our performance of humanity, we can always do so with a difference, some small resistance that pries at the cracks in the scaffolding. We cannot inhabit any subjectivity outside our humanity, but attending to animality in a way that resists its degradation does tend to make humanity appear all the more contingent, all the more plastic, all the more narrow and limited.

The rather extensive philosophical prolegomena above is necessary to support my theological claim that humanity—in its operation as an ideological apparatus—is the substance of original sin, a regime that entraps human beings in patterns of self-destructive and eco-destructive enmity with animality. As a step toward that theological claim, I would like to highlight a number of features of traditional accounts of original sin that resonate with the mechanistic metaphors for subject formation described just above.

Theological accounts of original sin emphasize several points:[33] First, human depravity is radical. Outside of the grace of God, human beings cannot attain moral or spiritual purity because even the most noble and honorable aspects of human life are, in some manner, corrupted. Sin is rooted in the very structure of human subjectivity. Second, human sin is universal and affects every human being. There is no community to which one could flee and escape from sinfulness, which is not to say that sinfulness is distributed evenly across peoples and cultures. Third, human sin is structural rather than merely intentional. This is to say that sin affects human thought, will, and desire prior to any conscious decision to sin *and* that individuals are complicit in social forms of sin even where they remain ignorant of (or even opposed to) sinful social structures. Fourth, human sin is accidental to human nature and not essential. God neither creates human beings as sinful creatures nor desires human beings to be sinful. Despite its pervasiveness within human life, sin is something "added" to (or subtracted from) human life—a miasma or fog that obscures human nature, or a wound that weakens human beings. A redeemed and sinless human being—for all the difference that redemption makes—is still essentially a human being.

Agamben, Althusser, and Butler are not offering accounts of human sin and it would be deceptive to claim any simple equivalence between the formative operation of ideology and traditional Christian teaching on sin. Sin is a *problem* in Christian theology, a problem that originates in a "fall." As its counterpoint, salvation names a condition outside human sin and a solution that counteracts the negative effects of sin. In contrast, there is no time before the ideological structures of subject formation, nor any "fall" into them. There is also no "outside" and no "solution" to formative ideology—a human being who did not participate in any recognized form of subjectivity, knowledge, and sociality could only be psychotic or feral. Despite these important differences, I want to think constructively within the resonance between the notions of original sin and formative ideology.

In the following section, I argue that humanity is the substance of original sin insofar as it disavows human animality. Like original sin, humanity frames every human thought and action, it encompasses every human being, it is the matrix in which human subjectivity and agency is formed, and yet, as an ideological apparatus it can be distinguished from the life of the human being as such. The risk in this connection is one that I mean to face squarely: As the end of humanity and the end of sin, salvation must be madness itself (as seen from within any human discourse). It may nevertheless be described as a particular kind of madness: not the absence of subject formation altogether, but a mode of creaturely formation in which animality and divinity dwell together without any regard for humanity's hierarchies and disavowals. Such an account of sin and redemption reverse the polarity of the traditional hierarchy that always sets humanity above animality. In order to sketch such an account, I turn to Genesis 2–3, the classical textual site for describing humanity's "fall."

Genesis 2–3 and the Fall of/into Humanity

In the Christian tradition, Genesis 2–3 is the classic textual locus of humanity's fall into sin. The doctrine of the fall describes a transformation of human nature from a state of original perfection (for the Augustinian tradition) or a state of original immaturity and innocence (for the Irenaean tradition) into a state of spiritual and moral decay. In addition to serving as a textual site for the doctrine of the fall, Genesis 2–3 have often functioned as an origin myth that explains and reinforces the difference between human beings and other creatures.[34] It is remarkable, however, how seldom the Eden narrative is read *simultaneously* as the narrative of the fall and as an account of human differentiation.[35] The two uses or two meanings of the text have been carefully kept apart. When we cross the wires and short-circuit these two uses of Genesis 2–3, then the marks of human exceptionalism begin to appear as the substance of human moral and spiritual sickness. Assertions of human uniqueness cannot be so easily distinguished from the condition of human fallenness.

The classical Christian interpretation of Genesis 2–3—as the story of a change from original innocence or perfection to perversity, sickness, and spiritual decay—is far from the only viable reading. Nevertheless, it is very difficult to hear this story otherwise because this traditional interpretation of Genesis 2–3 has been repeated so often and the concept of the fall lies so deep within the structure of Christian theology. Stepping off the well-established interpretive track for a moment may shed fresh light on a too-familiar text. The traditional Christian reading of Genesis 2–3 as the story of humanity's fall into a state of inescapable corruption is far from the *only* viable interpretation.

It is hard to find a theme more pervasive in the Hebrew scriptures than human disobedience of God's instructions, yet the Hebrew scriptures never refer back to the Eden narrative as the origin of human wickedness.[36] Nor does the rabbinic tradition read Genesis 2–3 as the story of a cataclysmic transformation of human nature. The taking of the forbidden fruit seems to be one instance of disobedience among many, evidence of the "wicked inclination" of the human heart, but not its origin.[37] Likewise, historical-critical scholarship on Genesis regards the notion of the fall as a theological accretion that overdetermines the details of an enigmatic and loosely woven narrative. Claus Westermann claims, "The common opinion that the passage describes 'the fall' reads into the narrative its own understanding of sin and then finds it there step-by-step."[38] For these Jewish and historical-critical interpreters, the question is not whether Genesis 2–3 describes a tragic act of human disobedience (never in doubt), but rather, whether that act of disobedience can be marked as the *origin* of sin and evil in human life. Reading Genesis 2–3 as the origin of sin requires a theological reading that retrojects a Pauline account of sin and death in human nature back onto an older text whose outline can certainly bear such an overlay, but whose details do not convey it.[39]

It is important to establish that Genesis 2–3 *can* (and perhaps *should*) be read otherwise precisely because this chapter offers an adjustment of the traditional interpretation—but it does not do so through a historical-critical argument pressing toward the original meaning of the text. Insofar as the fall is absolutely essential to the edifice of Christian theology and its various conceptions of redemption, the dominant theological reading of Genesis 2–3 has too much cultural momentum to be effectively corrected on historical-critical grounds. However, the recognition that reading Genesis 2–3 as the story of the corruption of human nature is, from a historical critical perspective, already a misreading opens up space for a catachrestic misreading of my own. To repeat the dominant theological misreading with a few critical differences unsettles that traditional interpretation on its own terms by calling attention to the connections that the traditional reading must overlook and misrecognize.[40]

If Genesis 2–3 does indeed narrate humanity's fall, I will suggest, the sinfulness into which humanity falls is not enmeshment in animality but pretension to a transcendent exceptionalism within creation. Again, this theological reinterpretation does *not* uncover the authentic historical-critical meaning of Genesis 2–3, but resists the habitual association of animality and sinfulness from within the framework of the predominant Christian theological interpretation itself. The dominant theological misreading begins to collapse under its own weight once one sees how this text refuses to associate sinfulness with animality.

Genesis 2–3 contain a veritable catalogue of the traits and capacities that cut the human-animal distinction in Western theological/philosophical discourse: knowledge of death; language; personal sexual intimacy (over against mere reproduction); moral reasoning; affinity for the divine; nudity, shame, and clothing; and self-reflective consciousness. Remarkably, as each of these traits distinguish humanity from animality in the narrative, they are *simultaneously* linked to human disobedience and expulsion from Eden. Thus, Genesis 2–3 does not authorize anthropological exceptionalism but offers a lament for humanity's "fall" into self-differentiation, a mythic countertestimony that resists humanity's pretension to transcendence.

Genesis 2–3 is not a perfectly clear window with a view into a prelapsarian past, nor a divinely revealed escape hatch from the cognitive enclosure of human fallenness. If these chapters describe a fall then this account, too, is written in the language of fallen humanity, a retrospective record of a change long past. The text is more a lament for all that has gone wrong than a suspense-filled thriller whose ending remains uncertain until the very last moment. From the moment of the prohibition against eating from the tree of the knowledge of good and evil, one knows that the fruit will be taken. All of the story's elements build momentum toward the tale's tragic conclusion in transgression and banishment.[41]

God sets the human in a garden full of good food, prohibiting only the fruit of the tree of the knowledge of good and evil in the middle of the garden. The consequences are clear: "for in the day that you eat of it you shall die" (2:17). The nature of this death has always puzzled interpreters because the humans do not fall dead when they eat from the tree, but continue to live. So this death has been variously explained as a spiritual death, a loss of original immortality, a living death, or a new existential knowledge of death. Without trying to adjudicate precisely what sort of death is attached to the transgression, it is worth noting that death and knowledge of death have long functioned in philosophy and theology as a mark of categorical human uniqueness. For Heidegger, humanity (*Dasein*) is structured by a being-toward-death, while animals merely pass away without any awareness of death as such.[42] Other thinkers argue that humanity alone possesses foreknowledge of death and lives in anticipation of death.[43] Even as it may be a generative source of creativity and cultural accomplishment, humanity's unique anticipation of death appears in Genesis 2–3 as a function of human transgression.

When the solitude of the human appears as a problem, God says, "It is not good that the human should be alone" (2:18). God resolves to make a partner and helper for the human and creates all the animals of the field and the birds of the air, expectantly bringing them forward "to see what [the human] would call them" (2:19). Traditionally, this naming scene has been taken as a sign of humanity's dominance over the other animals.[44] Without disputing this basic interpretation, I want to suggest that the story's narrative frame might cast an air of lament rather than triumphalism over the episode. The human being, sole possessor of language, stands back in a posture of sovereignty and assigns names to the creatures while God listens. Animal life is transformed into meaning before God through the words of the human being. In order to evade the idea that the human ought to find genuine community among the other animals, the traditional interpretation must assume that God brings the animals before the human in naivety or pedantry. Either God cannot see the (obvious?) human superiority that would prevent real human community with other animals or God must demonstrate this superiority one animal species at a time. If one does not evade the possibility of genuine creaturely community, however, then this first use of language appears suddenly tragic. The human does not call any of the animals "friend" or "partner," but instead stands back, using language to set the abyss of sovereignty between himself and the animals, objectively giving the creatures names, so that "whatever the human called every living creature, that was its name" (2:19). Contravening God's efforts to incorporate the human within a creaturely community, human language (carnivorous even in its first instance) structures human life around claims to sovereignty, mastery, and order.[45] Bonhoeffer writes, "It was Adam's first occasion of pain that these brothers and sisters whom Adam loved did not fulfill the human being's own expectation. They remained a strange world to Adam; indeed they remain, for all their nature as siblings, creatures subjected to, named by, and ruled over by Adam. The human person remains alone."[46] Human language sets the deadening distance of objectivity between the human and the other animals. Human language—in all of its distinctiveness—drives humanity to the brink of the fall.

Curiously, the origin of sexual difference stands within the same narrative episode as the naming of the animals.[47] Because the human finds neither helper nor partner among the other creatures, God splits the human being in two: *ha'adam* becomes *ish* and *ishah*; the human is man and woman. Hans Urs von Balthasar offers a traditional interpretation of this conjunction, asserting the uniqueness of (heteronormative) human sexuality: "Even Adam, according to the legend of Paradise, although created in the fullness of God's grace, had an unsatisfied longing until God had given him Eve. Adam transcended and sought through the whole of nature—naming and hence knowing it—looking for that which would bring him fulfillment and completion. He did not find it. It is strange that human nature, obviously quite different from the animals which were already created two by two, has to long for the other."[48] However, another reading remains possible. If, with Bonhoeffer, we read the Eden narrative as a kind of lamenting prehistory of the fall, then the origins of sexual difference and marriage are not straightforwardly celebratory.[49] Up to this point in the text it has not been possible to identify the human (*ha adam*) as male or female. The man (*ish*), however, pulls off a retrospective gendering of the sovereign subject who named the animals by claiming to have been there first all along, "This at last is bone of my bones and flesh of my flesh; this one shall be called Woman, for out of Man this one was taken!" (2:23). There is something ominous even in this "honeymoon" phase of relations between man and woman. Following the refusal of community with the animals, the man's celebratory recognition of the woman's sameness expresses entitlement, appropriation, and control. The text is capacious enough to carry a subtle lament about the problematic ordering of relations between men and women, even as it was written in patriarchy and is used to cement patriarchal order.[50] Adam's pretensions to sovereignty and primacy inscribe hierarchy across both animal difference and sexual difference—fractures in the creaturely community that are only exacerbated in the history of human transgression.[51] Humanity will leave the garden wearing the skins of the creatures with whom they could not make genuine community (3:21).

The tree that is forbidden to the humans is called the tree of the *knowledge of good and evil*.[52] Prudential wisdom and moral reasoning have frequently been claimed (inaccurately) as capacities for which there are no counterparts among nonhuman animals. Ostensibly, knowing good and evil sets the human above the animals, who remain amoral and lack prudential foresight. Bonhoeffer identifies knowing good and evil with human ethics, and regards ethics itself as a system that usurps the judgment and grace that properly belong to God. Thus Bonhoeffer paradoxically claims that "the first task of Christian ethics is to supersede that knowledge."[53] If humanity's unique capacity for moral reasoning is what allows humans to judge one another good and bad, engage in self-condemnation and self-approbation, and presume to know what is best for creation, then humanity's knowledge of good and evil is a false pretension to sovereign transcendence.[54] Similarly, after God constitutes the human being as a living creature (*nephesh*) like the other animals with the divine breath/spirit (2:7), the serpent tempts Eve with the promise that transgression will make her "like God, knowing good and evil" (3:5, 3:22).[55] God's recognition that the human beings are "like one of us" instigates the decree that banishes the human beings from the garden. In this light, humanity's claims on a God-like capacity for moral discernment are the mark of pretension. Dissatisfied with being a living creature like the other animals (*nephesh*) sustained by the very breath of God, humanity transgresses God's commands in order to grasp at a God-like transcendence over fellow creatures.

Whereas once the humans were "naked and not ashamed" (2:25), as the humans ate the fruit of the tree of the knowledge of good and evil, "the eyes of both were opened, and they knew that they were naked; and they sewed fig leaves together and made loincloths for themselves" (3:7). The "problem" of nudity appears almost exclusively on human bodies—an unclothed animal does not generally appear "naked." Yet the problem of nudity is intimately bound up with human animality. We are inclined to say that someone stripped naked in public has been dehumanized and that someone who shamelessly bares their body in public lacks a self-respect that belongs properly to human dignity.[56] If we resist the traditional interpretive move to spiritualize original nudity as a cipher for innocence and shame as a cipher for moral guilt, then the uniqueness of the nudity, modesty, shame, and clothing complex among human beings is not a mark of human dignity but a primary consequence of human transgression.[57]

In a maneuver closely related to their new shameful self-awareness, the humans hear God walking through the garden and run to hide themselves. On the traditional Christian reading, their hiding has been understood as a sign of self-consciousness and a guilty conscience. Previous chapters have examined claims that self-consciousness and self-reflectivity are marks of human uniqueness relative to the animals. If these capacities are manifest in human hiding, Genesis 3 hardly celebrates them. Bonhoeffer connects self-reflective conscience to the knowledge of good and evil as a mark of fallenness rather than exaltation:

> This flight, Adam's hiding away from God, we call conscience. Before the fall there was no conscience. . . . Conscience chases humankind away from God into its secure hiding place. Here, far away from God, humankind itself plays the role of being judge and in this way seeks to evade God's judgment. Humankind now lives truly out of the resources of its own good and evil, its own innermost dividedness from itself. . . . Conscience is not the voice of God within sinful human beings; instead it is precisely their defense against this voice.[58]

Bonhoeffer understands this hiding not as the act of a guilty conscience *avoiding* the judgment of God, but rather as a sovereign self-reflective effort to *preempt* God's judgment, rendering it redundant and unnecessary.[59] The structure of fallen human subjectivity, in all its unique self-reflexivity, then, has rendered God unnecessary precisely by way of sovereign self-consciousness.

Finally, the humans are cast out of the garden under a stern pronouncement of God. The woman hears of the pain of childbirth and of subjection to the rule of her husband; the man hears that from now on he will not feed himself by reaching out for fruit from the earth, but will labor over crops with his sweat dripping into thorns and briars. Insofar as labor, toil, and the (re)production of surplus are taken to be distinctive human traits, Genesis 2–3 presents them as the consequences of human transgression rather than as a height of human exceptionalism. Humanity's unique conception of itself standing over against nature as a store of resources to be exploited or as a danger to be fought betoken a presumption to (false) transcendence and a network of broken relations. The Eden narrative is a lament for these strained relations rather than a celebration of human labor's transformative potential.

Even though a majority of the Christian theological tradition regards sin as a descent into animality, Genesis 2–3 links every defining characteristic of anthropological exceptionalism to transgression and the breakdown of an original community. If—mythologically or otherwise—the Eden narrative contains a fall of the sort theorized under the name of original sin, then such a fall cannot be easily distinguished from assertions of human uniqueness. Put otherwise, Genesis 2–3 is not the story of humanity's fall *into* animality but its fall *out* of animality.

Genesis 2–3 as Origin of Sovereign Differentiation

All the pieces are now in place to draw connections between the chapter's initial discussion of humanity as an ideological regime in which human subjects are interpellated, the doctrine of original sin, and the rereading of Genesis 2–3. Through culturally pervasive and rhetorically effective associations between fallenness and animality—whether through metaphors of beastly desires or of self-discipline as taming, tightening the reins, or shepherding—traditional theological discourse of the fall denigrates human animality in order to establish anthropological exceptionalism. The theoretical distance between an idealized, unfallen humanity and actually existing fallen human beings is projected as an abyss between proper humanity (with all its exceptional capacities untarnished and intact) and the animals (along with debased human animality).[60] Yet Genesis 2–3 construes humanity's self-proclaimed uniqueness and sovereignty with fundamental ambivalence. Such self-important claims are implicated in human transgression and expulsion from paradise. While human uniqueness has often been read as a fact written into the natural order of creation, here it appears as a function of human fallenness, an ideological assertion of sovereignty, and a (false) pretense to transcendence.

The theological discourse of the fall and fallenness helps to establish a certain homology between the internal political struggle between humanity and animality and the ecopolitics through which human sovereignty governs the lives of subjected creatures/resources as far as it is able. The unpredictable world and its goods are ordered to serve human needs and the unpredictable animality within human life is ordered for the sake of conformity to proper humanity and its social order.[61] In both registers, animal disorder becomes a trope through which properly humanized order is maintained and enforced.

To write that ideological claims on uniqueness are the substance of human fallenness is to take sides with those theologians who identify sinfulness with humanity's uniquely destructive refusal to find its place on a plane with other creatures rather than above them.[62] This account also takes sides against those anthropologies in which authentic humanity is realized by subjecting animality to regimes of management that lead to the grace-enabled transcendence of the limits of finitude—particularly where proper human uniqueness effectively leaves animality behind.[63] My rereading of Genesis 2–3 stands in continuity with the traditional interpretation by claiming that human fallenness affects the structure of human subjectivity all the way down. Human fallenness is more than a set of destructive habits or a (conscious?) choice to refuse kinship with fellow creatures. Because humanity is founded in the disavowal of animality, ecocidal tendencies are endemic to the structure of human subjectivity. The logic of transcendence at the subjective level repeats itself in the logic of governance at the ecopolitical level, where humanity's transcendence (sovereignty) is expressed as stewardship—divine sovereignty deputized and transferred onto human sovereignty for the (supposedly) proper management of animality and created resources. Original sin and proper humanity are two sides of the same coin.

In Christian theology, accounts of sin and redemption are always linked. The movement of thought runs dialectically from fallenness to redemption (or from redemption back to an account of the fallenness that preceded it). Having identified the ideology of humanity with a fallen condition of human beings, the next section carries on by thinking of the incarnation of the Logos and God's redemption of creation as an intervention on behalf of animality (including human beings) against fallen humanity, rather than the isolated redemption of a humanity that already transcends the rest of creation.

The Incarnation of the Logos as the End of Humanity

John's gospel claims: "The light came unto its own; but its own did not receive it" (1:11). In Christian doctrine, the "Word becoming flesh" has served as the scriptural starting point for the incarnation as much as Genesis 2–3 has been the textual site of the fall. John's gospel begins by placing a Logos at the very beginning, a Word sounding out the earliest origins of creation and measuring up even to God. After expansively asserting that everything in existence resonates with echoes of the Logos, having come into being through it, John narrows his view and writes that this Logos is life (*zōē*), and that this life is the light of human beings. Human life (*zōē*) radiates as light from the Logos of God.

Almost from the beginning, however, something is amiss; all is not light and life. John quickly modulates into a minor key and writes of a darkness that refuses the light. The Logos receives—at best—a mixed reception in the world created through it. The Logos is neither recognized nor received by its very own. The world of humanity, the cosmos, wraps itself in darkness; humanity fails to recognize the Logos as its very life.

Despite John's ominous tone, logos has been highly esteemed within the history of Western thought. Whether the term is rendered Reason, Speech, Argument, Thought, Logic, or Discourse, it hardly seems a marginal and under-valued human capacity. Contrary to John, logos has not historically lacked for recognition, prestige, and honor. But perhaps there are two radically different logoi in play here?

The crucifixion of the Logos-in-flesh by a world that nevertheless highly esteems logos can be explained if it is another, specifically human logos that rejects the light and life from the divine Logos. In point of fact, the remainder of John's gospel goes on to describe a deep antagonism between the Logos of God and the Reason, Speech, or Discourse of humanity. Humanity's own logos stands in opposition to the *zōē* with which the Logos illuminates human life. The luminous *zōē* of John's text cuts between Logos and logos. Humanity lives out of a light and a life that never quite fits into human thought or language. Humanity bends around an abyssal *zōē* which it can never understand but which nevertheless animates it.

As with the rereading of Genesis 2–3 in the previous section, I am not recovering John's original meaning here, whatever that may have been.[64] Rather, inasmuch as John's prologue functions as a locus classicus for the doctrine of the incarnation, the text haunts every account of God becoming flesh. The whole Christian theological tradition labors under the weight of John's first chapter. Christian thinkers quickly took advantage of affinities between John's vocabulary and the philosophical vocabulary of the Stoics. The embedding of Stoic arguments within Christian theological discourse produced assumptions of continuity between human *logos* and the divine *Logos* and the assumption that nonhuman animals universally irrational.[65] Indeed "irrational" (*alogoi*) became a substantivized adjective commonly used to refer to animals generally.

In chapter 1, I examine Gregory of Nazianzus's assumption of continuity between the divine Logos and human logos, arguing that Gregory had to displace *zōē* (life) from the illuminating work of the Logos in order to establish this continuity. But the (quasi-Stoic) assumption of a unique affinity between divinity and humanity in logos extends long after Gregory in the Christian tradition. Even an antiphilosophical theologian such as Martin Luther presumes that human life must be categorically different than animal life, for otherwise one would be led to the (to him, completely absurd) conclusion that God would share something with the animals.[66] The incarnation is one doctrinal linchpin of anthropological exceptionalism; God redeems humanity because of something like a familial obligation.[67] Whatever the quantitative excess of divine Logos over human logos, a qualitative continuity remains one of the bedrock assumptions of traditional Christian anthropology rooted in the Johannine vocabulary of incarnation.

If we depart from this Stoic logic and suppose that there is an abyss between human logos and divine Logos which prevents humanity from recognizing and accepting the *zōē* of the divine Logos as its own, then from an ecological standpoint we can say that the logos of humanity is destructively bent around its own ideological delusions.[68] At present, the dominant logos of humanity presents a great threat to the integrity of *zōē* on the planet. Judging by its operation humanity's logos neither recognizes nor values the *zōē* of the world, not even the life of future human generations. As the interdependent relations between populations of living creatures are irreparably dismantled—in an instant through nuclear war or gradually through a warming climate and material exploitation—it is the celebrated heights of human *logos*, its cultural, technological, economic, and political accomplishments that are responsible for this destruction, and not momentary lapses and oversights. If, as John claims, the Logos of God is the *zōē* of human beings, then the operations of human logos are significantly endangering the future of that human *zōē*, to say nothing of the even greater dangers facing nonhuman creatures.

Val Plumwood argues that a crisis of rationality—a problem of logos—underlies the pluriform anthropogenic ecological crisis, rather than a more superficial problem with the use and misuse of technology.[69] She explains that the dominant forms of reason and rationality in Western global capitalism are systematically distorted and myopic.[70] For instance, within economic discourse, presumptions about "rational" profit-maximizing behavior justify exploitative labor practices, externalized production costs (through pollution and public subsidy), and shortsighted efforts to raise quarterly profits for the sake of shareholders. Driven by a need to sustain perpetual growth, the rationality of the market and the rationality of geopolitics are constitutively blind to the long-term well-being of the earth's ecosystems and therefore also to the long-term well-being of most living creatures, human beings included.[71] Where "rational" behavior requires constantly deferring questions of ecocide and species-level suicide until they are met unavoidably in disaster and crisis, there is a strange rationality at work.[72] The dominant forms of human reason, then, are ideologically self-enclosed, delusional, and self-destructive. Plumwood emphasizes that her sustained critique of "rationality" in its current form is not a rejection of reason altogether nor an embrace of a kind of absurd primitivist anti-intellectualism. It is, rather, a recognition of the need for different forms of reasoning, patterns of rationality embedded in the long-term integrity of complex ecosystems rather than short-term gain.[73]

If the "world" (*kosmos*) that misrecognizes and rejects the divine Logos-in-flesh is ordered by human logos, then we can read John's prologue as suggestive of a chasm between the logos of humanity and the divine Logos who is also the light (*phōs*) and the life (*zōē*) of the world. With a different vocabulary, Plumwood's ecological analysis—exemplary among many others—marks a dysfunctional mismatch between the logos of humanity and the Logos through whom all creatures were made. This reading of John's text correlates well with the rereading of Genesis 2–3 offered above. The hallmarks of anthropological exceptionalism—including the logos of human thought and speech—are signs of original sin insofar as they are disavowals of the animality/life (*zōē*) of the divine Logos.

Inasmuch as the incarnation is the site where Christian theology works out an account of redemption, the remainder of this chapter grapples with the meaning of the incarnation in the context of this fundamental rupture between Logos and logos—the living Word-in-flesh and the ideological apparatus of humanity. The incarnation of the Logos in specifically *human* flesh has often figured as an endorsement or ratification of humanity's uniqueness in creation, an affirmation of a special bond between humanity and God that is not shared with the other creatures. In contrast, my goal here is to sketch a counterreception of John's prologue that would refigure the place of animals and animality within Christian thinking about the incarnation. The incarnation of the Logos should be understood as divine judgment upon humanity's ideological presumption to sovereign uniqueness and the redemptive means by which humanity might be turned from its destructive ideology.

The stakes of this interpretive argument emerge in these questions: Should God's incarnation be understood as a celestial endorsement of the exceptional status of humanity over against all other creatures, or as the deconstruction of humanity from within, a salvifically subversive maneuver undertaken for the sake of all God's beloved creatures? If the divine Logos is the life (*zōē*) of the world, would we better understand John's "eternal life" (*zōē aiōnios*) as an extension and exaltation of the unique logos of humanity, raised into an exclusive fellowship with God? Or, should we understand "eternal life" (*zōē aiōnios*) as the life of the *zōon* (animal), a redemption that first and foremost concerns animality?

As the incarnate *zōē*-Logos of creation, the becoming-human of the Logos does not validate humanity's ideological projects but brings near God's judgment upon humanity. David Clough has argued persuasively that the incarnation of God in flesh has salvific significance for all creatures and cannot establish a boundary between human beings and other animals.[74] Just as the particularity of Jesus's male, Palestinian, Jewish flesh has not (over the long term) been understood to restrict the boundaries of the redeemed community to those who share these particular characteristics, it is a falsely narrow view that cuts other creatures off from redemption on the basis of Jesus's human flesh.[75] Clough takes recourse to Karl Barth's expansive notion of election (while resisting the ecological erasure inherent within Barth's anthropological exceptionalism) to argue that all creatures are elect, chosen by God and beloved.[76]

In order to work out a narrative of sin and redemption that reverses the traditional alignment of animality with sin and proper humanity with redemption, I would like to suggest yet another use of Barth's understanding of election—one that, admittedly, moves against a more restrictive line of Barth's own exposition.[77] Barth too begins his discussion of the incarnation and divine election with John's prologue. All of humanity is elected in God's choice to take human form through becoming incarnate as Jesus Christ.[78] Barth quickly distinguishes two forms of this one election, positing a difference in God's relationship to Israel from God's relationship to the church even as both are contained within God's single election of humanity. God elects Israel as a chosen people *for the sake of* humanity as a whole but elects the church *as the form of* a new humanity. God elects Israel in order to manifest the divine judgment upon humanity that God has chosen to shoulder in Jesus Christ.[79] In other words, God reveals Godself as an incarnate Israelite—and elects Israel as the chosen people—not in order to endorse Israel's (previously) exclusive relationship with God and to entrench Israel's social identity over against the gentiles, but in order to make manifest the judgment from which God rescues the world.[80] God's incarnation as an Israelite, for Barth, breaks Israel open for the sake of a new form of life for the community of God, which includes Israel but is most clearly manifest in the church.

Even as I would resist its supercessionism, Barth's account of the incarnation in relation to the election of Israel provides a model for thinking about God's becoming human. For Barth, God's becoming Israelite in Jesus of Nazareth does not endorse Israel's exceptionalist self-understanding relative to the nations. Similarly, God's becoming human need not validate anthropological exceptionalism. The love that motivates the incarnation of the Logos in human flesh has been too long mistaken for a love that sets humanity above other creatures. Barth opens a way to see the incarnate election of humanity as a love that extends far beyond human beings alone, a love that must break humanity open for the good of creation. The Logos of God sounds out a thundering "Nein!" to humanity precisely by taking on human flesh.[81] God elects and bears humanity not to set humanity above creation in a new and alien holiness, but to turn the wayward creature back toward the beloved creation for the sake of the reconcilliation of all creatures.[82] Humanity is specially chosen because human beings have become especially obdurate and dangerous (not because human beings are especially deserving). The incarnation of the Logos as a human being is judgment upon the logos of humanity, not validation. God inhabits human subjectivity in order to rekindle within it (and against it) the flame of *zōē*/animality, a light long threatened but not yet snuffed out. The incarnation is the messianic *zōē* of a new realm within the very heart of the old; it is a redemptive divinanimality unraveling the disavowal of animality in the structure of human subjectivity.[83]

A few other considerations bolster the claim that God's incarnation as Jesus of Nazareth loosens the theological knots that hold anthropological exceptionalism together.

Although the Logos bears specifically human flesh, Jesus's alignment with humanity rather than animality is less secure than it might appear at first. The Logos imparts life to human beings at the particular places to which humanity relegates animals: Jesus offers himself as the flesh-meal around which humanity unites (John 6; Matthew 26; 1 Corinthians 11), the sacrificial lamb slaughtered for ritual purity (Revelation 5), the scapegoat cast out by the fury of human sin, and the symbolic lion whose ferocity lends courage to the disheartened. By symbolically and sacramentally redeeming human beings from positions usually forced upon animals (meat, sacrifice, outcast, mascot) Jesus stands in solidarity with "all flesh" and exposes the ongoing violence of anthropological exceptionalism.

On this account, the "self" that Jesus asks his disciples to "deny" as a condition of following him (the hinge-point of the synoptic gospels) is the proper human self formed through the ideology of humanity.[84] Inasmuch as Jesus knows that the world of humanity has no room for him, he asks his disciples to negate their investment in this social world—not for the sake of an otherworldly kingdom, but for the sake of a living realm of God "on earth as it is in heaven."[85] Returning to the Johannine vocabulary, this is to say that the *zōē* with which Jesus the Logos illumines human beings should not be regarded as the enlightenment of a more proper humanity, but as an animality that escapes, resists, and utterly transforms the logos of humanity. The light of divine *zōē* breaks apart the ideological regime of proper humanity for the sake of human animality and the integrity of the earth's ecopolitics. The becoming-flesh of the Logos is not the endorsement of human subjectivity in its present structures, but an effort to knock loose the gears of the destructive apparatus that reproduces humanity. The Logos, then, from the closest proximity to humanity's own logos, opposes it for the sake of animality.

Although the incarnation of the Logos does redeem human beings from their fallen condition on this account, redemption works differently than is usually assumed. After humanity's fall into a destructive obsession with self-differentiation, the redemption wrought in the incarnation turns human beings back to the life (*zōē*) of the world.

On this understanding, the Logos of God is no longer the Master Signifier, the keystone that anchors the logos of self-reflective human thought and speech in a stable economy of meaning.[86] Instead, relative to the logos of humanity and its pretension to creaturely superiority, the Logos of God is negatively transcendent. God's Logos is the charged silence over which humanity finds itself interminably babbling. The logos of humanity can find no entryway into the Logos of God; it tries to speak its way over a communicative abyss rather than being immersed in the silence of divinanimality. Icons of the mystery of the *zōē* of God, the unsettling eyes of animals—whose gazes have so little regard for human discourse—are unsettling not because they lack meaning, but because they convey an excess of meaning that always remains opaque to human logos. The living silence of the divinanimal Logos offers (or threatens) to swallow whole the logos of humanity—and no one can guess what kind of new *zōē* might emerge from this end.

For very different reasons, Gregory of Nyssa recognized the limits of human reason and discourse on the journey toward God. At the point where the excess of divine mystery breaks open humanity's rationality and humanity's language, Gregory argues that perfected forms of desire (a function of animality in his anthropology) orient human beings and draw them closer to God. To set Gregory's insight into the vocabulary of this chapter: Divine grace draws human beings into redemptive communion through their commonality with other creatures and for the sake of creation's common good. Perhaps, with Gregory, we have been looking "up" too long for the limits of human language and rationality; perhaps the Logos of God has been too close to recognize, already at work in the pluriform *zōē* of the world. Greater conformity to the Logos of God might teach us to communicate not in the tongues of angels but within the animal interdependencies that sustain every living creature.

Within John's Gospel, the work of the Logos in and through Jesus is named as eternal life (*zōē aiōnios*). In the light of the connection between *zōē* and animality, the work of the Logos might be understood as animality without end. In such an account, *zōē aiōnios* is not an abstract temporality added to one isolated creature (the human) upon the extraction of that creature from the whole network of living relations in the world.[87] *Zōē aiōnios* is rather the reeducation and reintegration of an alienated creature for the sake of the common good—what Colossians calls the reconciliation of all things (Colossians 1:15–19). In order to redeem the groaning creation, God becomes a human being so that human beings might become-animal with God through the limitless life of the Logos. The incarnation of the Logos is the inspirited dismantling of humanity from within, a divine deconstruction that refuses containment in any single form of flesh; the work of the Logos is a *zōē aiōnios* that can sustain all God's beloved creatures.

In the face of such a vision of redemption, clinging to humanity's parochial logos (in its self-assured superiority) is no theological virtue, but a darkened refusal of the Logos's work in creation. The question of the life of the world evades human discourse, looming instead in the haunted silences where the logos of humanity pauses, ever so briefly, for breath.

Conclusion

Where the discourse of sin and redemption invokes a vertical spatiality in which humanity falls and is raised again, animality traditionally appears beneath authentic humanity. This chapter has reversed the traditional polarity of humanity and animality in the narrative of human sin and redemption so that, paradoxically, the fall is marked by false transcendence and God's work to lift human beings out of sin through redemption actually sinks human beings more deeply into their animal relations. Althusser, Agamben, and Butler provided a framework for talking about the formation of human subjectivity within a pervasive cultural-ideological regime and demonstrated that human subject formation depends on the supposition of a human-animal difference that subsequently orders the subject's world around a categorical distinction. A theological rereading of Genesis 2–3 as the narrative of the fall connected original sin to ideological subject-formation in the regime of proper humanity. On this reading, human beings fall into humanity, a condition structured around a constitutive disavowal of their own animality. The incarnation of God as Jesus of Nazareth is the means of redemption, not because one species of flesh is privileged above the rest and extracted from relationships with other creatures, but because the chasm between human logos and the life (*zōē*) of creation is exposed and confronted in the person of the divine Logos. A reconsideration of John's prologue demonstrated that God's being-human disrupts humanity from within for the sake of creation; God's choice to reveal Godself as a human being should not validate humanity's pretensions to categorical uniqueness, even if it has traditionally done so. The redemption of human beings, then, does not produce an ethereal "eternal life," a spiritual existence abstracted from the material context of creation, but an endless animality (*zōē aiōnios*) in which human beings live in the breath of God.

6

Animality in Eschatological Transformation

> And these measures shall reveal all the secrets of the depths of
> the earth,
> And those who have been destroyed by the desert,
> And those who have been devoured by the beasts,
> And those who have been devoured by the fish of the sea,
> So that they may return and rely on the day of the Chosen One;
> For no one shall be destroyed in the presence of the Lord of Spirits,
> And no one is able to be destroyed.
>
> —*1 Enoch 61:5*[1]

An oft-repeated tradition in Christian antiquity held that God will resurrect animals on the last day so that they can vomit out the human beings they have eaten.[2] Just as the "devouring grave" spits out the dead, so also the animals who consumed human flesh are compelled to give it back. Byzantine iconography depicts fish, eagles, vultures, wolves, lions, and bears looking submissively to heaven with human body parts protruding from their open mouths. The resurrection of these animals, however, serves no purpose other than to return human flesh, and, having done so, they die a second death and return to the soil. Tertullian attempts to talk his readers out of their assent to this vomiting animal scheme, but he does so precisely by presuming that the notion of an animal resurrection is absurd.[3]

This image of animals disgorging body parts so that God can reassemble human beings poignantly illuminates the problem of human animality in the theology of the resurrection. First, it illustrates an early shift in Christian thinking about resurrection. Jewish and New Testament notions of resurrection emphasized the return of a whole person who, having died, tarried in a kind of sleep until the final day when God calls all people back to life. Gradually, Christian thinking shifted toward conceptual problems with the material continuity of the resurrected body after death, decay, and reassembly. These conceptual problems only arise where identity itself is located primarily in a mind or soul that "possesses" a body (so that the soul must be sure it has the right one).[4] The vomiting animal trope—or Athenagoras's suggestion that animals are physiologically incapable of digesting human flesh—are solutions to a conceptual problem that did not arise for earlier thinkers.[5] Second, this image neatly crystalizes a broader pattern: the eschatological divergence of humanity and animality, that is, a tendency to leave animals (and eventually, human animality) behind. For the bulk of the Christian tradition, God's only real concern in resurrection lies with human beings; God resurrects anthropophagic animals so that they will disgorge the humans they have eaten. Yet where animals are excluded, human animality sits in a precarious position. The image of vomiting animals powerfully affirms the resurrection of the human body, but does so at the expense of animality—and although this trope eventually faded from prominence, Christian theology of the resurrection found other, more subtle ways to leave animality behind.

From Paul's argument in 1 Corinthians 15 onward, the eschatological resurrection of a material human body has been a boundary-defining conviction of Christian theology. For example, the vilification (however inaccurate) of Valentinian Christians and Origenists centered on questions of the resurrection of the body. Yet, it has been commonplace in theological history to imagine the eschatological transformation of the human being as the cessation of physiological functions such as digestion and sexual expression, so that the associated organs become vestigial reminders of a former life. It is no coincidence that eating and sex are the activities in which human and animal life are most obviously alike, nor that these activities are most likely to trigger shame and disgust. The evacuation of animality from the resurrected body secures the conceptual integrity of corporeal resurrection by excising shame-laden aspects of bodily life while still allowing for strong affirmations of eschatological corporeality.

What would resurrected animality be like? This chapter takes the mainstream disavowal of human animality in eschatological transformation as an opportunity go down an alternate path, one in which human animality (concentrated in digestion and sexual expression) is the point at which divine grace operates in human life, the point at which (or through which) human beings participate in the triune life of God. As with previous constructive chapters, this argument reverses a familiar subordination of animality beneath proper humanity, but in surprising ways the theological tradition already places animality at the center of eschatological transformation, even though it generally goes unnamed. Digestion and sexual expression are the corporeal anchors for Christian ideas about how human beings live with God, so this chapter's work is more about insisting on the theological seriousness of traditional language than devising new ways to involve animality in the eschaton.

The chapter is divided into three sections: First, I argue that evacuating digestion and sexual expression from transformed human bodies disavows human animality in a way that fails to account for the centrality of animal imagery within biblical texts regarding the eschaton. Second, I take up digestion in particular, arguing that a theological disavowal of human animality has produced a false dissociation of the eucharist from the messianic banquet in the new creation. Overcoming this false separation allows us to imagine sharing in divine life through glorified and transfigured relations of ecological interdependence—consuming and being consumed. Third, I will address sexual expression and the frequent sublimation of erotic desire within theological and mystical discourse, in order to argue that describing eschatological union with the corporeal register of concepts such as instinct and desire better encompasses creaturely freedom than concepts from the intellectual register (comprehension and understanding, for example).

Digestion and Sexual Expression in the Life of the Resurrection

In efforts to concretely articulate the hope of the resurrection and offer pastoral comfort, theologians have speculatively ventured answers on a wide range of conceptual problems. For example: Will those who die as infants be resurrected as infants or at a mature age that they never attained in bodily life? Will heavenly hair and fingernails continue to grow as a living part of the human body? Will those who are born with physical deformities or cognitive abnormalities be resurrected in a "whole" and "healthy" state, or as the embodied persons they were? Will the martyrs wear their wounds as a sign of glory, or will these wounds be cast aside along with suffering and death?[6]

Even more basic problems have attended resurrected bodies insofar as life-sustaining corporeal activities such as eating and reproduction seem superfluous for eternal life and also, somehow, beneath the dignity of heavenly glory.[7] Agamben draws on Thomas Aquinas in introducing the mainstream position on digestion and sexual expression in resurrected bodies:

> It is with regard to two principal functions of vegetative life—sexual reproduction and nutrition—that the problem of the physiology of the glorious body reaches its critical threshold. If the organs that execute these functions—testicles, penis, vagina, womb, stomach, intestines—will necessarily be present in the resurrection, then what function are they supposed to have? [Thomas writes,] "The end of procreation is to multiply the human race, while the end of nutrition is the restoration of the individual. After the resurrection, however, the human race will reach the perfect number that had been preordained by God, and the body will no longer undergo either diminution or growth. Procreation and nutrition will therefore no longer have any reason for being."[8]

In the life of glory, the organs associated with digestion and sexual expression remain "idle and empty" since there is no need for the purposes toward which they are directed.[9] The exclusion is logical insofar as heaven will be "full" of the elect (obviating the need for reproduction) and resurrected bodies will not need energy from food in order to stave off death. However, a secondary reason (or retrospective justification) for the exclusion is the aesthetic impropriety of excretion, bodily fluids, and eroticism within the sphere of heavenly glory. Jerome, Augustine, and Thomas Aquinas all deny that resurrected bodies will engage in digestion and sexual expression.[10] Asserting a radically plastic view of the body, Gregory of Nyssa (perhaps following Origen) famously goes a step further, asserting that glorious bodies will, like the angels, lack genitals altogether.[11]

Eating and sex are the most obvious points of commonality between human beings and other animals, so the exclusion of digestion and sexual expression also functions as an eschatological excision of human animality. By excluding digestion and sexual expression, theologians imagine an anatomically complete resurrected body, but one that is free from the shame of secretions, involuntary movements, and unexpected desires. The mores and standards of decorum that regulate eating and sex—even though they differ widely from one cultural context to the next—inscribe difference between human eating and sex and that of the animals. It is hardly surprising, then, that regulations on eating and sex extend into an eschatological exclusion that removes the very possibility of indiscretion from a setting where barbarity would be unthinkable. The evacuation of animality from human bodies allows for an affirmation of the full corporeal integrity of resurrected humanity while simultaneously safeguarding heavenly glory against contamination. In such accounts, animality becomes expendable without anything "essential" being lost; human bodies spring free of their own animality just as surely as—in this chapter's opening image—the animals themselves vomited up human bodies only to fall back into the soil.

To be clear, I am taking up questions of glorious digestion and sexual expression because these physiological functions are a condensation of human animality—a kind of synecdoche. The attention paid in this chapter, then, to digestion and sexual expression derives from the recognition that these functions are an index for animality more generally. As these functions are included or (more frequently) excluded, the ultimate significance of ecological relations of interdependence rises and falls.

The purpose of my argument, then, is not to establish certainty about the details of the eschaton but to address a deficiency in Christian theology's collective imagination. The argument here undoubtedly crosses into the territory of imaginative speculation. The exclusion of digestion and sexual expression, however, is no less speculative and no more consistent with scripture and tradition. I will argue that the eschatological transformation of digestion and sexual expression coheres with central Christian convictions regarding the eucharist, the resurrected body of Christ, and the communion of the new creation with God. Again, the purpose of demonstrating such coherence is not so much to establish a seamless theological system as to put additional pressure on the incoherence of the commonsense devaluation of animality. Wherever Christians imagine an eschaton in which animality and other animals are absent, the lives and deaths of animals can never be a matter of ultimate concern. In such schemes (hardly a rarity in the theological mainstream) animals and animality are captive within the limits of history while proper humanity finds its final home in eternity. Imagining digestion and sexual expression at the heart of eschatological transformation, then, suggests that animality, nonhuman animals, and the whole ecology of creaturely life are matters of primary spiritual and theological concern, rather than a boutique specialization. The goal of this chapter is not to convince readers that my particular description of the eschaton is accurate down to the gritty details, but to persuade readers that, whatever the eschaton entails, God's grace transforms and welcomes animals and animality into the divine life rather than leaving them on the abandoned shore of history.[12]

Although it is certainly well-covered ground in ecological theology, a reminder of the centrality of animals within the eschatological imagination of the scriptural canon highlights the oddity of the theological tradition's exclusion of animality.[13]

Isaiah's eschatological images frequently invoke the verdant renewal of parched landscapes as a sign of peace in the land.[14] Most famously, Isaiah invokes a vision of predators, livestock, and children napping together:

> The wolf will lie with the lamb, the leopard will lie down with the goat, the calf and the lion and the yearling together; and a little child will lead them. The cow will feed with the bear, their young will lie down together, and the lion will eat straw like the ox. Infants will play near the hole of the cobra; young children will put their hands into the viper's nest. They will neither harm nor destroy on all my holy mountain, for the earth will be filled with the knowledge of the LORD as the waters cover the sea.[15]

In contrast, Daniel's apocalyptic visions are filled with terrifying hybrid beasts, symbols of the empires oppressing Israel.[16] The author of the book of Revelation adopts Daniel's bestial imagery, with beasts and dragons causing great destruction.[17] But Revelation also depicts animals as the figures dwelling closer to God than any others. Where the author of Revelation rewrites the scene of Isaiah's vision of the divine throne room, the circling seraphs who cry "Holy, holy, holy!" return as animals.[18] The crucified and resurrected Christ appears as a lamb who opens the seals (chs. 5–8), leads the 144,000 righteous (chs. 14 and 17), and is the bridegroom of the new Jerusalem—the home of the redeemed in a "new heavens and new earth" that echoes Eden (ch. 21).[19]

The Pauline corpus is arguably the most anthropocentric portion of the New Testament, yet the eschatological vision therein is never restricted to humanity alone. The inspirited groans of the whole creation—animals included—express a longing for a redemption whose reach extends beyond the human community.[20] And the deutero-Pauline vision of Colossians honors a Christ whose cross and resurrection are effective to reconcile all things to God.[21]

The eschatological visions of scripture stands in contrast to the sterile squeamishness around animals and animality exhibited in the theological tradition. While apocalyptic literature is certainly marked by an exuberant use of imagery, the erasure of animals and animality from theological accounts of glory runs deeper than any chaste regard for the limits of metaphor.[22]

This Is My Flesh, Take and Eat

> Leave me to be a meal for the beasts, for it is they who can provide my way to God. I am His wheat, ground fine by the lions' teeth to be made purest bread for Christ. Better still, incite the creatures to become a sepulcher for me; let them not leave the smallest scrap of my flesh, so that I need not be a burden to anyone after I fall asleep. When there is no trace of my body left for the world to see, then I shall truly be Jesus Christ's disciple.
>
> Ignatius of Antioch[23]

In the New Testament Gospels, the resurrected Christ appears to his disciples and eats with them, sharing bread and fish.[24] Although theologians mention these passages as evidence that the bodies of the resurrection will be transfigured versions of the bodies of this age, many nevertheless go on to argue that consumption and digestion will be absent from the life of eternal glory. Their reasons for this exclusion generally fall into three kinds.[25]

One set of reasons is physiological: If God perfects human bodies in the resurrection, then it stands to reason that starvation and hunger should be banished. Moreover, since the very root of hunger lies in the body's dependence on the external energy derived from food, a perfected body should be spared from the dependence that bears the possibility of deprivation. Likewise, bodies inhabiting God's eternity will neither grow nor age; nutrition seems superfluous where human bodies are nourished directly by the life of God.

Another set of reasons is anchored in a respect for divine holiness and strong notions of purity/contamination. Since digestion ends in defecation, cutting off from the beginning any process that might produce heavenly feces safeguards heavenly purity against contamination. The association of feces and holiness is difficult to bear. Agamben tells of a tradition (he attributes it to Basil of Caesarea) in which Jesus's body digested food so completely and efficiently that he never had any need to expel waste.[26] If the life of glory does not include sewers and catholes, then, resurrected bodies would need to share this condition. Digestion is excluded from the new creation because its result—feces—is strongly associated with decay, putrefaction, disease, and finally death, all of which are also banished.[27]

A third set of reasons derive from the conviction that death is the final enemy, decisively conquered in the realm of God. Every form of eating involves weakening or killing another creature—even if only severing the vital connection of a leaf to its stalk and roots. The eradication of death, therefore, strongly implies the end of consumption.

Theologians exclude digestion from resurrected bodies because of associations with suffering, decay, and death. Rather than the parsimonious logic of theologians, however, Christian liturgy has taken guidance from pervasive biblical references to the eschaton as a great feast. Isaiah, for example, describes a celebration marking the end of death: "On this mountain the LORD Almighty will prepare a feast of rich food for all peoples, a banquet of aged wine—the best of meats and the finest of wines. On this mountain he will destroy the shroud that enfolds all people, the sheet that covers all nations; he will swallow up death forever."[28] Likewise, the synoptic gospels attribute a number of parables to Jesus in which the eschaton is figured as a great wedding banquet.[29] At the last supper, Jesus instructs his disciples to remember him by means of the new covenant in his flesh and blood, but also tells them that he will not eat or drink again until they are reunited in the realm of God. Luke's account is the richest: "He said to them, 'I have eagerly desired to eat this Passover with you before I suffer. For I tell you, I will not eat it again until it finds fulfillment in the kingdom of God.' After taking the cup, he gave thanks and said, 'Take this and divide it among you. For I tell you I will not drink again of the fruit of the vine until the kingdom of God comes.'"[30] Drawing on such passages, Western liturgy takes up Jesus's promise by celebrating the eucharist as a "foretaste of the feast to come," and Orthodox liturgy makes an even stronger connection, figuring the bread and wine of the eucharist as the substance of the heavenly feast itself, food that draws celebrants into the eschaton—if only for an anticipatory moment.[31]

Where theologians cut digestion out of the life of glory, the messianic banquet becomes, ironically, an empty signifier of heavenly fullness. The biblical and liturgical visions of a divine feast, if taken seriously in a way that the theological tradition has seldom done, would place animality and digestion at the very heart of the eschatological relationship between God and God's redeemed creatures. What description of the eschaton would emerge if theological reflection took its cues in this matter from liturgy and scripture, despite the foreseen problems around suffering, decay, and death?

In order to work out the problems of glorious consumption, I am first going to amplify the problem with some ecological considerations. As theologians in recent decades have turned to a vision of salvation as the renewal of the whole creation—a "new heavens and new earth" in Revelation's words—they have encountered new questions about the lives of gloriously transfigured creatures.[32] Predators and parasites, in particular, raise a thorny set of problems. What might the eternal life of a tiger, a wolf, a falcon, or a shark look like? The problem of heavenly predation clarifies the problem of resurrected consumption by raising the stakes.[33]

One of the highest excellences of tiger-ness, for example, must lie in the skills, instincts, and physical endowments (claws, teeth) that enable tigers to be silent, ruthless, and efficient killers. Although hunting and killing are not the *only* activities in the life of a tiger, the physiology of the tiger from nose to tail tells an evolutionary story about the refinement of an ability to stalk and dispatch prey. Even as Pannenberg restricts the practice of religion to human beings alone, he notes that animals are oriented toward God in their vital functions, quoting the Psalmist's claim that lions seek their meat from God.[34] If tigers and other predators are indeed oriented to God through the excellence of their ability to hunt and kill, then any new creation that strips them of these activities would also strip them of their fundamental orientation to God. A heaven in which tigers sing hymns and chant psalms transforms tigers into "humans in furry suits" rather than glorifying the excellence of the tigers themselves.[35] Isaiah's vision of the peaceable kingdom, in which lions and lambs lie down together is a poignant image of cosmic transformation and the end of conflict, but for the lions involved, such a vision of heaven must be nearly as dystopically dull as Dante's vision of endless, well-lit clouds. Can the new creation be the heaven of tigers if their basic instincts are denied, thwarted, or rewired? Is a glorious tiger still a tiger if it does nothing more than nap and cuddle?

Just as clearly, however, the maiming, tearing, and slaughter involved in predation are incompatible with a new creation in which "death will be no more; mourning and crying and pain will be no more."[36] If the heaven of tigers is also the home of wild pigs, deer, and antelope, then setting glorious tigers loose to practice their deadly craft on glorious ungulates seems to turn heaven into hell for prey species. The incompatibility of predation with the life of the resurrection has led Christian theologians who picture resurrected animals to insist that the animals of the resurrection will be entirely vegetarian (and, often, domesticated beneath human command).[37] To eradicate suffering and death, it seems, God must surely eradicate predation, at whatever cost to heavenly tigers.

These considerations on heavenly predation are linked to a wider conversation regarding ecotheology. Lisa Sideris argues that ecotheologians misappropriate terms such as *interdependence* and *community* from biology by redeploying the same terms with very different connotations in ethical and theological discourse.[38] To transfer *interdependence* and *community* from a descriptive ecological register into the value-laden ethical register without addressing the resulting equivocation erases the bloodiness of these relations.[39] Biologists describe relations of dependence without any implication that dependent creatures will actually receive what they vitally depend on; often enough, they do not.[40] Sideris argues the emphasis on relationality in ecotheology derives from an eschatological vision of harmonious coexistence rather than (as often claimed) ecology and evolutionary biology.[41] *Interdependence* names ecological relations of predation, parasitism, or scavenging—acts that we would name "murder," "robbery," and "opportunism" if they took place in the human community. Sideris persuasively disconnects the ecological ethics put forward by Moltmann, McFague, Ruether, and Cobb from claims that this ethic can be grounded in evolutionary biology. If ecological theology is not to constitutively rely on terminological equivocation then ecological theologians need to explicitly address the bloodiest forms of interdependence in which creatures live and die. However, Sideris does not demonstrate that these theologians have their eschatology wrong. Theological assertions of interdependence and community may reach toward an eschaton that, taking

Sideris's critique to heart, transfigures (rather than eradicates) relations of predation and parasitism.

The problem of heavenly consumption—made concrete in the figure of a glorious tiger—is bound up with the ecology at the heart of ecological theology insofar as it presses the question of just which relations of interdependence theologians valorize. If glorious human consumption raises problems involving suffering and death, then the tiger's hunting and killing considerably ups the ante. Having folded the anthropological problem of glorious digestion into the ecological problem of heavenly predation, I suggest that eucharistic theology provides a way to think through both problems at once.

Let us start with relatively uncontroversial points of Christian doctrine. First, Jesus of Nazareth, the very same man who was crucified and died, rose bodily from the grave to new life through the power of God's Spirit and ascended to God's right hand. Second, according to Orthodox, Catholic, and Lutheran eucharistic theology, the bread and wine of communion really are the flesh and blood of Jesus Christ. The exact contours of this identity relationship have been the subject of interminable argument, but the longest-lived confessional traditions of Christianity agree that for the faithful, Christ's body and blood are shared and consumed "in, with, and under" the bread and wine (to use a Lutheran formulation).

We can draw these points of doctrine together. In the resurrected body of Christ, we are confronted with a glorious body that is endlessly broken, divided, and consumed; we are confronted with a glorious body that provides transformative nourishment to those who consume it; and we are confronted, for all that, with a body raised beyond death and suffering. The resurrected wholeness of Christ's body is not contradicted by its endless consumption. There is precisely one body that Christian theology affirms as already having been resurrected, and that body is also endlessly eaten. The broken, betrayed, abandoned, and executed body of Jesus—*a body preyed upon*—is also a body whose flesh and blood continues to be consumed, even as Christ surely lives beyond suffering and death, because through resurrection the Spirit has transformed the agony of the cross into glory. At the heart of eucharistic theology, then, stands a resurrected body torn and consumed, yet undiminished in its glory.

The eucharist is a sacrament of memory, a participatory remembrance of the life and death of Jesus; but it is also a sacrament of eschatological anticipation, a "foretaste of the feast to come." It is a meal that draws its eaters into a new reality. Irenaeus writes of the eucharist as the "medicine of immortality" because sacramentally sharing in the bodily life of the resurrected Christ restores and transforms human bodies subject to mortality and corruption.[42] In three dimensions of a single movement, God's Spirit raises Jesus from the grave, unites the gathered church through a sacrament that begins from grapes and grains, and transforms creation by drawing creatures together into the life of God. The Spirit's work in Jesus's resurrection and the church's sacraments, in other words, cannot be separated from the inarticulate groans of the Spirit moving through a creation awaiting transformation.[43]

The eucharistic paradox in which Christ is consumed but not diminished offers a theological bridge across the problems of glorious consumption and predation. If the problem of glorious predation is irresolvable, then receiving the eucharist raises questions about the ongoing bodily suffering of the resurrected Christ. Conversely, if Christians already consume a body that lives beyond the reach of death, then the paradoxes involved in thinking about heavenly predation and consumption hardly present an insurmountable conceptual problem. Rather than a problem, heavenly predation and consumption provide a richly concrete way of imagining creation's eternal participation in the life of God in substantial continuity with God's sacramental work in the present.

The resurrected body of Jesus must be the beginning and end of all Christian reflection about resurrected bodies. The living Christ is the whole substance of Christian hope for resurrection. What faith can know about resurrection rests on a messianic promise: "What we do know is this: when he is revealed, we will be like him, for we will see him as he is."[44] This Johannine expression echoes Paul's understanding of Jesus's resurrection as the gathering of a "first fruits"—a gift to God of the first part of the harvest, in gratitude for the whole, which is shortly to be harvested. The power of Paul's harvest metaphor turns on the assumption of continuity between the risen Christ and the resurrection of Christ's followers.[45] Christ is the first fruits, so Christians may know in faith that their resurrection will follow in like manner.[46] The logic of the New Testament's teaching on resurrection regards Jesus's resurrection as the path-breaking manifestation of a general eschatological promise meant for all.

Insofar as the body of Jesus is broken and consumed daily without suffering or death, we can speculatively imagine other resurrected bodies participating in the same form of life. In such a vision, eucharistic theology no longer pertains only to a ritual taking place within the walls of the church (a misconception in any case), but sacramentally outlines the ecology of the eschaton. Indeed, the eucharist—generalized in the Spirit through the resurrection—becomes the means of grace through which creatures share together in the life (*zōē*/animality) of the triune God. As Peter Scott argues, Christ's resurrection not only promises to transform human nature but to reorder the human relationship to nature generally by drawing the human-nature relation into the Trinitarian life of God.[47] Somewhat similarly, Robert Jenson argues that the "space" of the resurrected community of God—the answer to the question "Where is heaven?"—is found in the spatiality of the eucharist, the availability of Christ's flesh to the gathered creatures who, together, become the body of Christ.[48] Together, these arguments begin to depict a eucharistic renewal of the whole creation. Resurrection does not transform individual creatures in isolation, but draws the entire network of ecological interdependence into the life of God. Through the broken body of the resurrected Christ, "God was pleased to reconcile to himself all things, whether on earth or in heaven, by making peace through the blood of his cross."[49]

I can now make a claim for the eschatological unity of three theological themes that are usually connected only along tangents: the eucharist, the "new heavens and new earth," and the messianic banquet. As noted, Christian liturgy already speaks of the eucharist as a "foretaste of the feast to come." Such language clearly refers to the messianic banquet, the great wedding feast of the eschaton. But what of the food on the table? Is this messianic feast to be conjured up deus ex machina? If the messianic banquet is an empty metaphor for eschatological fullness, then the consumption of the eucharist is a hollow foretaste of a feast which will never come. Is it not simpler to imagine that the messianic banquet is the fruit of the new heavens and new earth? There is, of course, a danger that such a picture could redouble anthropocentrism by allowing someone to imagine that the new heavens and new earth are an infinitely renewable resource meant for human consumption—renewed creatures are waiting only for the honor of being carved up on human plates. Instead, I suggest that we imagine the eschatological transfiguration of the entire food chain, human beings included, such that created ecology is suffused with the ecology of the divine Trinity, in an endlessly expansive rehearsal of eucharist. The messianic banquet cannot be confined to any single table.[50]

The major objection to such a scheme is obvious: how can creatures consume one another without perpetuating the economy of death that the eschaton is supposed to eradicate? We cannot imagine any form of consumption that does not involve some degree of fear, suffering, injury, and death. In response to such an objection, it would be possible to appeal to mystery along the lines of Balthasar's claim that "there is no common measure" between the life that is subject to death and the life of the resurrection, so that the ecology of the new creation may simply lie beyond our understanding.[51] There is a stronger response than Balthasar's appeal to mystery, however, since the body of Jesus Christ is the common measure between this life and the life of glory. I argued earlier that fears about ongoing consumption inflicting death and injury are misplaced—at least regarding Christ's own body. In an ongoing expression of his mission as the Son of the Father, Jesus shares his body and blood daily through the work of the Spirit, and yet for all that consumption, lives undiminished by the fear and pain that such consumption would "normally" entail. If we are to imagine resurrection by starting with the body of Christ, then we must imagine the compatibility of resurrected life with consumption. If the resurrected body of Jesus Christ is consumed without being trapped in suffering and death, then—though it strains reason and imagination—the promise of eternal life in Christ is not of a life free from consuming and being consumed. Eternal life in Christ *just is* an economy of sharing in flesh and blood, but now we can picture this eucharistic economy multiplied into ecological dimensions.[52]

Nor would such an eschaton be the privileged paradise of predators alone. Grazers and browsers may find and feast upon vibrant greens; nut gatherers and berry pickers may collect the fullest fruits; plants themselves may reach their roots into the richest soil; even microscopic life may thrive on the fecundity of glorious "waste." If the life of the new creation is indeed the *zōē aiōnios* of God—eternal animality—then the body of the resurrected Christ demonstrates that divine life cannot be diminished, divided, or threatened simply by being torn and consumed. The Spirit who groans with creatures in their current suffering does not abandon this commitment of solidarity at the eschaton, but exults, as companion and midwife, in animating the richest diversity of creaturely life as it fills the new heavens and the new earth.[53]

Consuming the body and blood of Christ in faith is—in the present age—a grace-given means by which human creatures participate bodily in the life of God. Similarly, in the age to come, when all creatures participate in Christ's resurrection through the life of the Spirit, creaturely relations of consumption (including being consumed), will be the grace-given means by which creatures share together in the love of God. Creatures no longer eat and drink because they must incorporate energy from outside their bodies to survive. Rather, creatures eat and drink because sharing in another's flesh is the gracious means by which God has chosen to share the divine life with creation. Consuming the flesh and blood of others, and likewise being consumed by others, constitutes the eucharistic ecology of the divine life, a circulating economy of flesh and blood that mirrors, in a created fashion, the circulating, self-giving economy of the Trinity. The messianic banquet spreads across every hill, forest, and wave of the new creation.

Gregory of Nazianzus's trajectory of contemplative ascent in Oration 28 draws near to God by way of attention to the divine Logos in animals and other nonhuman creatures. Participating in divine life through consumption and digestion is not entirely dissimilar to Gregory's scheme, although there has been a change in the organ through which one best traces one's way back to the Logos. For Gregory, the Logos meets the human mind in the appreciation of plants and animals. If the Logos is present in resurrected flesh, then in addition to their minds, creatures will encounter God through their stomachs and intestines. Gregory's cerebral ascent becomes fully sacramental in a gustatory and gastrointestinal communion of the Spirit.

To be clear, there are no exemptions for human beings in the life-giving economy of consumption and predation. Heavenly tigers may hunt and consume human beings as readily as they hunt and consume deer. In Christ, God's own flesh stands at the center of the ecology of divine *zōē*, and there can be no categorical distinction between flesh liable to consumption and flesh that is beyond this limit. The life of God infuses the glorious life of resurrected creatures precisely through a sacramental ecology of sharing in flesh.[54] If the eschaton reveals that the new creation, eucharist, and messianic banquet are finally identical, then humans participate corporeally in the divine life precisely through their place in the ecological economy of consuming and being consumed. Christians too, in conformity to Christ, may at last know what it is to impart life to other creatures through body and blood.

Rather than otiose organs that are entirely superfluous in glorious bodies, resurrected mouths, teeth, stomachs, and intestines will join resurrected bodies into the communion of divine life. If, in the present age, the Spirit imparts life to human beings through their faithful consumption of the body and blood of Jesus, is it not strange to think that the age to come will leave consumption altogether behind? Where eschatological transformation centers on human animality (in digestion and consumption) we find the intersection of eucharistic theology with an ecologically attuned eschatology. At this intersection, it is possible to describe a vision of participatory communion in the triune life of God in which human beings are in no way privileged over other creatures. This vision fulfills and completes the suggestion in the previous chapter that the incarnation of the Logos as a human being accomplishes salvation precisely by restoring human beings to their own disavowed animality, undoing the ideological knots of proper humanity. God shares divine life (*zōē*) through the very bonds that join all created lives (*zōa*) together—perfecting nature rather than abolishing it.

At the very point where human animality has been traditionally excluded from accounts of eschatological transformation in order to safeguard anthropological exceptionalism—that is, in the cessation of a common creaturely consumption, digestion, and nutrition—there lies the forgotten possibility of an anthropology that embraces human animality and embeds human redemption more deeply into the renewal of the whole cosmos. Once this forgotten anthropology is uncovered, however, profound resonances with biblical, liturgical, and theological themes burst out upon the properly attuned ear. In the passage at the beginning of this section, Ignatius longs to approach God through beastly bellies. His strange desire is closer to the heart of the sacramental tradition than has yet been acknowledged. The hope and promise of the resurrection of the body is the hope and promise of the messianic banquet, the wedding feast of the lamb, the meal that makes the Church, the foretaste of the feast to come, the new heavens and the new earth, endless animality (*zōē aiōnios*), and the whole creation's participation in the triune life of God. If human animality is not cast aside, such promises are no longer hollow metaphors for an inscrutable and ethereal fullness, but a nourishing hope that bears the weight and substance of creaturely life.

Sexual Intimacy in the Life of the Resurrection

Western thought has fixated upon the necessity to incorporate food and drink to sustain life as one primary point of commonality between human and animal life. The other point at which Western thought persistently worries over the commonality of human and animal life is in bodily reproduction. As with digestion, the majority of the Christian theological tradition has denied that there will be any sexual expression in the life of glory—in large part because of associations between sexual activity and animality.[55] While Gregory of Nyssa argued that resurrected human bodies will lose their genitals entirely, other theologians strip resurrected genitals of any sexual function whatsoever.[56] One of Jesus's statements in the synoptic gospels apparently supports this exclusion: "When they rise from the dead, they neither marry nor are given in marriage, but are like angels in heaven."[57] In this case, resurrected genitals will be only vestigial markers of a long-abandoned function. Thomas Aquinas argues, for example, "The instrument serves not only to execute the agent's operation, but also to show its virtue."[58] Once resurrected genitals have no "operational" purpose, they serve to manifest the virtue and glory of God's gift of sexual activity (precisely by refraining from it).

Even Stanley Grenz, whose entire theological anthropology centers upon human sexuality, suspends corporeal sex acts in favor of a sublimated "sexuality" composed of a drive toward wholeness and unity: "Sexuality is the sense of incompleteness together with the quest for wholeness that provides the impulse—the drive toward bonding. This impulse leads ultimately to the eschatological community that constitutes the new humanity in fulfillment of Gods' intentions from the beginning. . . . Although the community of male and female is its primal expression, marriage is neither the only nor the highest embodiment of bonded community."[59] Grenz's concept of sexuality relegates corporeal interaction to a secondary and peripheral status for the sake of a higher, spiritual unity and wholeness. Whatever role corporeal interaction plays in the ultimate form of sexuality, genital sexual expression ceases: "Even though genital sexual expression is left behind, the dynamic of bonding . . .

is at work in constituting humans as the community of the new humanity within the new creation in relationship with the triune God."[60] Grenz reduces sexuality to an abstract drive toward bonding, only loosely linked to corporeal expression. Although it is true that sexual expression cannot be restricted to any particular pattern of bodily contact, the term *sexuality* seems arbitrary where it no longer signifies bodily interaction at all. Despite his assertion that sexuality lies at the very heart of eschatological communion, Grenz does not provide any reasons why resurrected bodies have any particularly important role in this eschatological sexuality.[61] Moreover, once Grenz's eschatological sexuality has no reproductive function, his claim that only heterosexual intimacy holds an *analogia relationis* for trinitarian unity-in-difference begins to appear inexplicably narrow.[62]

Most theologians explain the cessation of sexual activity by appealing to a kind of eschatological population control. If reproduction carried on throughout eternity, the number of creatures in the new creation would approach infinitude, straining spatial logic. Beyond these spatial and mathematical cavils, however, theologians such as Augustine and Aquinas find the idea of sexual expression in glory somehow indecent, too absorbed in finitude, too animal. The strong connections between animality, sexual desire, and sexual interactions grate against many conceptions of holiness. Therefore, the new creation excludes sexual expression.

Nevertheless, sexual expression cannot be excised from the resurrection as easily as it might seem. Alongside the widespread negation of sexual expression in resurrected bodies, both scripture and the theological/mystical tradition employ sexual metaphor as a figure for creaturely union with God.

Repeatedly, Jesus describes the eschaton using images of marriage and marriage feasts.[63] At the center of the new heavens and new earth in Revelation, descends a "New Jerusalem, prepared as a bride" who is to be married to the lamb.[64] The consummation of this wedding is the life of the redeemed in the renewed holy city, a union evoked by the claim that the light emanating from the lamb's throne fills the entire city so completely that there is no need for the sun or stars. The root of these images lies with prophetic metaphor in the Hebrew Scriptures likening the relationship between YHWH and Israel to the relationship between a husband and wife. Jeremiah, Ezekiel, and Hosea lean heavily on metaphors of sexual fidelity in calling Israel to faithfulness.[65] In this framework, the restoration of

Israel figures as a final, once-for-all marriage between God and God's people.

Ascetics, monks, and mystics of the Christian tradition have long imagined themselves bound within a spiritual marriage to Christ, ultimately consummated in perfect union at the eschaton. The notion that celibacy is a kind of marriage to Christ appears already in Tertullian with reference to dedicated (female) virgins, but soon enough this spiritual marriage was inhabited by men as well.[66] Bernard of Clairvaux's meditations on the Song of Songs are an erotic celebration of union with God celebrating the details of the bridegroom's body (taken to be Jesus) in lavish detail. Bernard longs for the "kiss of his mouth," an image from the Song in which he finds both erotic energy and a picture of the Trinity (two lips pressed together in a loving kiss are like the Father and Son held together by the Spirit).[67] Bernard presses toward the consummation of this union. Gerard Loughlin relates a medieval tradition of interpretation, represented in both text and manuscript illumination, in which the marriage taking place at Cana, the site of Jesus's first miracle in John's gospel, was actually a wedding between Jesus and John. According to this tradition, when Jesus arrived at the wedding, John—who was preparing to marry someone else—was so deeply taken with Jesus that the first marriage was called off and John married Jesus instead.[68] The whole discourse of mystical marriage assumes an analogy between spiritual union with God and the sexual union between bodies.

Notably, the theological-metaphorical usefulness of sexual expression depends on *uniting* power of sexual intimacy rather than its reproductive function. In fact, in describing eschatological union through metaphors of sexual intimacy, reproduction generally drops out altogether. As evident above, where sexual metaphor illuminates notions of sanctification, union, and the fulfillment of spiritual desire, it need not rely on heteronormative assumptions (even if, in practice, it often has). Gender norms, too, loosen substantially in ascetic and mystical discourse as God and humans trade stereotypical gender roles quite fluidly.

Significant tension exists, then, between the exclusion of sexual expression from resurrected bodies and the prominent role of sexual metaphor in Christian imagination of the eschaton. Even the erasure of corporeal sexual expression for the sake of a sublimated, spiritual union still relies on sexual metaphor and thus leaves resurrected bodies suspended in a strange, liminal space. Under the influence of sublimation, the glorious "consummation" of history in the realm of God effectively drains resurrected bodies of animality by insisting that these bodies have nothing to do with union, consummation, and intimacy. Eschatological consummation, in this picture, trades the animality of material sexual interactions for an anemic sexuality involving perfected personalities, spirits, and subjectivities. Animality and corporeality are relegated to a secondary and passive participation.

Addressing the conceptual tension between bodies resurrected whole and intact and the evacuation of the physiological functions of those intact bodies, Agamben frames the question as one of "use": "The ostensive body of the elect, no matter how 'organic' and real it may be, is outside the sphere of any possible use. There is perhaps nothing more enigmatic than a glorious penis, nothing more spectral than a purely doxological vagina."[69] It is paradoxical to insist on the wholeness and integrity of the resurrected body while also asserting the suspension of its functions. Yet Paul claims: "Those parts of the body that seem to be weaker are indispensable, and the parts that we think are less honorable we treat with special honor. And the parts that are unpresentable are treated with special modesty, while our presentable parts need no special treatment."[70] Perhaps the "special honor" that belongs to "less honorable" parts lies in the transfiguration of the "use" of human animality, rather than its cessation. Agamben asks, "Is it possible, then, to speak of a different use of the body, on the basis of the glorious body's useless or unusable organs?"[71] The speculative maneuvers of this chapter counteract theological disparagement of human animality as a kind of residue of earthly existence by demonstrating the coherence of an eschaton in which human animality is the ineradicable means of participation in God's eternal life.

In order to support the claim that sexual expression (and therefore human animality) is not sidelined by eschatological transformation, but central to human communion with God, I want to fold in a discussion of the conceptual pairs intellect/instinct and freedom/determinism insofar as these, too, function as dividing lines between humanity and animality. The full dignity of proper humanity—as traditional eschatology imagines it—rises above the animality of sexual expression; likewise the free exercise of the mind sets proper humanity apart from instinct-driven animals. If, as Augustine's *non posse peccare* assumes, resurrection eradicates temptation toward sin, eschatological transformation brings the final silence of the urges and instincts that distract from a basically intellectual connection to God.[72] For large swaths of Christian thought, sexual desires and instincts have functioned as a conceptual condensation of temptation more generally, the point at which human nature stands conflicted. Accounts of eschatological transformation frequently resolve human complexity by taming human instincts—particularly sexual urges—simplifying the consciousness of the resurrected subject so that thoughts no longer arise from multiple conflicting internal sources. Eschatological freedom is freedom *from* the drives of instinct *for* the pursuit of a rarified knowledge of God.

Mary Midgley helpfully breaks down the opposition between intellect and instinct as a false dichotomy. Unspecified, the term *instinct* codes for a register of determinism, implying the channeling of a creature's agency; in contrast, the term *intellect* belongs to the register of freedom. In descriptions of nonhuman animals, language frequently overdetermines inquiry on this point: the category *instinct* tends to generate mechanistic accounts of behavior while discussions of *intellect* tend toward accounts of behavior focused on motive and strategy. But these answers should not diverge so strongly. Most animate creatures, humans included, have a combination of closed instincts (startling and looking around after a loud noise or a sudden flash of light, for example) and open instincts (the urge to flee danger, whether by climbing a tree, running away, or concealing oneself). Closed instincts may predominate in anemones and slugs, but it is open instincts that shape most behavior in vertebrate species. Closed instincts produce involuntary reactions, but open instincts propel creatures toward particular kinds of responses while allowing for a great deal of creativity in the responsive action. That is to say, open instincts require intelligence. Intelligence and instinct are not mutually exclusive, nor do instincts suddenly turn into intelligence at a certain threshold of complexity.[73] Rather, Midgley argues, complex instincts take the form of desires and interests—predictable concentrations of a creature's attention.[74] Instinct shapes the orientation of intelligence in its deployment. Because intelligence is always oriented by particular needs, interests, and desires, intelligence never displaces instinct.

If instinct names the fundamental orientation of intelligence, however, the way is open for an account of eschatological transformation in which divine grace operates in human life by shaping instinct (rather than freeing human beings from it). Once the binary opposition between intelligence/freedom and instinct/determinism is abandoned, the perfect creaturely freedom of resurrected life no longer requires a realm of intelligence unfettered by instinct. Eschatological freedom consists, rather, of instincts that orient creatures to the values of the realm of God. Robert Jenson describes the substance of God's eschatological promise: "We will live in this love [that is, God's triune love] as we are together the Body of the Son; therefore this same love must be the being also of our human [and creaturely] community with one another. We will be as different from one another as the Father is different from the Son; just as such we will be perfectly united to one another by the Spirit."[75] To see the love of God as the substance of the resurrected community provides a framework for the role of instinct within the lives of glorious creatures. Where the love of God is the substance of creaturely instinct, creaturely interests and desires refract divine love throughout the creaturely community in expressions as complexly differentiated as creatures themselves.

Intelligence—the subjective aspect of a creaturely life oriented by instinct—is not a homogeneous substance distributed in varying amounts to different creatures. Just as whale instincts appropriately direct whale interests, so whale intelligence will creatively express the glorious life of God in ways that reflect the love of God in whale-shaped experience. Assigning instinct the central role in creaturely appropriation of the love of God multiplies the ways in which God's love is understood and reflected in creaturely life. In other words, with instinct rather than intelligence at the center of divine-creaturely communion the range of eschatological freedom increases greatly—especially because intelligence often names a uniformly quantifiable capacity operating in a narrowly instrumental mode. Exclusively epistemological descriptions of eschatological communion—the beatific vision as the revelation of a perfect knowledge of God, for example—impoverish the new creation through the relegation of corporeal diversity (each body with its own modes of knowledge, attention, and response) to a peripheral concern. The refraction of divine love through the multiplicity of creaturely instincts manifests God's infinite generosity through endlessly creative creaturely performance. As the substance of instinct, the love of God orients creaturely life toward unity in virtue without any restriction on the range of creaturely agency.

The bees, ants, and spiders that infest Gregory of Nazianzus's 39th Oration can now rejoin the discussion. For Gregory, the productivity and order evident in these tiny creatures' homes is evidence of the intelligence of the divine Logos as it is mechanically expressed through irrational instinct. The "intelligence of unthinking creatures" does not belong to the creatures themselves but is externalized and attributed to the transcendent Logos. Although he does not recognize the link, Gregory describes the pinnacle of contemplative union with God as a participation in the divine Logos that is structurally identical to the externalized intelligence of spiders and ants. My account of eschatological transformation embraces this link between animal instinct and the creative expression of divine love so that human contemplative union with God becomes a function of the transformation of human instinct, rather than a function of a rarified intelligence that leaves instinct behind.

Where the Spirit enfolds creatures in the triune life of God, the resulting transformation of creaturely instinct refracts the love of God through the incalculable diversity of creaturely forms.[76] The diversity of creaturely expressions of divine love sounds out finite echoes of an infinite love in the constitutive exchange between God's three persons. One established name for creaturely formation in the love of God is *virtue* (although virtue is often falsely distinguished from instinctual patterns of behavior).[77] Augustine argues that sin will be an impossibility in the eschaton—*non posse peccare*—not because God artificially constrains human freedom, but because human attentions and desires will be so thoroughly saturated in the love of God that alienation cannot gain a moment's consideration.[78] Here, the language of instinct better captures the comprehensively corporeal significance of virtue than alternative definitions focused on habit or practice.[79] Training for virtue in the present age anticipates the full eschatological transformation through which the generative creativity of the Spirit will allow human beings (and other creatures) to reflect the life of the Logos. Human virtue, of course, differs from the virtues of tigers and elephants as much as tiger and elephant sociality differ from each other, but when perfected virtue is linked to instinct, human virtue no longer divides one supposedly moral species from an amoral creation. Instead, human virtue is one unique register of creaturely excellence among many others.[80] Just as Gregory recognizes the Logos in spiders and ants, so too we might imagine every species instinctually conformed to the Logos in its own peculiar way. Human intelligence participates in the divine life whereas the differing intelligences of other creatures participate in equal measure, but diverse ways. Without negating the multiplicity of creaturely intelligence, centering eschatological freedom in instinct shatters any single hierarchical scale of creatures by insisting that God's creativity multiplies its own expression through the diversity of creaturely life.

At this point, I would like to focus again on one particular kind of instinct—the interests, attentions, and desires that we call sexual—as a site of human participation in the divine life. The Christian tradition has a long history of sublimating the energy of erotic discourse by directing it toward union with God. Earlier, I described the breakdown in Gregory of Nyssa's sublimation scheme as it ultimately fails to parse truly human desire from the sexual impulsiveness of animality. Gregory's sublimation is complex, and not subject to any easy division of body from spirit, even as the very shape of the corporeal seems constantly to shift in his texts.[81] Human contemplation draws closer to the divine darkness through the alluring attraction of God's corporeal appearances—the divine back shown to Moses, or the bridegroom leaping away as a deer.[82] Moreover, even as Gregory clearly thinks that human genitals will not accompany human bodies into the life of the resurrection, Gregory's new creation is still sexually charged insofar as erotic desire stretches out toward a God whose infinite presence also infinitely recedes.[83] And this stretching out, it would seem, is precisely what it means to live "like the angels." The solid ground of human discursiveness must give way to the sea of erotic passion to be carried beyond the grasp of reason and language by the allure of divine beauty.[84] Gregory's sublimation doubles back on itself in its dependence on the animalized sexuality that it seeks to transfigure. Even if it does so unwittingly, Gregory's theology demands an account of sexual expression as it persists within eschatological transformation.

Counteracting theological claims that resurrected human bodies will lack genitals or that human genitals will lack any function, an account of eschatological sexual expression can certainly begin in agreement with Mark Jordan:

> We get our bodies back again and stay with them for eternity. We get them back as the best human bodies there are, which means, as bodies with genitals. Unless you regard human genitals as a sort of cancerous affliction, a disease, a deformity, that

> came upon us after sin, then you cannot regard them as something that will be missing from our bodies after resurrection—any more than you can hold that Jesus' resurrected body was a eunuch's body. Here again, take the organs as emblem of deeper powers. The erotic powers with which we were created were given not only for this world, hence not only for reproduction. They were given as instruments and enactments of intimate union. That union culminates in union with God.[85]

Nevertheless, while the unitive power of sexual expression frequently concentrates upon the genitals, sexual expression plays a much larger role in human life than genital stimulation or any set of activities hived off from the rest of human life in the privacy of a bedroom.[86] Like most other species, human beings use the repertoire of bodily interactions that, in some contexts, forge sexual intimacy to establish connections in relationships that are not straightforwardly sexual.[87] The examples are numerous: we greet one another with hugs and kisses; we hold hands with our friends (more in some cultures than others); we comfort one another by sitting close or massaging each other's shoulders and neck; we prolong eye contact with one another to share the significance of a moment. In some non-Western cultures, even affectionately touching another person's genitals is not taken as a sexual advance so much as the expression of trusting friendship.[88] The semiotic plasticity of sexual behavior generates a huge range of functions for corporeal intimacy that betray any hermetic separation of "sexuality" as an isolated sphere of human interaction. Recognizing that contextual factors determine whether or not an act is legible as "sexual" or not also forces us to recognize that the corporeal repertoire of sexual expression can communicate personal bonds of trust through "nonsexual" interaction. *Union*, then, need not be narrowly constrained to any particular set of bodily acts.

While maintaining an apophatic reserve with regard to the explicit details, with this broad view of sexual interaction it is entirely appropriate to affirm, with Robert Jenson, that the uniting and bonding power of sexual interaction may be constitutive of human participation in divine love in its social and interpersonal forms. Jenson notes that the reproductive function of (heterosexual) sexual expression may cease, but that the function of sexual expression to create deep interpersonal bonds may persist, even adding that sexual intimacy is a figure for the more general bondedness of the whole human community in Christ in the eschaton.[89] And although Jenson clearly refers narrowly to sexual intimacy within heterosexual marriage, if the final telos of sexual expression does not involve reproduction, this restriction becomes entirely questionable. It would hardly be wise to bring narrowly straight expectations to the marriage of the lamb and the New Jerusalem.[90] Wholehearted human love for God does not detract from love for neighbors, but focuses and intensifies it. Likewise, the transformation of human sexual instinct as a reflection of the love of God will focus and intensify the whole range of sexual expression that bonds human beings together. The desires that draw human beings into corporeal intimacy will manifest the glory of God within the richly diverse corporeal bonds that knit the human community together.

Conclusion

Agamben writes of *profanation* as a process that restores to common use something which has been locked into a specialized function.[91] Agamben regards the glorious body of the resurrection—in which both digestion and sexual expression have been rendered superfluous—as the human body profaned, restored to a common use: "In the glorious body it became possible for the first time to conceive the separation of an organ from its physiological function. But the possibility of discovering another use of the body—which this separation allows us to glimpse—has remained unexplored."[92] This chapter's speculations have put theological imagination to work in discovering a range of eschatological uses for human bodies. For Agamben, the eschatological suspension of the physiological function of the digestive and sexual organs opens up the space of a separation, the space of the possibility of profanation.[93] Just as a dancer's stylized movements evoke common activities, but also lend them additional beauty by stripping them of their ordinary context and function, so also the superfluity of heavenly digestion and sexual expression may be the most profound creaturely expressions of divine glory in the new creation—"the hieroglyphs or the arabesques that divine glory inscribes onto its own coat of arms."[94] Neither digestion nor sexual expression are, in this vision of the eschaton, necessary to sustain life. They are set free—precisely in their stylized superfluity, precisely in their uselessness—for the common use of sharing divine life and divine love.[95]

The traditional denial of resurrected digestion and sexual expression safeguards corporeal materiality while simultaneously sanitizing the resurrected body from its animal associations. Insisting upon the animality of resurrected human bodies provides momentum for thinking about an eschatological ecology. If the new heavens and new earth are replete with a new ecology and not merely an assemblage of creatures living hermetically side by side, then the concrete relations named in consumption and sexual intimacy represent a substantial overlap between theology and ecology. Eucharistic theology (insofar as it always pushes toward an eschatology) and the theology of eschatological union with God demand an ecological articulation that pushes beyond a narrowly anthropocentric vision of the new heavens and new earth. Insofar as eschatology provides the ethical horizon for Christian thought, a fully populated eschatological ecology calls to account the settled patterns of oppression in which so many creatures presently suffer confinement, encroachment, exploitation, or extinction. The Spirit may take up these animal bodies, after all, as reflections and extensions of God's own superabundant life and love, so that the most mundane bodily acts perform God's grace for the common good.

Conclusion

Our basic human self-understanding, inextricable from conceptions of humanity and animality, is a primary engine of ecological degradation in all its myriad forms, from loss of biodiversity and habitat destruction to climate change and ocean acidification. The wager of this book is that ecological concerns must ultimately be addressed vis-a-vis a reconfiguration of our notions of our own humanity, our notions of the animality shared among all sentient creatures, and our relations with nonhuman animals themselves. Of course, at the level of ethics and politics, concerns for environmental problems and for animal rights and welfare are not only separate matters, but frequently in opposition. A thick cloud of ethical disagreements leads to Tom Regan's accusation that Aldo Leopold is a proponent of "environmental fascism."[1] Nevertheless, I am convinced that, conceptually prior to these ethical concerns, there is a layer of thought at which problems of ecology, humanity, and nonhuman animal life are thoroughly enmeshed. Unraveling conceptions of humanity rooted in anthropological exceptionalism would simultaneously turn human attention toward transforming our overwhelmingly exploitative role in earth's ecosystems, but also reconfigure the terrain of our moral sensibilities regarding nonhuman neighbors. In other words, examining and reconstructing relations between humanity and animality at the level of cosmology and basic self-conception (that is, at the level of theological anthropology) remains a necessary step for a deep transformation of both the ethical and ecological relations between human and nonhuman animals. A theological reconsideration of animality, then, provides a fresh angle into ecotheology.

The foregoing chapters demonstrate that ideas about humanity and animality do not just shape relations between species, but structure relations between human thoughts, bodies, desires, social relations, and subjects—not to mention human differences along the boundaries of class, gender, sexuality, race, citizenship, and ethnicity. The mobile border between proper humanity and human animality correlates with distinctions made between human beings and nonhuman animals. Our intrahuman distinctions and internal "parts" end up dividing the perceptible world too. As such, the construction of a categorically exceptional proper humanity is not only a disavowal of our own human animality, and a denigration of people who are associated more closely with animality (arbitrarily), but also the symptom of a kind of ecological death drive.[2] In the Anthropocene era, not only human beings but the whole collective of earth's living creatures are trapped and threatened within the ideological regime of proper humanity.

The distinction between human animality and humanity proper is a conceptual knot that generates, justifies, and perpetuates anthropogenic ecological degradation. This internal distinction produces a categorical distinction between human beings on the one hand and all other animals on the other.[3] When all living creatures are divided into these two categories, the whole natural world (the spaces and places that other animals inhabit) is lumped in with the animal side, while the home, the town, and the city are conceptually hived off from the "natural" world and become the proper space of humanity. Nature and animality are both ambiguously subordinated beneath proper humanity, which defines itself by superiority over nature and animality. Animality and nature both nominally include humanity, but humanity's self-definition performs its exclusion by denying that authentic humanity is governed by these categories. The sustained ideological production of a nonnatural, nonanimal space for humanity is the knot that inescapably binds human beings to the ecological degradation we cause.

Of course, we recognize our alienation from the natural world and have made efforts to respond. Yet in the United States, the conservation movement is nearly a century and a half old, and the popular environmental movement is over four decades old, and these movements are very clearly fighting a losing battle.[4] The victories won (for example, the establishment of National Parks and congressionally designated Wilderness areas, the ban of DDT, and the reintroduction of wolves) deserve genuine celebration. But energy consumption, species extinction, and wildland encroachment have only increased in the last four decades.[5] In aggregate, we are exacerbating the problems rather than adequately addressing them. Corporate and state power gladly supports local recycling programs, organic options, and isolated wildlife preserves as long as nothing impedes the "liberation" of capital "frozen" in forests and oil deposits, the intensification of agriculture in its quest for maximally efficient livestock and soil, and the externalization of production costs through shoddy waste treatment and pollution. These compromises are a suicide pact. Systemic political and economic disregard for ecological integrity cannot be adequately addressed through individual behavior modification, conscientious consumerism, and piecemeal reform movements. All of these approaches only scratch the surface of our ideological, antiecological human self-understanding. Proper humanity has a momentum all its own, untethered from the ecosystemic rhythms that it has disavowed. The deep alienation of proper humanity from creation supports the link between proper humanity and original sin in chapter 5.

Proper humanity is most at home in the world of finance, industry, entertainment, and statecraft. The spaces of our interaction with nonhuman animals—what we call *nature*—appears almost as another planet. The difference between these worlds is only the distinction between proper humanity and human animality amplified institutionally. Like all our neighbors, human beings vitally depend on air, water, and an intricate network of biodiversity. Yet, the human world perpetually operates as if our lives were more tightly bound up with our vocational identity, our standard of living, and our social status than with ecological politics. The antagonistic division between the human world and the natural world is so patently false that stating it explicitly manifests its incoherence. But we do not sustain the division between our creaturely lives and our human livelihoods because it is true; we sustain the division because it *works*. It works by authorizing the ongoing destructive exploitation of fellow creatures for short-sighted economic ends. We are the animals whose lives are at stake in the sacrifices we make to keep our markets growing.[6] Proper humanity will finally kill us off, but it will destroy animality (human and nonhuman) first.

This destructive conceptual opposition between humanity on the one hand and animality and nature on the other persists (despite its increasingly alarming consequences) because of a deep ideological investment in proper humanity. The very structure of Western subjectivity builds upon the disavowal of animality. In boardrooms and government chambers the pressure to make "rational," "innovative," and "path-breaking" decisions is a pressure to participate in a mode of human progress that is untethered from the constitutive ecological relations in which we live as creatures. At the interpersonal level, the short-term consequences of any failure to perform humanity properly press more urgently than the long-term consequences of ecological degradation. So we reproduce the norms of proper humanity despite our best intentions. The human-animal distinction is the mirror in which we recognize ourselves, not an idea with which one might agree or disagree. It is an ideological structure integral to our identity formation. It is written in every norm that delimits civilization and holiness. It has become a basic fact about the world, a truth that we inscribe into a political order that keeps every creature in its place. All this is to say that the boundary between humanity and animality can be destabilized; but insofar as it holds our personal and societal formation together, it remains impossible to simply opt out.

All this verges on a counsel of despair. Nevertheless, piecemeal resistance to the boundary between humanity and animality leaves traces of hope. Fleeting zones of suspension that temporarily jam the anthropological machine occasionally set common creaturehood above proper humanity and make visible the politics of creaturely life. Jane Goodall, Dian Fossey, and Biruté Galdikas famously negotiated zones of suspension that endured longer than most, but smaller zones open up wherever someone frees a trapped raccoon, honors the dignity of a road-killed squirrel by moving it off the highway, feels the vulnerability of sharing a hillside with a bear, or negotiates domestic relations with a dog or cat. In spaces where the politics of creaturely life are unavoidable, we recognize more easily the stranglehold that proper humanity has on us. Standing witness to the precarity of creaturely lives—and feeling our own precarity in connection with theirs—gives hints of a different configuration of creaturely politics. Chapters 4 and 6 offered arguments for regarding these moments as the proximity of the *basileia theou*, the realm of God.

While bodily solidarity with other creatures is undoubtedly the most effective form of resistance to proper humanity, resistance might also take conceptual form. There is no escape hatch in proper humanity, no way to simply opt out. But the ideology itself is built on constitutive contradictions. Proper humanity thrives on the insularity that it creates for itself. For this reason, destabilizing the integrity of humanity as a category historicizes and denaturalizes the particular formations that govern our collective self-conception. Since proper humanity aspires to a pure transcendence over nature and animality, demonstrating that it is inescapably contaminated with animality (even and especially where it pretends to extricate itself into transcendence) can relax the hold that its norms have upon us, and allows us to inhabit both our humanity and animality differently.

Sadly, theological discourse—and theological anthropology in particular—has labored mightily to safeguard humanity as a natural category that transcends animality and nature. This fact would be particularly damning if most other Western discourses had not been wholeheartedly engaged in the same project. Certain strains of feminism and decolonial resistance are notable exceptions. Despite theology's complicity, the problem of human animality must be addressed at the level of a world-building discourse like theology because proper humanity and its disavowal of human animality is part of the elemental story that we tell about ourselves, the narrative structure that orients us to the world, providing a frame for our ambitions and our day-to-day experience. Narratives that describe human nature and purpose operate in the background of consciousness; these narratives cannot be retired without setting another narrative of a similar magnitude in its place. Even though theology now lacks the cultural influence that imbedded theological concepts in the foundations enlightenment thought—the image of God, for example—theology remains an apt discourse to take on such a critical and constructive project.

This project exposes the contours of the problem of human animality in the contours of Christian theology in order to build resistance to the commonplace disavowal of animality. The critical and historical work demonstrated several instances of a generally applicable principle: insofar as animality is finally ineradicable from human life, any effort to cut a categorical human-animal distinction inevitably produces contradictions surrounding unacknowledged disavowals of human animality. Where theologians disavow animality in order to safeguard human uniqueness, animality returns unnamed and uncredited. The historical inquiry carried out in the early chapters could be fruitfully repeated with other theologians and philosophers to provide a much richer picture of the ways that animality performs unmentioned functions within accounts of human nature and human transformation.

The ineradicability of human animality in the work of theologians such as Gregory of Nyssa, Gregory of Nazianzus, Karl Rahner, and Wolfhart Pannenberg also leaves traces useful for those seeking out a different path. The moment in which thought disavows animality, upon a carefully considered return, can become a moment in which another, radically different relationship to animality becomes visible. Once they are recognized, animality's disavowed theological roles may be honored and centered. Where human animality is the contact point for divine grace, human beings' ecological relations cannot be excluded from theological reflection and the longstanding erasure of nonhuman creatures from the theological narrative becomes easier to resist.

This project grew out of a relatively simple question: What has prevented Christianity from becoming a site of effective resistance to ecological degradation? My answer: Christian theology is so thoroughly committed to a categorical human-animal distinction that the narrative structures of subject formation in societies with Christian heritage pervasively minimize the enmeshment of human beings within the ecological politics of creaturely life. Failing to see our enmeshment within networks of creaturely interdependence, we fail to resist their degradation. We imagine that moral and spiritual politics take place on a higher level than that of corporeal creaturely interaction, rendering interactions with other creatures basically irrelevant to one's standing before God. Until Christian theology surrenders its investment in a categorical human-animal distinction and correctively centers its theological anthropology on human animality, Christian resistance to ecological degradation will be ineffective and contradictory. This project represents only a few steps along that road, a prolonged gesture in a new direction; but similar efforts could extend the trajectory through other historical texts and other constructive loci—resisting the valorization of proper humanity and exposing the hidden disavowals of human animality. Where humanity surrenders its propriety, however, and enters an apprenticeship in *zōē aiōnios*—the animality of God—we may at last hear the voice of the Spirit rising through the lives of creaturely neighbors in expressions more hopeful than inarticulate groans.

Acknowledgments

This project has occupied my mind and my heart for an inordinate number of years and I owe a tremendous debt of gratitude to all of those who have helped to see it through with me. Elizabeth Johnson's wisdom, impeccable theological instincts, and incisive critique have shaped this project more than I can express. Benjamin Dunning is the single most generous and generously critical person I have met in academic circles. I can only aspire to pay forward his unsurpassed contributions to my thought and writing. Time and again, Aristotle Papanikolaou encouraged the project along with well-timed questions and illuminating conversations. My cotravelers at Fordham heard more than one version of these ideas and helped to sharpen them along the way. Thanks to Daniel Reginald Soowong Kim, John Penniman, the Reverend Mother Kathryn Reinhard, Brianne Jacobs, Tom Jacobs, Jack Downey, Catherine Osborne, Erica Olsen, Beth Pyne, Scott MacDougall, Malik JM Walker, Emily Cain, Michael Azar, Mara Brecht, Jon Stanfill, Zach Smith, Monica Danae Pierce, Krista Stevens, Allan Georgia, Jeannine Hill-Fletcher, Larry Wellborn, Samir Haddad, and Crina Gschwandtner. Through the project's middle years, the Theological Studies Department at Loyola Marymount University made a wonderful academic home. Special thanks to Jonathan Rothchild, Molly Gower, Matt Pereira, Mugdha Yeolekar, Nirinjian Khalsa, Will Britt, Anna Harrison, Gil Klein, Chris Chapple, Amir Hussain, and Cecilia González-Andrieu for personal, intellectual, and collegial accompaniament. Finally, I am deeply grateful for my colleagues at Carroll College—John Ries, Eric Hall, and Katherine Greiner—whose theological conversations have been so fruitful. More to come!

Many of the ideas in these pages first saw the light of day at academic conferences. The work that goes into planning and pulling off such events is rarely appreciated, but their intellectual fruit and personal connections have been inexpressibly important to me. Thanks especially to Beatrice Marovich, Anthony Paul Smith, Donovan Schaefer, Aaron Gross, Adam Kotsko, Ellen Muehlberger, David Clough, Alison Covey, Jenny Barry, Peter Mena, Virginia Burrus, Marika Rose, Amaryah Armstrong, Alex Dubilet, David Aftandilian, Jennifer Koosed, Dan Barber, Catherine Keller, Karen Bray, and Becky Artinian-Kaiser, whose far-flung intellectual community has both shaped and sustained me.

Family and friends, equally far-flung, have been instrumental in my ability to imagine and write these pages. Thanks to Mark and Kim Meyer, Karen and Willy Rust, Patrick and Christopher Meyer, Shelley Kerr, Nancy Adams, Marjorie and Grosvenor Rust, David and Kim Meyer, Casey Bailey, David Kerns, Elinor and Stephen Gottschalk, Dave Willis, Dwight Kroll, Aaron Sparks, Lois Lorentzen, Jon Linton, Brad and Sara Johnson, and Tom Fikes.

Finally, to Carolyn, Lupine, and Avery—the pack with whom I affiliate—my deepest love, admiration, and joy is yours, here again as always.

Notes

Introduction

1. Aristotle, *Politics*, 10.

2. Derrida, *Animal*, 32.

3. A sampling of accounts of human self-understanding vis-a-vis animality: Agamben, *The Open*; Calarco, *Zoographies*; Derrida, *Beast and the Sovereign*, vol. 1; Gilhus, *Animals, Gods and Humans*; Midgley, *Beast and Man*; Oliver, *Animal Lessons*; Osborne, *Dumb Beasts and Dead Philosophers*; and Sorabji, *Animal Minds and Human Morals*.

4. Oliver, *Animal Lessons*, 1–22; Gross, "Question of the Creature," 122, 128.

5. Agamben, *The Open*, 33–38, 79–80.

6. Plato, *Phaedrus*, §§246–54.

7. Many authors take note of the connection between intrahuman distinctions and the human animal distinction; this project's contribution lies in sustained theological analysis of the relation between these distinctions. See Haraway, *When Species Meet*, 71–72; Keller, *From a Broken Web*, 24; Kelsey, *Eccentric Existence*, 117; and Midgley, *Beast and Man*, 40, 197.

8. The question of the integrity of the human being was at the center of the fourth- and fifth-century Christological controversies as well as controversies over Origenism.

9. Wolfe, *Animal Rites*, 17.

10. In the helpful typology outlined in Calarco's *Thinking through Animals*, I am working out a theological version of an "indistinction" model of human-animal relations.

11. Gross, "Question of the Creature," 121.

12. This broad historical claim is a condensation of the argument set forward in White's classic article, "The Historical Roots of Our Ecologic Crisis."

13. A representative sampling of environmental texts that take the separation of humanity from all other earthly life as the root source of ecological irresponsibility: Abram, *Spell of the Sensuous*; Plumwood, *Environmental Culture*; and Cronon, "Trouble with Wilderness."

14. Derrida, *Animal*, 32.

15. Gross, *Question of the Animal and Religion*, 102; Gross, "Study of Religion After the Animal," 71; Peterson, "Posthumanism to Come," 134.

16. Calarco, *Zoographies*, 140–41. More narrowly, it also responds to Celia Deane-Drummond and David Clough's call for an effort to "engage in detail with figures in the Christian tradition and its neighbors with attentiveness to the implications of their thought for the construal of what it means to be human and non-human" ("Postscript," in *Creaturely Theology*, 267).

1. Gregory of Nazianzus: Animality and Ascent

1. Gregory of Nazianzus, Orat. 28.30, *PG* 69c. All citations of Gregory's orations will be given according to the oration and the section number, followed, for convenient reference, by the column number in Migne's *Patrologia Graece* [hereafter, *PG*], vol. 36. The text of Oration 28 is from *Grégoire de Nazianze: Discours 27–31*; the *Sources Chrétiennes* volumes also contain marginal references to *PG*. All translations from the Greek are my own. A complete English translation is available in Gregory of Nazianzus, *On God and Christ*.

2. McGuckin, *Saint Gregory of Nazianzus*, 192; Michel Foucault's 1983 lectures on parrhesia are transcribed and compiled in *Fearless Speech*.

3. Christopher Beeley takes up the same two orations jointly in *Gregory of Nazianzus on the Trinity and the Knowledge of God*, 69, 88.

4. For example: Ep. 101, *To Cledonius*, §6, *PG* 37:181d–184ab; §9, *PG* 188ab. The text of Gregory's theological letters is from *Grégoire de Nazianze: Lettres Théologique*; English translation is available in Wickham, *On God and Christ*. Ruether, *Rhetor and Philosopher*, 130. For Gregory, the mind is the site of subjectivity, whereas the soul is the site of subjectivity for Origen. Gregory's human soul functions in the way that animal souls function for Origen—as the source of animation and instinctive drives. Compare Origen of Alexandria, *On First Principles*, 1.1.6; 1.4.1; 2.8.2–3; 3.6.7. See also O'Laughlin, "Anthropology of Evagrius Ponticus and its Sources," 357–73, especially 364–68. See also Beeley, *Trinity and Knowledge*, 272.

5. Gregory of Nazianzus, Ep. 101, *To Cledonius*, §4, *PG* 177bc; Orat. 28.22, *PG* 56–57a. Ellverson, *Dual Nature of Man*, 20–32. The soul (*psyche*) plays only a minor role in Gregory's texts; his anthropological narrative focuses on ongoing tensions between mind and flesh; see Richard, *Cosmologie Et Théologie*, 268–69.

6. Gregory of Nazianzus, Ep. 101, *To Cledonius*, §12, *PG* 189c.

7. Wesche, "'Mind' and 'Self' in the Christology of Saint Gregory," 45. On the alignment of intra-anthropological divisions with the boundary between humanity and animality see Agamben, *The Open*, 15–16.

8. Richard, *Cosmologie et Théologie*, 265–66; Wesche, "'Mind' and 'Self,'" 36.

9. Gregory of Nazianzus, Orat. 28.12, *PG* 40d–41a.

10. Gregory of Nazianzus, Orat. 39.7, *PG* 341bc.

11. Gregory of Nazianzus, Orat. 39.10, *PG* 344d; 39.18, *PG* 356c.

12. Norris, *Faith Gives Fullness*, 110; also 122.

13. Richard, *Cosmologie et Théologie*, 260.

14. Gregory of Nazianzus, Orat. 39.8, *PG* 344a.

15. Gregory of Nazianzus, Orat. 28.12, *PG* 41b; see also Orat. 28.11, *PG* 40b; Orat. 28.13, *PG* 41cd-44a.

16. Gregory of Nazianzus, Orat. 28.13, PG 41c. See also F. Norris, *Faith Gives Fullness*, 118.

17. Barbel, *Gregor von Nazianz*, 284. See also Norris, *Faith Gives Fullness*, 37; Wesche "'Mind' and 'Self,'" 50.

18. Gregory of Nazianzus, Orat. 28.31, *PG* 72a–c. See also Orat. 38.9–11, *PG* 36:320d–324b; Orat. 40.5, *PG* 364bc; Orat. 45.2, *PG* 36:624bc–625ab; Orat. 45.5–7, *PG* 629a–632b; "On the Soul," ll. 65–80, *PG* 37:452; "In Praise of Virginity," ll. 30–55, 80–95, *PG* 524–525, 528.

19. Joseph Barbel, *Theologischen Reden*, 283. See also Orat. 28.12, *PG* 41b; Orat. 28.16, *PG* 45d–48ab; Orat. 28.17, *PG* 48cd; Richard, *Cosmologie et Théologie*, 127.

20. Gregory of Nazianzus, Orat. 28.28, *PG* 65d–68a. The luminous communion of divine, angelic, and human minds that one finds in Gregory's texts, of course, resonates with contemporary Neoplatonic thought. See Richard, *Cosmologie et Théologie*, 127; Beeley, *Gregory of Nazianzus*, 66, 103–4.

21. Gregory of Nazianzus, Ep. 101, *To Cledonius*, §9, *PG* 188ab; see also §7, *PG* 185ab.

22. Gregory of Nazianzus, Orat. 39.7, *PG* 341bc; see also Orat. 38.12, *PG* 324bcd.

23. In fact, Gregory refers to human subjection to death as the "condemnation of the flesh"—as if death were a problem of the flesh, rather than the mind; Orat. 39.13, *PG* 349b; see also Ep. 101, *To Cledonius*, §9, *PG* 188a.

24. It is also known by the title "On the Baptism of Christ." The text is from *Grégoire de Nazianze: Discours 38–41*. An English translation is available in Gregory of Nazianzus, *Festal Orations*. Translations from the Greek are my own.

25. McGuckin, *Biography*, 337.

26. Most significantly, in front of the Emperor Theodosius, Gregory is to baptize Athanarich, the Gothic leader whose alliance has helped Theodosius to victory over a rival band of Goths. Ibid., 241, 337, 343.

27. Gregory of Nazianzus, Orat. 39.7, *PG* 341c; see also Orat. 28.15, *PG* 45bc; Orat. 39.6, *PG* 341a.

28. Gregory of Nazianzus, Orat. 39.6, *PG* 341a.

29. Gregory of Nazianzus, Orat. 39.11, *PG* 345b–d.

30. Gregory of Nazianzus, Orat. 39.8, *PG* 344a.

31. See Beeley, *Gregory of Nazianzus*, 71.

32. Gregory of Nazianzus, Orat. 40.23, *PG* 389a.

33. John 1:9.

34. Thinking of baptism as illumination is not unique to Gregory, but was a fairly common trope in the fourth century. Harrison, *Festal Orations*, 90n74; McGuckin, *Biography*, 337; Beeley, *Gregory of Nazianzus*, 109; Ruether, *Gregory of Nazianzus*, 63n4.

35. "What came about through this one [the Word] was life, and this life was the light of human beings." John 1:4.

36. "I am the light of the world, Whoever follows me will never walk in darkness, but will have the light of life." John 8:12. See also 12:44–46.

37. For example: Gregory of Nazianzus, Orat. 39.8, *PG* 341d; Orat. 39.10–11, *PG* 344d–345c; Orat. 39.11, *PG* 345bc, Orat. 39.20, *PG* 360a. See also Beeley, *Gregory of Nazianzus*, 103–4.

38. Gregory of Nazianzus, Orat. 39.10, *PG* 344d–345d.

39. For example, in a more extended engagement with John's prologue (specifically John 1:9, quoted earlier) at the beginning of Oration 31, God's illumination is clearly equated with the knowledge of the Trinity, *zōē* appears nowhere in the passage. Gregory of Nazianzus, Orat. 31.3, *PG* 136a–137a.

40. Barbel, *Theologischen Reden*, 284.

41. Gregory of Nazianzus, Orat. 40.5, *PG* 364bc. See also Orat. 39.11, *PG* 354bc, Orat. 39.20, *PG* 360a; Orat. 38.9-10, *PG* 320d–321c.

42. Ruether, *Rhetor and Philosopher*, 153; see also Bynum, *Resurrection of the Body*, 112–13.

43. Beeley, *Gregory of Nazianzus*, 83; Richard, *Cosmologie et Théologie*, 282–84. Beeley and Richard rightly correct Ruether on Gregory's understanding of the resurrection (see *Rhetor and Philosopher*, 136, 149), but miss his erasure of animality. See also Ellverson, *Dual Nature*, 32.

44. This reading of Gregory stands in some tension with that of Bergmann, *Creation Set Free*, 14, 138–39.

45. Gregory of Nazianzus, Orat. 38.11, *PG* 321c–324b.

46. Gregory of Nazianzus, Orat. 39.13, *PG* 348d.

47. Richard, *Cosmologie et Théologie*, 227.

48. Gregory of Nazianzus, Orat. 39.13, *PG* 348d–349ab.

49. Gregory of Nazianzus, Orat. 39.13, *PG* 349b.

50. Gregory of Nazianzus, Orat. 39.18, *PG* 356b.

51. Ruether, *Rhetor and Philosopher*, 132.

52. Gregory of Nazianzus, Orat. 28.31, *PG* 72b; Orat. 38.9, *PG* 321a; Richard, *Cosmologie et Théologie*, 155; Otis "Cappadocian Thought as a

Coherent System," 107. For an extended consideration of the theological problem of the angelic fall and angelic mutability, see Kotsko, *Prince of this World.*

53. Gregory of Nazianzus, Orat. 39.18, 356b.

54. McGuckin, *Biography*, 240–41, 276–78.

55. Gregory of Nazianzus, Orat. 28.1, *PG* 25d.

56. Gregory of Nazianzus, Orat. 28.2, *PG* 28a–d.

57. See Gross, *Question of the Animal and Religion*, 8–10; Derrida, "White Mythology"; Derrida, "'Eating Well' or the Calculation of the Subject."

58. Gregory repeats the violent imagery from Sinai/Exodus 19 at the beginning of Orat. 31, *PG* 133b.

59. Beeley, *Gregory of Nazianzus*, 66–68.

60. Gregory of Nazianzus, Orat. 28.12, *PG* 41b; 28.13, *PG* 44ab. Norris, *Faith Gives Fullness*, 113.

61. Gregory of Nazianzus, Orat. 28.23, *PG* 57b.

62. Gregory of Nazianzus, Orat. 28.24–25, *PG* 57d–61a.

63. Discussion of the ordered habits of bees, ants, and spiders in particular is a trope in Late Antiquity. Aristotle mentions them together (*Historia Animalium*, 1) Philo brings them into the theological tradition (*De providentia*, 1.25; *De animalibus*, §17–21) Origen discusses them (*Contra Celsum* 4.81), as do Gregory's contemporaries Basil of Caesarea (*Hexaemeron*, 8.4), Nemesius of Emesa (*De natura humana*, §43), Evagrius of Pontus (*Ont the Faith*, §39; *On the Eight Thoughts*, §11), and Jerome (*Life of Malchus*, 7). For discussion, see also Gilhus, *Animals, Gods and Humans*, 73–74; Dickerman, "Some Stock Illustrations of Animal Intelligence"; and Grant, *Early Christians and Animals*, 29.

64. Gregory of Nazianzus, Orat. 28.25, *PG* 60cd.

65. Gregory of Nazianzus, Orat. 28.24, *PG* 60b.

66. Gregory of Nazianzus, Orat. 28.25, *PG* 60c.

67. That is to say, there is a kind of autoimmune structure within Gregory's spirituality. At the eschatological limit, personal knowledge of God—insofar as I claim it as *my* knowledge—is actually an impediment to lived intimacy with God. On the logic of autoimmunity, see Derrida, *Rogues*, 35–36, 86.

68. Gregory of Nazianzus, Orat. 28.30, *PG* 69c.

2. Gregory of Nyssa: Reading Animality and Desire

1. Gregory of Nyssa, *Gregorii Nysseni Opera*, 8.1:179; hereafter cited as *GNO*. All translations from the Greek are my own. A complete English translation is available in Gregory of Nyssa, *Fathers of the Church*, vol. 58.

2. The text has come to be known by the title *On Calling Oneself a Christian*; *GNO*, 8.1; English translation in Callahan, *Ascetical Works*.

3. Gregory of Nyssa, *GNO*, 8.1:132–33.

4. Ibid., 8.1:136.

5. Ibid., 8.1:137. Gregory is likely alluding here to Plato's *Republic*, 588b.

6. The homilies were commissioned by Olympias, a wealthy young widow in Constantinople, and delivered during the lenten season in one of the years between 391 and Gregory's death ca. 394. See Gregory of Nyssa, *GNO*, 6:3; Norris, *Homilies*, xvi; Daniélou S.J, "La chronologie des oeuvres de Grégoire de Nysse," 159–69. The text of Gregory's homilies are in Gregory of Nyssa, *GNO*, vol. 6. I have benefitted from Norris, *Gregory of Nyssa*. Both Norris's translation and the older McCambley translation contain marginal reference to the page numbers in *GNO*, which I provide for convenience throughout the chapter.

7. Derrida, *Animal*; with occasional reference to the original French text, *L'animal que donc je suis*.

8. Gregory's mention of "some clerics" is often taken to refer to Diodore of Tarsus and his student Theodore of Mopsuestia, though Gregory does not name anyone specifically; Gregory of Nyssa, *GNO*, 6:4. See Heine, "Gregory of Nyssa's Apology for Allegory," 366–69.

9. Gregory of Nyssa, *GNO*, 6:5.

10. Gregory's relationship to Origen, his primary influence in the practice of theological interpretation, has been the subject of several excellent studies. See, in particular, Dünzl, *Braut und Bräutigam*; Norris, "Soul Takes Flight"; and Ludlow, "Theology and Allegory."

11. Gregory of Nyssa, *GNO*, 6:19–23.

12. Dünzl refers to this as the *Stichwort* (keyword) method of exegesis, in which sense is brought to a difficult word through connections made to other instances of the same word in scripture; see *Braut und Bräutigam*, 54; for contrast with Origen, see Ludlow, "Theology and Allegory," 55–56, 58.

13. Gregory of Nyssa, *GNO*, 6:105–6.

14. Norris, "Soul Takes Flight," 531–32; Ludlow, "Theology and Allegory," 50–51, 53, 63–64; see also Torjesen, *Hermeneutical Procedure*, 71–72.

15. Norris, "Soul Takes Flight," 520–21.

16. Gregory of Nyssa, *GNO*, 6:14.

17. Norris, *Homilies*, xxxiii; Laird, "Fountain of His Lips," 40.

18. Gregory, *GNO*, 6:15.

19. Ibid., 6:17. See also Ludlow, "Theology and Allegory," 54.

20. Norris, *Homilies*, xx.

21. Gregory's unique understanding of the doubleness of creation stands in the tradition of readings of Genesis 1–3 significantly informed by Plato's *Timaeus*. Prominent predecessors would include Philo (*De opificio mundi*) and Origen (*De principiis*).

22. Gregory of Nyssa, *GNO*, 6:22–23; cf. 27. While Gregory's theological interpretation undoubtedly places the Song of Songs into a patriarchal

framework in which the (female) bride longs after and is commanded by the (male) bridegroom who stands in for God, this patriarchal framework is not ironclad for Gregory; it is incidental to this particular text. To read Gregory's commentary as a normative effort to ontotheologically ground patriarchal gender roles in an understanding of an arche-male God would be tendentiously anachronistic. Gregory's default androcentrism is unquestionable, but his understanding of gender and human nature is so fluid (as seen earlier) as to call ontological gender hierarchy into question—the "bride" has been a "son" and the "bridegroom" has been woman Wisdom. See also ibid., 6:183, 212–13 for Gregory's considered use of feminine imagery for God and his defense of the practice.

23. Gregory repeatedly uses *hypographomenon* and *hypographe* in clearly pedagogical (or mystagogical) contexts, although he can also use it in the more general sense of a "description" or "outline." In any case, it always refers to the "lower," material meaning of a text which is to be transposed into a spiritual register. See ibid., 6:19, 39, 144–45, 146–47, 180, 188, 190, 384.

24. The agency of the text itself and the agency of God are difficult to separate: "The anagogical interpretation here aligns with the thought already examined, for the discourse [or the Logos] accommodates human nature to God by an ordered sequential road." It is not clear in context whether *Logos* refers to the discourse of the Song of Songs (as McCambley's translation has it), or to the second person of the Trinity (as Norris's translation reads). At any case, there is a transformative divine agency at work upon the reader in and through the sequential development of the text. Ibid., 6:145; see also 278–79, 294–96 and Ludlow, "Theology and Allegory," 63–64.

25. Nonna Verna Harrison refers to Gregory's style of exegesis as "iconic," in that attention to the surface of the text ultimately involves the reader in the scene described; as with an icon, the text looks back at the reader. Harrison, "Allegory and Asceticism in Gregory of Nyssa," 125; likewise, Martin Laird coins the term "logophasis" to try to capture the sense that the text affects the reader in her relationship to God in ways other than simply communicating content or concepts, "it is not language in search of God (kataphatic), but language that is full of God (logophatic)." Laird, "'Whereof we Speak,'" 4; see also Mosshammer, "Disclosing but not Disclosed," 99; Ludlow, "Theology and Allegory," 62; Dünzl, *Braut und Bräutigam*, 335; and Norris, *Homilies*, xx, xli.

26. Gregory of Nyssa, *GNO*, 6:11.

27. Gregory of Nyssa, "De hominis opificio," §18. Translation available in Gregory of Nyssa, *Writings and Letters*.

28. Gregory of Nyssa, *GNO*, 6:15.

29. Norris, *Homilies*, xxiii.

30. Gregory of Nyssa, *GNO*, 6:12.

31. See also Gregory of Nyssa, *GNO*, 6:27–29, in which Gregory relies on the same violent stoning of animals from Exodus 19 that Gregory of Nazianzus took up in Oration 28.

32. "La vérité de la pudeur sera finalement notre sujet." Derrida, *L'animal*, 70; cf. *Animal*, 45. Derrida also claims that the essay is about "response" and "limitrophy," although all of these themes are arguably bound up together. Ibid., 8, 29.

33. Derrida, *Animal*, 20, 45. For Derrida's earlier investigation and definition of the notion of "proper"-ness, see Derrida, "White Mythology," 246–50.

34. My interpretation of humanity's "fault" differs slightly from that of Lawlor, *This Is Not Sufficient*, 29, 40; for yet another interpretation, see Calarco, *Zoographies*, 18.

35. The subject constructed through an opposition between humanity and animality simultaneously builds upon the hierarchical opposition between masculinity and femininity. See Derrida, "Eating Well," 280–81.

36. Derrida's articulation of the constitutive role of "the animal" in Western philosophical discourse about the human and Giorgio Agamben's concept of the "anthropological machine" are mutually illuminating and deeply consonant. See Agamben, *The Open*, 15–16, 21, 29, 37.

37. The exceptions here are the lion/leopard and the raven, which are taken to symbolize how far the bride (or in the case of the raven, Jesus's apostles and prophets) has come from a dissolute life of sin. Gregory of Nyssa, *GNO*, 6:250–53, 391–93.

38. For a more explicit picture of Gregory's understanding of the connection between animality and sexuality (as unnatural to humanity as such), see *De hominis opificio*, §14–16. Substantial secondary literature has been written on this passage from *De hominis opificio*. My understanding of the passage aligns closely with Zachhuber, *Human Nature in Gregory of Nyssa*, 169–72.

39. Gregory of Nyssa, *GNO*, 6:25.

40. See also ibid., 6:250–52, where the former association of the bride with lions and leopards is taken as indicative of a shamefully sinful past, and 6:15, 104, 391–93, 423–24.

41. Song 5:4 LXX; Gregory of Nyssa, *GNO*, 6:332.

42. Gregory of Nyssa, *GNO*, 6:333; see also Dünzl, *Braut und Bräutigam*, 169.

43. Gregory of Nyssa, *GNO*, 6:23.

44. Another excellent example of this dynamic is found in Gregory's comments on the extended praise of the Bride's beauty (Song 4:1–5, 6:5–9), in which her hair is compared to a flock of goats, her teeth are likened to twin sheep, her lips to a thread, her cheeks to pomegranates, her neck to a tower, and her breasts to grazing fawns. The passage is repeated twice in the Song and receives extended commentary in Gregory's exegesis. Gregory, *GNO*, 6:218–42 and 450–56; cf. 78, 85, 140, 175, 178–79, 377.

45. Ibid., 6:84.

46. Ibid., 6:359–61. See also Dünzl, *Braut und Bräutigam*, 179.

47. Gregory of Nyssa, *GNO*, 6:379.

48. Ibid., 6:327–28. Gregory begins the first homily with an invitation to the discerning listener to strip off the garment of sin and enter the intimacy of the bridal chamber in pure, white garments, thus evoking the nudity of baptismal rituals. See ibid., 6:14.

49. Burrus, "Queer Father," 158.

50. Derrida, *Animal*, 47–49.

51. Ibid., 54–55.

52. Ibid., 12. See Kelly Oliver's notion of "animal pedagogy," *Animal Lessons*, 20–21.

53. Derrida, *Animal*, 47–51.

54. The depth of this formation (and not some apolitical attachment to the human-animal distinction for its own sake) is the reason why Derrida refuses to deny or negate the human-animal distinction altogether. Matthew Calarco criticizes him for this refusal (*Zoographies*, 137–49 and *Thinking Through Animals*, 51), but perhaps does not reckon with the impossibility of simply setting aside the human-animal distinction for a human subject whose identity is irreparably formed by that distinction both at an individual and collective level. Calarco rightly recognizes that Derrida makes any attempt to draw a categorical distinction between humanity and animality nonsensical, but this is because his engagement deconstructs such a distinction from within its own assumptions rather than denying it more straightforwardly. See Derrida, *Animal*, 29–31 for the relevant passage. See also Gross, *Question of the Animal and Religion*, 141–44; and Peterson, "Posthumanism to Come," 127–28, 134.

55. Derrida, *Animal*, 5–6, 31–32, 54–60; see also Gross, *Question of the Animal*, 121–26.

56. Gregory of Nyssa, *GNO*, 6:178; 6:139–40. Cf. Song 2:8–9; 2:17; 8:14. Gregory reads the verb ἥκει in Song 2:8 as signifying that the bridegroom has "come" into sight in order to draw the bride further on, rather than—more straightforwardly—that the bridegroom is actually coming toward the bride.

57. Gregory of Nyssa, *GNO*, 6:139; see also 6:137–42, 170–71, 178, 356, 378–77.

58. See Louth, *Origins of the Christian Mystical Tradition*, 90–92; Daniélou, *Platonisme et théologie mystique*, 291–307.

59. Gregory of Nyssa, *GNO*, 6:104.

60. Ibid., 6:27–29, 63; Burrus, "Queer Father," 147, 155.

61. Dünzl, *Braut und Bräutigam*, 366–67; see also Laird, "Under Solomon's Tutelage," 79; and Ludlow, *Universal Salvation*, 58–59, 63.

62. Gregory of Nyssa, *GNO*, 6:247; cf. 323–24, 356, 425–26.

63. Gregory "identifies love with the appetitive faculties of our irrational nature," that is, with *epithumia*. See Smith, *Passion and Paradise*, 191.

64. Harrison, "Allegory and Asceticism," 124.

65. Derrida, *Animal*, 67.

66. For example, Gregory of Nyssa, *De hominis opificio*, §14.

67. One paradigmatic example of this dynamic is Warren J. Smith's text *Passion and Paradise*. In the first part of the book Smith meticulously traces Gregory's effort to distinguish humanity from other animals along the lines of rationality/discursiveness, sexual procreation, desire, and passion/emotion. Yet, when desire returns to play a positive theological role in human salvation, its essential connection to animality is pervasively effaced. See Smith, *Passion and Paradise*, 37, 69, 77–78, 87, 104–6, 183, 187, 219, 227.

68. Dünzl takes stock of the ambivalence in Gregory's treatment of erotic desire; *Braut und Bräutigam*, 357, 364–69.

69. See Deleuze and Guattari, *Thousand Plateaus*, 238–39.

70. Gregory of Nyssa, *GNO*, 6:29.

71. Ibid., 6:21.

72. Smith, *Passion and Paradise*, 183.

3. The Problem of Human Animality in Contemporary Theological Anthropology

1. Karl Marx, *Capital*, 1st edition, quoted in Žižek, *Less Than Nothing*, 410. This sentence was removed from the second edition of *Capital*.

2. Wallace, *Infinite Jest*, 694.

3. Although he describes a slightly different dynamic, David Clough also sees a pervasive spread of what he calls "not-animal anthropology" in contemporary accounts; "Not a Not-Animal," 10. For other articulations of a contemporary consensus, see Pannenberg, *Anthropology in Theological Perspective*, 63; and Huyssteen, *Alone in the World?*, 140.

4. Jenson, *Systematic Theology*, 2:56–57.

5. Ibid. Such an argument is an even more insidious inversion of Kant's already pitiless claim that we should not mistreat animals only because doing so will make us more likely to mistreat other humans. It is hard to imagine how willful indifference to the unprecedented regimes of animal suffering offers reminders of the high value of human life.

6. Jenson, *Systematic Theology*, 2:59, 130; *Systematic Theology*, 1:79.

7. Jenson, *Systematic Theology*, 2:61–63, 79, 95.

8. Ibid., 2:57–58, 130.

9. Zizioulas, *Being As Communion*, 35, 44, 50–51, 56.

10. Ibid., 42–45; Zizioulas, "Human Capacity and Human Incapacity," 408.

11. Zizioulas, "On Being a Person," 44.

12. Zizioulas "Priest of Creation," 286. Zizioulas echoes Martin Heidegger at this point, whose three-fold scheme classified the stone (that is,

material objects) as "without world" (*weltlos*), animals as "poor in world" (*weltarm*), and human beings as "world making" (*weltbildend*); Heidegger, *Fundamental Concepts of Metaphysics*, 176–77; *Die Grundbegriffe der Metaphysik*, 263.

13. Zizioulas, "Priest of Creation," 290.

14. Zizioulas, "Human Capacity and Incapacity," 415.

15. David Clough provides invaluable analysis on questions of human uniqueness, election, and the place of animals in the theology of Karl Barth; see *On Animals*, 1:89–100.

16. Barth, *Church Dogmatics*, III/2, 136; III/1, 18, 44.

17. Barth, *The Humanity of God*, 52. See also Clough, "Not a Not-Animal," 9.

18. Barth, *Humanity of God*, 53.

19. Barth, *Church Dogmatics* III/2, 224.

20. Ibid., III/2, 14–15; III/1, 207–8.

21. Balthasar, *Theo-Drama*, 2:322, 339.

22. Ibid., 2:343; *Theological Anthropology*, 85.

23. Ibid., 2:339.

24. Tillich, *Courage to Be*, 81; *Systematic Theology*, 180. Much of Tillich's vocabulary with regard to the difference between humans and animals manifests a debt to Heidegger's *Fundamental Concepts of Metaphysics*, see note 12 supra.

25. Tillich, *Systematic Theology*, 175.

26. Ibid., 191, 205, 209.

27. Ibid., 175.

28. Ibid., 259–60.

29. Ibid., 170–72.

30. Ibid., 260.

31. Comblin, *Retrieving the Human*, 70, 88, 229–30.

32. Ibid., 92, 229–30.

33. Ibid., 73, 88, 92.

34. Ibid., 88-89; see also 94–95, 193.

35. Ibid., 98, 160.

36. Peacocke, *Theology for a Scientific Age*, 244; see also 217, fig. 3; 230–31.

37. Ibid., 238–39, 242, 248; and Peacocke, *Creation and the World of Science*, 72–73.

38. Peacocke, *Theology for a Scientific Age*, 252–53.

39. Tanner, *Christ the Key*, 9, 11.

40. Ibid., 16, 25, 28.

41. Ibid., 48; on the plasticity of human nature, see 37–42.

42. Grenz warrants this claim by reference to Genesis 1:26–27; only human beings are explicitly created "male and female." Grenz, *Social God and the Relational Self*, 273; see also 199–201, 324; and Grenz, *Theology for the Community of God*, 130.

43. Grenz, *Social God*, 302, 324.
44. Ibid., 280; see also 283.
45. Grenz, *Theology for the Community*, 130–31.
46. Ruether, *Sexism and God Talk*, 87.
47. Ruether, *Gaia and God*, 5, 30; *Sexism and God Talk*, 20, 73.
48. Ruether, *Gaia and God*, 43.
49. Ruether, *Sexism and God Talk*, 88, 91–92.
50. See also Sideris, *Environmental Ethics*, 46–60, esp. 59.
51. Kelsey, *Eccentric Existence*, 30–31, 162–63, 200, 255–56. While I entirely concur with David Clough's criticism of Kelsey's anthropology—that he proceeds as if humanity could be described solely in relation to God without any reference to other creatures—I wonder whether Kelsey's account has actually succeeded in avoiding a contrastive account of humanity; see Clough, "Not a Not-Animal," 9.
52. Kelsey, *Eccentric Existence*, 291–92.
53. Ibid., 286–89.
54. Ibid., 252–53; see also 117, 256, 271–72.
55. Deane-Drummond, *Wisdom of the Liminal*, 26–29.
56. Kelsey, *Eccentric Existence*, 718, 837–40, 864–65, 1025, 1043.
57. See, for example, Kelsey, *Eccentric Existence*, 84.
58. Rahner, *Foundations of Christian Faith*, 119.
59. Kilby, *Karl Rahner*, 20.
60. Rahner, *Foundations*, 123–24, 127.
61. Rahner, "Theology and Anthropology," 28, 42; see also, Fischer, *Der Mensch als Geheimnis*, 101–2.
62. Rahner, "Christology within an Evolutionary View," 174; "Theology of Freedom," 180–81.
63. Rahner, *Foundations*, 77; see also Kilby, *Karl Rahner*, 59.
64. Rahner, "Christology in Evolutionary View," 170, 172; see also "Natural Science and Reasonable Faith," 40, 42; and *Foundations*, 54, 77.
65. Rahner, "Natural Science," 42–43.
66. Rahner, "Unity of Spirit and Matter," 169.
67. Rahner, *Foundations*, 140, 142; "Theology and Anthropology," 30.
68. Rahner, "Christology in Evolutionary View," 160.
69. Rahner, *Foundations*, 207.
70. Rahner, "Theology and Freedom," 188; "Christology in Evolutionary View," 168.
71. Rahner, "Theology of Freedom," 181.
72. Rahner, *Foundations*, 48; see also Buckley, "Within the Holy Mystery," 33.
73. Rahner, "Natural Science and Reasonable Faith," 45–46; see also, *Foundations*, 39.
74. Rahner, "Theology of Freedom," 190; see also *Foundations*, 35–36; see also Carr, "Starting with the Human," 23–25.
75. Fischer, *Der Mensch als Geheimnis*, 367, 373–74.

76. Rahner, *Foundations*, 42; see also McDermott, "Bonds of Freedom," 52.

77. Rahner, "Theology and Anthropology," 37; see also Fischer, *Der Mensch als Geheimnis*, 277.

78. Rahner, *Foundations* 208–12, 228–30, 235. Schüssler Fiorenza, "Theology: Transcendental or Hermeneutical," 332.

79. Rahner, *Foundations*, 118.

80. Ibid., 308.

81. Ibid., 309.

82. Rahner, "Unity of Spirit and Matter," 176.

83. Rahner, "Gnade als Mitte menschlicher Existenz," 83; quoted in Losinger, *Anthropological Turn*, 68.

84. Porter, "Moral Language and the Language of Grace," 178, emphasis added. See also the exchange between Jean Porter and Brian Linnane following the initial article in Porter, "A Response to Brian Linnane and David Coffey," 285–86; and Linnane, "Categorical and Transcendental Experience in Rahner's Theology," 201, 205–6.

85. Porter, "Moral Language and the Language of Grace," 174–75.

86. Metz, *Faith in History and Society*, 74; see also Díaz, *On Being Human*, 113; and Freyer, "Inwiefern sind ontologische Kategorien für eine theologishe Anthropologie unabweisbar?," 20.

87. Defending Rahner against Metz's claims, Paul Crowley and Francis Schüssler Fiorenza argue that Rahner's transcendental theology provides an account of human commonality across difference that actually enables dialogue and negotiation across major differences. See Crowley, "Encountering the Religious Other," 578, 583–85; and Schüssler Fiorenza, "Karl Rahner," 129–134.

88. The distinction here is borrowed from Kotsko, *Prince of this World*, 95.

89. Rahner, "Theology and Anthropology," 35, emphasis added. See also Rahner, "Theology of Freedom," 186; Linnane, "Categorical and Transcendental Experience," 205; Porter, "Moral Language and the Language of Grace," 176.

90. Kilby, *Karl Rahner*, 34; see also Losinger, *Anthropological Turn*, 61–62; Fischer, *Der Mensch als Geheimnis*, 275–76.

91. Rahner, *Foundations*, 20.

92. Rahner, "Unity of Spirit and Matter," 155–56, 177.

93. Rahner, *Foundations*, 98–99.

94. Rahner, "Christology in an Evolutionary View," 186.

95. Rahner, *Foundations*, 99–101.

96. Rahner, "Unity of Spirit and Matter," 177.

97. Pannenberg, *Anthropology in Theological Perspective*, 69. Other uniquely human characteristics for Pannenberg include symbolic communication (*Anthropology*, 186–87), a religious impulse (*Systematic Theology*, 2:134, 175.), plastic and malleable nature (*Anthropology*, 45,

59, 63, 500), abstract engagement with objects (*Anthropology*, 62, 72, 76; *Systematic Theology*, 2:192–93); and deputized authority over creation (*Anthropology*, 76–79; *Systematic Theology*, 2:190, 219, 231). For further analysis of the human-animal distinction in Pannenberg, see Wong, *Wolfhart Pannenberg*, 62; Onah, *Self-Transcendence*, 23; Grenz, *Reason for Hope*, 132; Dallmayr, "Politics of the Kingdom," 91; Galloway, *Wolfhart Pannenberg*, 14; and Saranyana, "Hacia una Antropologia Teologica," 1116–17.

98. Pannenberg, *Anthropology*, 109.

99. Fischer, "Fundamentaltheologische Prolegomena zur Theologischen Anthropologie," 56.

100. Pannenberg, *Anthropology*, 34/31; on the link between Pannenberg, Scheler, and von Euxküll, see Onah, *Self-Transcendence*, 17; on the concept of *Umwelt*, see Uexküll, *Umwelt und Innenwelt der Tiere*, and *Streifzüge*. For further analysis of Uexküll's *Umwelt*, see Agamben, *The Open*, 39–47.

101. Pannenberg, *Anthropology*, 33–34; see also Fischer, "Fundamentaltheologische Prolegomena," 48; Wong, *Pannenberg on Human Destiny*, 62; Tupper, *Theology of Wolfhart Pannenberg*, 70; and Dallmayr, "Politics of the Kingdom," 88.

102. Pannenberg, *Systematic Theology*, 2:229; see also *Anthropology*, 69–73.

103. Pannenberg, *Systematic Theology*, 2:135–36.

104. Pannenberg, *Anthropology*, 45, 59, 63, 186–87, 500.

105. Ibid., 225. See also Fraijo, *El Sentido de la Historia*, 135; Wong, *Pannenberg on Human Destiny*, 102.

106. Pannenberg, *Anthropology*, 61–62, 261; See also Wong, *Pannenberg on Human Destiny*, 76; and Galloway, *Wolfhart Pannanberg*, 32. David Polk suggests that Pannenberg has unnecessarily reified a subject/object distinction at this point; see Polk, *On the Way to God*, 113.

107. Pannenberg, *What is Man?*, 13.

108. Pannenberg, *Anthropology*, 108.

109. Pannenberg, *Systematic Theology*, 3:561–62.

110. For Pannenberg's development of the notion of a subjective pole and an objective pole see *Systematic Theology*, 2:194.

111. Wong, *Pannenberg on Human Destiny*, 103; Grenz, *Reason for Hope*, 125, 137–38; Galloway, *Wolfhart Pannenberg*, 23–24.

112. Pannenberg, *Anthropology*, 221, 225, 241; see also Tupper, *Theology of Wolfhart Pannenberg*, 73; Galloway, *Wolfhart Pannenberg*, 24.

113. Pannenberg, *Anthropology*, 109, quoted at length earlier.

114. Pannenberg, *Anthropology*, 142; see also Grenz, *Reason for Hope*, 128.

115. Pannenberg, *Systematic Theology*, 3:560; Schwoebel, "Theology in Anthropological Perspective?," 23; Wong, *Pannenberg on Human Destiny*, 104, 111, 114.

116. Pannenberg, *Anthropology*, 109.

117. Ibid., 105–7. Whether Pannenberg adequately distinguishes creatureliness from the state of sinfulness has been a point of contention among his readers. See Fischer, "Fundamentaltheologische Prolegomena," 53–54, 58; Olson, "Pannenberg's Theological Anthropology," 163–64; Wong, *Pannenberg on Human Destiny*, 105–7.

118. Pannenberg, *Anthropology*, 107; on solidarity and redemption, see Kotsko, *Politics of Redemption*, 3–5.

119. Pannenberg, *Anthropology*, 186–87, 261.

120. Pannenberg, *Systematic Theology*, 2:295, 304–5, 315, 419, 425–27, 430–31.

121. See Weheliye, *Habeas Viscus*, 3–12; see also my "Political Ecology of Dignity: Human Dignity and the Inevitable Returns of Animality," 549–69.

122. See, for example, Pannenberg, *Anthropology*, 165.

123. Pannenberg, *Anthropology*, 315.

124. Midgley, *Beast and Man*, 286.

125. Pannenberg, *Anthropology*, 34, 109.

126. *Natureculture* is a term adapted from Donna Haraway; see Haraway, *When Species Meet*, 15, 16, 25.

127. Midgley, *Beast and Man*, 197.

4. Animality and Identity: Human Nature and the Image of God

1. The "theological turn" in continental philosophy—particularly in the work of Jacques Derrida—is sharply contested. See, for example, Hägglund, *Radical Atheism*; Naas, *Miracle and Machine*; and Caputo, *Prayers and Tears of Jacques Derrida*.

2. Agamben, *The Open*, 16.

3. Ibid., 92; emphasis added.

4. Derrida, *Animal*, 62.

5. Ibid., 132.

6. Ibid., 101.

7. For Derrida's invocations of messianicity, see his *Specters of Marx*, 33; and "Faith and Knowledge," 55. For commentary on the concept, see Laclau, "Time Is Out of Joint," 92–93; and Ware, "Dialectic of the Past," 110–11.

8. Derrida, *Animal*, 12.

9. Deleuze and Guattari, *A Thousand Plateaus*, 252–53.

10. See the discussion in Sherman, "No Werewolves in Theology?," 1–7; with reference to Hallward, *Out of this World*.

11. Barber, "Ideology and Apocalyptic," 172.

12. Deleuze and Guattari, *A Thousand Plateaus*, 238–39.

13. Versions of this taxonomy appear in many texts. For a few examples, see Hall, *Imaging God*, 89–108; Middleton, *Liberating Image*, 17–29; Huyssteen, *Alone in the World?*, 126.

14. Keller, *From a Broken Web*, 13. For other integrated relational accounts of human identity from feminist theologians, see Ruether, *Gaia and God*, 266; *Sexism and God Talk*, 112–13; McFague, *Body of God*, 86–87, 106; Daly, *Beyond God the Father*, 168, 178.

15. Keller, *From a Broken Web*, 86; see also Ruether, *Gaia and God*, 171.

16. Keller, *From a Broken Web*, 114, 134, 136.

17. Ibid., 203.

18. See Zizioulas, *Being As Communion*; LaCugna, *God for Us*; Moltmann, *Trinity and the Kingdom*; and Grenz, *Social God*.

19. Rahner, *Foundations*, 42; Pannenberg, *Anthropology*, 241, 446; Kelsey, *Eccentric Existence*, 296, 382; and Suchocki, *Fall to Violence*, 42–43.

20. David Clough, "Not a Not-Animal," 5.

21. For example, see McFague, *Body of God*, 38–47; Haught, *God After Darwin*, 57–80.

22. See also Midgley (*Beast and Man*, 197), who suggests that the evolutionary framework is capable of supporting the same species hierarchy, with "forward" replacing "up" in the logic.

23. Gross, "Introduction," in Gross and Vallely, *Animals and the Human Imagination*, 8.

24. The phrase appears three times within the primordial history of Genesis 1–11 (1:26–27, 5:1–3, 9:6 with a likely allusion in Psalm 8), yet Pannenberg, for example, claims that the image of God and human sin are the two organizing concepts of theological anthropology (*Anthropology*, 20).

25. Briggs, "Humans in the Image of God," 112, 119.

26. Examples of the *imago dei* serving these functions are manifold: Pannenberg, *Anthropology*, 59–65, 76, 79; *Systematic Theology*, 2:229, 231; and Kelsey, *Eccentric Existence*, 281, 286, 291–92, 837. Even J. Richard Middleton's liberative account, asserts that the *imago dei* is a democratizing notion because it indicates that *all* humans rule over other creatures (rather than just a monarch); see *Liberating Image*, 204–5, 289.

27. Keller, *Face of the Deep*, 136–38; Bauckham, *Bible and Ecology*; Kelsey, *Eccentric Existence*, 161; Cunningham, "Way of All Flesh," 106–10; Moltmann, *God in Creation*, 186–90; Clough, *On Animals*, 101; see also Fergusson, "Human Nature in Theistic and Evolutionary Perspectives," 446, 449, 451–52.

28. Lucas, *Daniel*, 102–3.

29. Ibid., 104, 118.

30. If there is any historical authenticity to the letter and the events that it describes, it is more likely to tell the story of one of Nebuchadnezzar's successors, Nabonidus, of whom we have a historical record of insanity. Hartman and DiLella, *Book of Daniel*, 178–80; Lucas, *Daniel*, 106–7; Lacocque, *Book of Daniel*, 74–75.

31. Hartman, *Book of Daniel*, 174; Lucas, *Daniel*, 104; Lacocque, *Book of Daniel*, 83; Nolan Fewell, *Circle of Sovereignty*, 75.

32. Deleuze and Guattari, *A Theousand Plateaus*, 238–39.

33. For example, Lucas, *Daniel*, 116–18; Lacocque, *Book of Daniel*, 86, 88.

34. Oliver, *Animal Lessons*, 226–27; Johnson, *Women, Earth, and Creator Spirit*, 34.

35. Agamben, *The Open*, 3.

36. Jürgen Moltmann works out some of the differences between a "messianic" and a "Christological" approach to Jesus in *The Way of Jesus Christ*, 1–27; see also Kerr, *Christ, History, and Apocalyptic*, 11–17. The revival of an apocalyptic view of Jesus's life and teaching has a long and distinguished pedigree in nineteenth- and twentieth-century biblical scholarship; see Weiss, *Jesus' Proclamation*; Schweitzer, *Quest of the Historical Jesus*; and Käsemann, "Die Anfänge christliche Theologie," 162–85. See also Bultmann, "Ist der Apokalyptik die Mutter der christliche Theologie?." For uses of an apocalyptic view of Jesus close to my purpose here, see Boff, *Jesus Christ Liberator*, 53; and Sobrino, *Jesus the Liberator*, 67.

37. "Realm of God" as a translation of *basileia tou theou* follows the lead of Peter Scott who argues for a "common realm of God, humanity, and nature"; see Scott, *Political Theology of Nature*, 30–32; see also Moltmann, *Way of Jesus Christ*, 97–98.

38. Gutiérrez, *Theology of Liberation*, 134–35.

39. Schüssler Fiorenza, *In Memory of Her*, 148; Boff, *Jesus Christ, Liberator*, 72–75, 282.

40. Similarly, the Lukan parable of Lazarus and the rich man (Luke 16) centers on the perspectival solidarity of God's realm with the oppressed.

41. Schüssler Fiorenza, *In Memory of Her*, 119–30, Sobrino, *Jesus the Liberator*, 81. For an extended discussion of Jesus's table-sharing practices, see also Tilley, *Disciples' Jesus*, 175–87.

42. Sobrino, *Jesus the Liberator*, 71–72, 79–84; Moltmann, *Way of Jesus Christ*, 99–102.

43. Sobrino, *Jesus the Liberator*, 72, 116, 126–27; Scott, *Anti-Human Theology*, 53.

44. Boff, *Jesus Christ, Liberator*, 280–81.

45. My account of immanence and transcendence is particularly indebted to Barber, *On Diaspora*, 171–72.

46. There is, of course, very thin evidence in the gospels that Jesus ever advocated for animals and animality against humanity's disavowal. See Bauckham, "Jesus and the Wild Animals"; Wennberg, *God, Humans, and Animals*, 291; and Linzey, *Christianity and the Rights of Animals*, 48. Nevertheless, the conceptual privilege of humanity over animality naturalizes and stabilizes forms of privilege which Jesus did confront directly: the casting aside of the poor, women, and "unclean" ordinary

folk in preference for purified, righteous, wealthy, men. If the realm of God cannot brook these latter forms of privilege, then the mutually implicated privilege of humanity over animality is called into question as well. For an extended account of human dignity grounded in animality, see my "Political Ecology of Dignity."

47. Scott, *Political Theology of Nature*, 54.

48. Meyer, "They Fell Silent When We Stopped Listening."

49. Derrida, *Animal*, 5–6.

50. Derrida, *Animal*, 18. Haraway criticizes Derrida for using his cat as a mere prop in a larger discourse, for failing to actually engage with the cat as subject; see *When Species Meet*, 20, 22. Although Haraway's criticism has merit, it collapses too quickly the difference between Derrida's personal, face-to-face interaction with the cat and his account of that interaction. Derrida might be understood to be *intentionally* laconic and spare in an attempt to avoid domesticating the cat's gaze and assigning it (false) meaning (Derrida, *Animal*, 9, 14–15). By means of its relative anonymity, the nameless cat functions as a symbol whose gaze catches Derrida's readers as well. His text is not abstractly explaining from a distance so much as exercising an authorial reserve that allows his readers to be captured within analogous relations.

51. Plumwood, *Environmental Culture*, 176.

52. Butler, *Frames of War*, 19–20.

53. Plumwood, *Environmental Culture*, 120.

54. Bailly, *Animal Side*, 15.

55. The textual layers run deeper. Sultan's story is told in the style of Franz Kafka's story about Red Peter; see Kafka, "A Report to an Academy," 250–59.

56. Coetzee, *Lives of Animals*, 28.

57. See the similar analysis of these same experiments in Midgley, *Beast and Man*, 230. On the use of anthropomorphism within scientific observation and explanation, see Bekoff and Pierce, *Wild Justice*, 42.

58. More specifically, 9.2 billion nonhuman animals for roughly 320 million Americans, according to statistics from the USDA Livestock Slaughter Annual Summary (http://usda.mannlib.cornell.edu/MannUsda/viewDocumentInfo.do?documentID=1097) and Poultry Slaughter Annual Summary (http://usda.mannlib.cornell.edu/MannUsda/viewDocumentInfo.do?documentID=1497). These statistics are summarized (and set in historical context) by the Humane Society of the United States (http://www.humanesociety.org/news/resources/research/stats_slaughter_totals.html).

59. Vatsal G. Thakkar, "Diagnosing the Wrong Deficit," *New York Times*, April 27, 2013, accessed May 8, 2013, http://www.nytimes.com/2013/04/28/opinion/sunday/diagnosing-the-wrong-deficit.html.

60. Midgley, *Beast and Man*, 197.

61. Pope Francis, *Laudato Sil*, §48–52, the text of the encyclical is available from the Vatican website or in *Encyclical on Climate Change and Inequality*; Val Plumwood, *Environmental Culture*, 68.

62. Derrida, *Animal*, 14, 33, 87, 92–94; Žižek, *Less Than Nothing*, 410.

63. See "Toward a Dialogical Inter-species Ethic," in Plumwood, *Environmental Culture*, 167–95.

64. Smuts, "Response," 109.

65. Ibid., 118.

66. See Willett, *Interspecies Ethics*, 249, 274–75; Deane-Drummond, "Are Animal Moral?," 207; de Waal, *Primates and Philosophers*; and Bekoff and Pierce, *Wild Justice*, 10, 16, 31.

67. Dillard, *Pilgrim at Tinker Creek*; Abram, *Becoming Animal*, 186–87; Abbey, *Desert Solitaire*, 22–25.

68. Battaille, *Theory of Religion*, 21–22.

69. Derrida, *Animal*, 7.

5. Animality in Sin and Redemption

1. Plato, *Republic*, 9, §571.

2. Baldwin, *Go Tell It on the Mountain*, 89.

3. Agamben, *Homo Sacer*, 8.

4. In a maneuver that has generated unfortunate amounts of confusion among Agamben's readers, he maintains Aristotle's conceptual distinction between bare life and the good life (*zēn* versus *eu zēn*), but replaces Aristotle's vocabulary with another pair of terms (*zōē* and *bios*). See Agamben, *Homo Sacer*, 1, 8–9, cf. 66. In basic agreement with Norris ("Giorgio Agamben and the Politics of the Living Dead," 45n.17), my essay ("The Logos of God and the End of Man: Animality As Light and Life") seeks, in part, to address confusion regarding Agamben's project on the part of both Finlayson, "'Bare Life' and Politics in Agamben's Reading of Aristotle," 99; and Derrida, *Beast and Sovereign*, 1:325–26.

5. Agamben, *Homo Sacer*, 2, 7–8.

6. Ibid., 181.

7. Ibid., 28–29, 83, 109, 181.

8. Ibid., 83.

9. Derrida, *Beast and Sovereign*, 1:324–34; Weheliye, *Habeas Viscus*, 35-43, 65-72.

10. Calarco, "On the Borders of Language and Death," 96–97. In a later text (*Zoographies*, 90–103), Calarco recognizes a broadening in Agamben's work—beginning with *The Open*—to include the politics of the human-animal boundary.

11. Agamben, *The Open*, 21, 26, 37–38, 78–80.

12. Ibid., 15-16; see also ibid., 37–38; and Durantaye, "Suspended Substantive," 7.

13. Agamben, *The Open*, 25–26.

14. Agamben, "What Is An Apparatus?," 13–14.

15. Again, see Weheliye, *Habeas Viscus*, especially the introduction and chs. 2 and 4.

16. Judith Butler, *Frames of War*, 76–77.

17. On this point, see also Michel Foucault's classic definition of biopolitics, *History of Sexuality*, 1:143.

18. On the second point, see also Gross, "Introduction," 1; Oliver, *Animal Lessons*, 4, 20–21, 128; and Derrida, *Animal*, 32; "Eating Well," 278, 280–81; on the fourth point, see also Singer, *Animal Liberation*, 211.

19. Agamben, "What Is an Apparatus?," 16. The enigmatic reference to the distinction between the economic and immanent trinity is explored more fully in Agamben's *Kingdom and the Glory*.

20. Althusser, *On Ideology*, 7.

21. For another application of Althusser's notion of ideological interpellation, see Butler, "Conscience Doth Make Subjects of Us All," 6–26.

22. Althusser, *Ideology*, 49–50. For the first five theses, see 36–47.

23. Althusser, "Freud and Lacan," in *Ideology*, 161.

24. Althusser, *Ideology*, 7.

25. Butler, "Conscience," 15.

26. Butler, *Frames of War*, 167.

27. The work of Sylvia Wynter powerfully indicts "humanity" as a racialized ideology that persistently locates people of color at the periphery, in closer proximity to animality. "Humanity" is an ideological game designed so that some people always lose; or in Wynter's words, "humanity" only ever names an overrepresented subset of humans. See Wynter and McKittrick, "Unparalleled Catastrophe for Our Species?," 9–89.

28. See my "Political Ecology of Dignity," 550–51.

29. Butler, *Frames of War*, xxv–xxvi, 19, 75–76.

30. Gross, "Study of Religion," 71.

31. Althusser, *Ideology*, 45–46; see also Gross, "Introduction," 7.

32. Butler, *Frames of War*, 7.

33. See, for example, Jenson, *Systematic Theology*, 149; Pannenberg, *Anthropology*, 119–21.

34. Against this interpretation, see Clough, "All God's Creatures," 145–61.

35. See, however, Quinn, *Ishmael*.

36. See, however, Wisdom 2:23–24, 2 Esdras 3:20–27, and the apocryphal *Life of Adam and Eve* for the pre-Pauline roots of this interpretation.

37. Freedman and Simon, *Midrash Rabbah*, 71–72.

38. Westermann, *Genesis 1-11*, 253; see also Brueggemann, *Genesis*, 41–42.

39. See Romans 5:12:21 and 1 Corinthians 15:20–22; for an overview of other issues emerging from Paul's reading of Genesis, see Dunning, *Specters of Paul*, 1–27.

40. This reading strategy bears some resemblance to that of Trible, "Depatriarchalizing in Biblical Interpretation," 30–48; and "Eve and Adam," 251–58.

41. Bonhoeffer, *Creation and Fall*, 95, 103, 117–18.

42. Heidegger, *Being and Time*, 291; see also Derrida, *Beast and the Sovereign*, 2:116, 180.

43. For example, Comblin, *Retrieving the Human*, 88–92.

44. Grenz, *Social God*, 276; Agamben, *The Open*, 22; Derrida, *Animal*, 16, 42; see also Georges Bataille's discussion of the "making object" of animal flesh that precedes human carnivory, *Theory of Religion*, 39. But cf., Bonhoeffer, *Creation and Fall*, 96–97.

45. Derrida, "Eating Well," 282.

46. Bonhoeffer, *Creation and Fall*, 96–97.

47. On this connection, see Oliver, *Animal Lessons*, 142–43; and Derrida, *Animal*, 16–18, 21, 42–44.

48. Balthasar, *Theological Anthropology*, 85.

49. Bonhoeffer, *Creation and Fall*, 103.

50. Trible, "Depatriarchalizing," 39–41; see also Shaw, "Reformed and Enlightened Church," 226.

51. Keller, *From a Broken Web*, 24; Adams, *Sexual Politics of Meat*, 219.

52. Westermann, *Genesis*, 242–45.

53. Bonhoeffer, *Ethics*, 299.

54. Bonhoeffer, *Creation and Fall*, 108–10, 113; *Ethics*, 246–50, 261–65, 276–77.

55. Bonhoeffer makes a strong distinction between humanity *sicut deus* (like God) and humanity in the *imago dei*. See *Creation and Fall*, 134.

56. See Derrida's lengthy discussion of animality, nudity, modesty, and shame in *Animal*, 5–6, 56–61.

57. Bonhoeffer, *Creation and Fall*, 101, 124.

58. Ibid., 128.

59. Ibid., 128; see also Butler, *Frames of War*, 13; Pannenberg, *Anthropology*, 85, 109.

60. Agamben, *The Open*, 15–16, 92.

61. Derrida, *Beast and Sovereign*, 1:182; *Animal*, 96. See also Stiegler, "Doing and Saying Stupid Things in the Twentieth Century," 161.

62. McFague, *Body of God*, 113, 119; Ruether, *Sexism and God Talk*, 160–61; Moltmann, *God in Creation*, 28, 186, 240–41; Shiva and Mies, "Decolonizing the North," 265, quoted in Scott, *Political Theology of Nature*, 222.

63. Peacocke, *Theology for a Scientific Age*, 238; Grenz, *Theology for the Community*, 131–39; Pannenberg, *Systematic Theology*, 175, 204, 229–31.

64. For another rereading of the conjunction of logos, flesh, light, darkness, and life in John's prologue, see Burrus, *Saving Shame*, 47–52.

65. Gilhus, "From Sacrifices to Symbols," 157; Sorabji, *Animal Minds and Human Morals*, 2–3; for examples of this embedding, consider Justin Martyr, *Apologies*; Clement of Alexandria, *Paedagogos*; Origen, *Contra Celsum*; and Athanasius, *De incarnatione*. For a contemporary echo see Tillich, *Systematic Theology*, 1:74, 80–81, 172, 259.

66. Clough, "Anxiety of the Human Animal," 58.

67. For resistance to this narrow view of the incarnation see Edwards, "Redemption of Animals in an Incarnational Theology," 81–99.

68. Derrida argues for the multiplicity of logos precisely in the context of John's prologue, setting the incarnate Logos over against the logos of the human as the Aristotelian *logon zōon echōn*; see *Beast and Sovereign*, 1:320–21; see also Žižek, *Less Than Nothing*, 410.

69. Plumwood, *Environmental Culture*, 97–98; *Feminism*, 193–95.

70. Plumwood, *Environmental Culture*, 16.

71. Loy, "Religion of the Market," 18–21.

72. Plumwood, *Environmental Culture*, 1–4, 67; see also Midgley, *Beast and Man*, 212–13.

73. Plumwood, *Environmental Culture*, 14; see also Ruether, *Sexism and God Talk*, 90–91; Coetzee, *Lives of Animals*, 23, 25, 66–67.

74. Clough, *On Animals*, 83; "Not a Not-Animal," 12.

75. Clough, *On Animals*, 84.

76. Clough, *On Animals*, 97; see Barth, *Church Dogmatics*, 2.1:101, 157; on the ecological erasure in Barth's theology see Smith, *A Non-Philosophical Theory of Nature*, 47. Clough puts this vision of ecological election/salvation in productive conversation with Agamben in "Putting Animals in Their Place," 219.

77. Barth's anthropological exceptionalism repeatedly erases every relation of ecological interdependence in which human beings live. For examples, see *Church Dogmatics*, 2.2:101, 169, 195, 196.

78. Ibid., 2.2:99–101.

79. Ibid., 2.2:206.

80. Ibid., 2.2:206–7.

81. Ibid., 2.2:122–3, 167.

82. Ibid., 2.2:206, 212.

83. Derrida, *Animal*, 132.

84. Mark 8:34

85. Mark 8:34–38; Matthew 16:24–28; Luke 9:23–27; Matthew 6:10.

86. Agamben, *Sacrament of Language*, 42–44, 49–50, 65.

87. Agamben, *Kingdom and Glory*, xiii, 259.

6. Animality in Eschatological Transformation

1. 1 Enoch 61:5. Text from Nickelburg and Vanderkam, *1 Enoch*, 77.

2. Bynum, *Resurrection of the Body*, 24, 32, 36, 42, 75; Endsjø, *Greek Resurrection Beliefs*, 208–12. For textual examples, see the Ethiopic text

of the *Apocalypse of Peter* in *New Testament Apocrypha*; Tertullian, *De resurrectione carnis*, §32, in *Tertullian's Treatise*; Ephraim the Syrian, *Des Heiligen Ephraem*, 13. The passage from Enoch quoted as an epigraph appears to be the textual anchor for this speculation.

3. Tertullian, *De ressurectione carnis*, §32.

4. Bynum, *Resurrection of the Body*, 13–14; drawing on the classic study of Cullmann, *Unsterblichkeit der Seele*.

5. Athenagoras, *De resurrectione*, §4–6, 8; text and translation in *Legatio and de Resurrectione*.

6. Augustine, *Civitas dei*, 22.12, text in *City of God*; Thomas Aquinas, *Summa theologiae* III (suppl.), q. 80–81, 86, text in *Summa Theologiae*.

7. Agamben, "Glorious Body," 91.

8. Agamben, "Glorious Body," 97–98; Aquinas, *Summa theologiae*, III (suppl.), q. 81, a. 4; see also Agamben, *The Open*, 19.

9. Agamben, *The Open*, 19.

10. Bynum, *Resurrection of the Body*, 83, 87, 111–12; Brown, *Body and Society*, 382–83; Jerome, *Liber contra Joannem Hierosalymitanum*, §31–32; Augustine, *De civitate dei*, 22.17, 22.24; Aquinas, *Summa Theologiae*, III (suppl.), q. 81, a. 4.

11. Gregory of Nyssa, *De hominis opificio*, §17.

12. I take this conviction to be a (perhaps unexpected) entailment of Pope Francis's calls for an ecological conversion and his insistence on situating human life ecologically; *Laudato Si'*, §99–100, 139, 218, 221

13. A small, representative sample might include: Bouma-Prediger, *For the Beauty of the Earth*, 110–16; Haught, "Ecology and Eschatology," 47–64; Keselopoulos, *Man and the Environment*, 141–52; McFague, *Body of God*, 197–202; Moltmann, *God in Creation*, 181–84; Moltmann, *Way of Jesus Christ*, 291, 302–5; Nash, *Loving Nature*, 124–33; Northcott, *Environment and Christian Ethics*, 202.

14. See, for example, Isaiah 34.

15. Isaiah 11:6–9; see also Isaiah 65:17–25; Jeremiah 31:12–14, Amos 9:11–15.

16. Daniel 7–8.

17. Revelation 13, 17.

18. Revelation 4:6–11; see also 14:1–4; cf. Isaiah 6:1–5.

19. Moore, "Ecotherology," 207–9.

20. Romans 8:19–23.

21. Colossians 1:15–20.

22. Edwards, "Every Sparrow That Falls to the Ground," 113; Ruether, *Gaia and God*, 140.

23. Ignatius of Antioch, "Letter to the Romans," §4; text in Staniford, *Early Christian Writings*, 86.

24. Luke 24:30, 24:41–43; John 21:13.

25. Bynum, *Resurrection of the Body*, 67, 83, 87.

26. Agamben, "Glorious Body," 101.

27. Bynum, *Resurrection of the Body*, 50–1; see also Ruether, *Gaia and God*, 53, 140.

28. Isaiah 25:6–8.

29. See, for example, Matthew 22:1–44, 25:1–13; and Luke 15:11–32.

30. Luke 22:15–17; cf. Mark 14:22–25, Matthew 26:26–29, and 1 Corinthians 11:23–26.

31. Schmemann, *Eucharist*, 110, 118; Schmemann, *For the Life of the World*, 39; Keselopoulos, *Man and the Environment*, 163–71.

32. See Denis Edward's typology of the different ways that theologians have handled the question of the resurrection of nonhuman creatures, "Every Sparrow," 115–17; I am assuming, with Christopher Southgate (*Groaning of Creation*, 85), that God's new creation will include members of every species. For one contrary position on this point see Edwards, "Every Sparrow," 119.

33. Southgate, *Groaning of Creation*, 88.

34. Pannenberg, *Systematic Theology*, 2:134; quoting Psalm 104:21.

35. The phrase is from Oliver, *Animal Lessons*, 32–33.

36. Revelation 21:4.

37. Clough, *On Animals*, 161–62; Bynum, *Resurrection of the Body*, 23.

38. Sideris, *Environmental Ethics*, 220.

39. Ibid., 69, 128–29, 175.

40. Ibid., 222.

41. Ibid., 83.

42. Irenaeus, *Contra haereses*, §22; text in *Ante-Nicene Fathers*, vol. 1.

43. Romans 8:22–25.

44. 1 John 3:2.

45. This continuity is also the point of Paul's Adam-Christ parallels in Romans 5 and 1 Corinthians 15.

46. 1 Corinthians 15:20, 23.

47. Scott, *Political Theology of Nature*, 7, 172–73.

48. Jenson, *Systematic Theologty*, 1:205; *Systematic Theology*, 2:355.

49. Colossians 1:20.

50. Edwards hints at an ecological connection between the eucharist and the life of the trinity, but does not develop it along the trajectory that is worked out here. See Edwards, "Every Sparrow," 121.

51. Balthasar, *Mysterium Paschale*, 50.

52. James Dickey's poem, "Heaven of Animals," imagines heavenly predation as a glorious exchange of life; see Dickey, *Staying Alive*, 221–22; quoted in full in Southgate, *Groaning of Creation*, 89.

53. Edwards, "Every Sparrow," 115.

54. Edwards, "Every Sparrow," 108; Keller, *Apocalypse Now and Then*, 175.

55. For example, Thomas Aquinas, *Summa theologiae*, III (suppl.), q. 80, a. 1.

56. Gregory of Nyssa, *De hominis opificio*, §17; Jerome, *Liber contra Joannem Hierosalymitanum*, §31–32; Augustine, *De civitate dei*, 22.17, 22.24; Aquinas, *Summa Theologiae*, III (suppl.), q. 81, a. 4; Bynum, *Resurrection of the Body*, 67, 83, 87, 111–12; Brown, *Body and Society*, 382–83.

57. Mark 12:18–27; Matthew 22:23–33; and Luke 20:27–40; see also Matthew 19:3–12.

58. Aquinas, *Summa theologiae*, III (suppl.), q. 80, a. 1; quoted in Agamben, "Glorious Body," 98.

59. Grenz, *Social God*, 283; see also 280–81.

60. Ibid., 302.

61. Ibid., 300–301.

62. Ibid., 294, 300-303, 321–22; see also 291, 293–94.

63. Matthew 9:14–17; 22:1–14; 25:1–15; Mark 2:18–22; and Luke 5:33–39; 12:35-36; 14: 6–24. Such images stand in tension with the teaching quoted above that resurrected persons will not marry.

64. Revelation 21:2, 21:9–10.

65. Jeremiah 2:2; 3:1–25; 31:1–6; Hosea 1–4; Ezekiel 16.

66. Tertullian, *De viriginibus velandum*, §16, text in *Ante-Nicene Fathers*, vol. 4. The gendering of mystical experience (and historical scholarship on it) is taken up in Amy Hollywood, *Sensible Ecstasy*, see especially 99, 207.

67. Loughlin, "Omphalos," 121; Bernard of Clairvaux. *Sermons*.

68. Loughlin, "Introduction," in *Queer Theology*, 1–4.

69. Agamben, "Glorious Body," 99.

70. 1 Corinthians 12:22–24.

71. Agamben, "Glorious Body," 99.

72. Augustine, *Enchiridion*, §118.

73. Midgley, *Beast and Man*, 331–32.

74. Ibid., 332.

75. Jenson, *Systematic Theology*, 2:319.

76. Johnson, *Ask the Beasts*, 149; Psalm 104, Psalm 148, Job 38–40.

77. MacInyre, *Dependent Rational Animals*, 87, 91–95.

78. Augustine, *Enchiridion*, §118.

79. MacIntyre, *After Virtue*, 191.

80. MacIntyre, *Dependent Rational Animals*, 87, 91, 96.

81. Burrus, "Queer Father," 147.

82. Gregory of Nyssa, *GNO*, 6:139; *Life of Moses*, 2.220–24; Burrus, "Queer Father," 157.

83. For a different reading of Gregory of Nyssa on the question of eschatological genitals, see Behr, "Rational Animal," 240–43; my reading substantially aligns with that of Zachhuber, *Human Nature in Gregory of Nyssa*, 170–72.

84. Burrus, "Queer Father," 158.

85. Jordan, "God's Body," 290.

86. Foucault, *History of Sexuality*, 1:155–56.
87. Midgley, *Beast and Man*, 333.
88. Greenberg, *Construction of Homosexuality*, 71.
89. Jenson, *Systematic Theology*, 2:357, 358.
90. Moore, "Ecotherology," 202.
91. Agamben, "What Is an Apparatus," 19.
92. Agamben, "Glorious Body," 100; see also 103.
93. Ibid., 98.
94. Ibid., 100, 102.
95. Burrus, *Saving Shame*, 133.

Conclusion

1. Regan, *Case for Animal Rights*, 396.
2. Meyer, "Political Ecology of Dignity," 560–63.
3. Agamben, *The Open*, 15–16.
4. I am dating the conservation movement roughly to the publication of Thoreau's *Walden Pond* (1854), the establishment of Yellowstone National Park (1871) and John Muir's move to California to take up residence in the Sierra Nevada mountains (approx. 1870). I am dating the environmental movement by the publication of Rachel Carson's *Silent Spring* (1962) and the establishment of Earth Day (1970).
5. For one example, the US per-capita energy usage in 2010 was essentially the same as it was in 1970 (310 gigajoules per capita in 1970 to 305 gigajoules in 2010); globally, per-capita energy consumption has risen over the same period (52 gigajoules in 1970 to 72 in 2010). The human population of both the United States and the earth have, of course, greatly increased over this period. From http://www.financialsense.com/contributors/gail-tverberg/world-energy-consumption-since-1820-in-charts.
6. Agamben, *Homo Sacer*, 188; Foucault, *History of Sexuality*, 1:143.

Bibliography

Abbey, Edward. *Desert Solitaire: A Season in the Wilderness*. New York: Ballentine, 1968.

Abram, David. *Becoming Animal: An Earthly Cosmology*. New York: Vintage Books, 2010.

———. *Spell of the Sensuous: Perception and Language in a More Than Human World*. New York: Vintage, 1997.

Adams, Carol. *The Sexual Politics of Meat: A Feminist-Vegetarian Critical Theory*. 20th anniversary ed. New York: Continuum, 2010.

Agamben, Giorgio. *Homo Sacer: Sovereign Power and Bare Life*. Translated by Daniel Heller-Roazen. Stanford, CA: Stanford University Press, 1998.

———. "The Glorious Body." In *Nudities*, translated by David Kishik and Stefan Pedatella, 91–103. Stanford, CA: Stanford University Press, 2011.

———. *The Kingdom and the Glory: For a Theological Genealogy of Economy and Government*. Translated by Lorenzo Chiesa and Matteo Mandarini. Stanford, CA: Stanford University Press, 2011.

———. *The Open: Man and Animal*. Translated by Kevin Attell. Stanford, CA: Stanford University Press, 2004.

———. *The Sacrament of Language: An Archaeology of the Oath*. Translated by Adam Kotsko. Stanford, CA: Stanford University Press, 2011.

———. *What Is an Apparatus? And Other Essays*. Translated by David Kishik and Stefan Pedatella. Stanford: Stanford University Press, 2009.

Althusser, Louis. *On Ideology*. Translated by Ben Brewster. New York: Verso, 2008.

Aquinas, Thomas. *Summa Theologiae*. Blackfriars ed. New York: McGraw Hill, 1964.

Aristotle. *Politics*. Translated by Ernest Barker. New York: Oxford University Press, 1995.

Athenagoras. *Legatio and de Resurrectione*. Translated by William Schoedel. Oxford: Oxford University Press, 1972.

Augustine. *City of God*. Translated by Henry Bettenson. New York: Penguin, 1984.

———. *Enchiridion on Faith, Hope, and Love*. Washington, DC: Regnery, 1961.

Bailly, Jean-Christophe. *The Animal Side*. Translated by Catherine Porter. New York: Fordham University Press, 2011.

Baldwin, James. *Go Tell It on the Mountain*. New York: Random House, 1952.

Balthasar, Hans Urs von. *Mysterium Paschale*. Translated by Aidan Nichols OP. San Francisco: Ignatius Press, 2005.

———. *Theo-Drama*. Vol. 2, *Dramatis Personae: Man in God*. Translated by Graham Harrison. San Francisco: Ignatius Press, 1990.

———. *A Theological Anthropology*. New York: Sheed and Ward, 1967.

Barbel, Joseph. *Gregor von Nazianz: Die Fünf Theologischen Reden—Text und Übersetzung mit Einleitung und Kommentar*. Düsseldorf: Patmos Verlag, 1963.

Barber, Daniel Colucciello. "Ideology and Apocalyptic: A Review of Nathan Kerr, Christ, History, and Apocalyptic." *Journal of Cultural and Religious Theory* 10, no. 3 (2010): 167–72.

———. *On Diaspora: Christianity, Religion, and Secularity*. Eugene, OR: Wipf and Stock, 2011.

Barth, Karl. *Church Dogmatics*. Vol. 2.2, *The Doctrine of God*. Edited by G. W. Bromiley and Thomas Torrance. Translated by G. W. Bromiley. Edinburgh: T. and T. Clark, 1957.

———. *The Humanity of God*. Translated by John Thomas and Thomas Wieser. Atlanta: John Knox Press, 1960.

Bataille, Georges. *Theory of Religion*. Translated by Robert Hurley. New York: Zone, 1989.

Bauckham, Richard. *Bible and Ecology*. Waco, TX: Baylor University Press, 2010.

———. "Jesus and the Wild Animals (Mark 1:13): A Christological Image for An Ecological Age." In *Jesus of Nazareth: Lord and Christ, Essays on the Historical Jesus and New Testament Christology*, edited by Joel B. Green and Max Turner. Grand Rapids, MI: Eerdmans, 1994.

Beeley, Christopher. *Gregory of Nazianzus on the Trinity and the Knowledge of God: In Your Light We Shall See Light*. New York: Oxford University Press, 2008.

Behr, John. "The Rational Animal: A Rereading of Gregory of Nyssa's *De hominis opificio*." *Journal of Early Christian Studies* 7, no. 2 (1999): 219–47.

Bekoff, Marc, and Jessica Pierce. *Wild Justice: The Moral Lives of Animals*. Chicago: University of Chicago Press, 2009.

Bergmann, Sigurd. *Creation Set Free: The Spirit as Liberator of Nature*. Translated by Douglas Stott. Grand Rapids, MI: Eerdmans, 2005.

Bernard of Clairvaux. *Sermons on the Song of Songs*. Translated by Kilian Walsh. Kalamazoo, MI: Cistercian Publications, 1971.

Boff, Leonardo. *Jesus Christ Liberator: A Critical Christology for Our Time*. Translated by Patrick Hughes. Maryknoll, NY: Orbis Books, 1978.

Bonhoeffer, Dietrich. *Creation and Fall: A Theological Exposition of Genesis 1–3*. Edited by John W. DeGruchy. Translated by Douglas Stephen Bax. Minneapolis: Fortress Press, 2004.

———. *Ethics*. Edited by Clifford Green. Translated by Reinhard Krauss, Charles West and Douglas Stott. Minneapolis: Fortress Press, 2005.

Bouma-Prediger, Steven. *For the Beauty of the Earth: A Christian Vision for Creation Care*. Grand Rapids, MI: Baker Academic, 2001.

Briggs, Richard. "Humans in the Image of God and Other Things Genesis Does Not Make Clear." *Journal of Theological Interpretation* 4, no. 1 (2010): 111–26.

Brown, Peter. *The Body and Society*. New York: Columbia University Press, 1988.

Brueggemann, Walter. *Genesis: Interpretation: A Bible Commentary for Teaching and Preaching*. Atlanta: John Knox Press, 1982.

Buckley, Michael. "Within the Holy Mystery." In *A World of Grace*, edited by Leo O'Donovan, 31–49. New York: Seabury Press, 1980.

Bultmann, Rudolf. "Ist der Apokalyptik die Mutter der Christliche Theologie?: Ein Auseinandersetzung mit Ernst Käsemann." In *Exegetica: Aufsätze Zur Erforschung des Neuen Testaments*, 476–82. Tübingen: Mohr, 1967.

Burrus, Virginia. "Queer Father: Gregory of Nyssa and the Subversion of Identity." In *Queer Theology: Rethinking the Western Body*, edited by Gerard Loughlin, 147–62. Malden, MA: Blackwell, 2007.

———. *Saving Shame: Martyrs, Saints, and Other Abject Subjects*. Philadelphia: University of Pennsylvania Press, 2008.

Butler, Judith. "Conscience Doth Make Subjects of Us All." *Yale French Studies*, no. 88 (1995): 6–26.

———. *Frames of War: When Is Life Grievable?* New York: Verso, 2010.

Bynum, Caroline Walker. *The Resurrection of the Body: In Western Christianity, 200–1336*. New York: Columbia University Press, 1995.

Calarco, Matthew. "On the Borders of Language and Death: Agamben and the Question of the Animal." *Philosophy Today* 44, no. 2 (2000): 91–97.

———. *Thinking Through Animals: Identity, Difference, Indistinction*. Stanford, CA: Stanford University Press, 2015.

———. *Zoographies: The Question of the Animal from Heidegger to Derrida*. New York: Columbia University Press, 2008.

Caputo, John. *The Prayers and Tears of Jacques Derrida: Religion without Religion*. Bloomington: Indiana University Press, 1997.

Carr, Anne. "Starting with the Human." In *A World of Grace*, edited by Leo O'Donovan, 17–30. New York: Seabury Press, 1980.

Clough, David. "All God's Creatures: Reading Genesis on Human and Nonhuman Animals." In *Reading Genesis After Darwin*, edited by Stephen Barton and David Wilkinson, 145–61. Oxford: Oxford University Press, 2009.

———. "The Anxiety of the Human Animal: Martin Luther on Non-Human Animals and Human Animality." In Deane-Drummond and Clough, *Creaturely Theology*, 41–60.

———. "Not a Not-Animal: The Vocation to Be a Human Animal Creature." *Studies in Christian Ethics* 26, no. 1 (2013): 4–17.

———. *On Animals*. Vol. 1, *Systematic Theology*. New York: T. and T. Clark, 2012.

———. "Putting Animals in Their Place: On the Theological Classification of Animals." In Deane-Drummond, Artinian-Kaiser, and Clough, *Animals as Religious Subjects*, 209–23. New York: Bloomsbury, 2013.

Coetzee, J. M. *The Lives of Animals*. Princeton, NJ: Princeton University Press, 1999.

Comblin, José. *Retrieving the Human: A Christian Anthropology*. Translated by Robert Barr. Maryknoll, NY: Orbis Books, 1990.

Cronon, William. "The Trouble with Wilderness; Or, Getting Back to the Wrong Nature." In *Uncommon Ground: Rethinking the Human Place in Nature*, edited by William Cronon. New York: W. W. Norton, 1996.

Crowley, Paul. "Encountering the Religious Other: Challenges to Rahner's Transcendental Project." *Theological Studies* 71, no. 3 (2010): 567–85.

Cullmann, Oscar. *Unsterblichkeit der Seele oder Auferstehung der Toten?* Stuttgart: Kreuz, 1964.

Cunningham, David. "The Way of All Flesh: Rethinking the *Imago Dei*." In Deane-Drummond and Clough, *Creaturely Theology*, 100–20.

Dallmayr, Fred. "Politics of the Kingdom: Pannenberg's Anthropology." *Review of Politics* 49, no. 1 (1987): 85-111.

Daly, Mary. *Beyond God the Father: Toward a Philosophy of Women's Liberation*. Boston, MA: Beacon Press, 1973.

Daniélou, Jean. "La Chronologie des Oeuvres de Grégoire de Nysse." In *Studia Patristica*, 159–69. Berlin: Akademie Verlag, 1966.

———. *Platonisme et Théologie Mystique: Doctrine Spirituelle de Saint Grégoire de Nysse*. Paris: Aubier, 1954.

de Waal, Franz. *Primates and Philosophers: How Morality Evolved*. Princeton, NJ: Princeton University Press, 2009.

Deane-Drummond, Celia. "Are Animal Moral? Taking Soundings Through Vice, Virtue, Conscience, and *Imago Dei*." In Deane-Drummond and Clough, *Creaturely Theology*, 190–210.

———. *The Wisdom of the Liminal: Evolution and Other Animals in Human Becoming*. Grand Rapids, MI: Eerdmans, 2014.

Deanne-Drummond, Celia, and David Clough. "Postscript." In Deane-Drummond and Clough, *Creaturely Theology*, 266–69.

Deane-Drummond, Celia, and David Clough, eds. *Creaturely Theology: On God, Humans, and Other Animals.* London: SCM Press, 2009.

Deane-Drummond, Celia, Rebecca Artinian-Kaiser, and David Clough, eds. *Animals As Religious Subjects: Transdisciplinary Perspectives.* New York: Bloomsbury, 2013.

Deleuze, Gilles, and Felix Guattari. *A Thousand Plateaus: Capitalism and Schizophrenia.* Translated by Brian Massumi. Minneapolis: University of Minnesota Press, 1987.

Derrida, Jacques. *The Animal That Therefore I Am.* Edited by Marie Louise Mallet. Translated by David Wills. New York: Fordham University Press, 2008.

———. *The Beast and the Sovereign.* Vol. 1. Translated by Geoffrey Bennington. Chicago: University of Chicago Press, 2009.

———. *The Beast and the Sovereign.* Vol. 2. Translated by Geoffrey Bennington. Chicago: University of Chicago Press, 2011.

———. "'Eating Well' or the Calculation of the Subject." In *Points . . . Interviews 1974–1994,* edited by Werner Hamacher and David Wellbery, translated by Peter Connor and Avital Ronell, 255–87. Stanford, CA: Stanford University Press, 1995.

———. "Faith and Knowledge." In *Acts of Religion,* edited by Gil Anidjar, 40–101. New York: Routledge, 2002.

———. *L'animal que donc je suis.* Edited by Marie-Louise Mallet. Paris: Éditions Galilée, 2006.

———. *Rogues: Two Essays on Reason.* Translated by Pascale-Anne Brault and Michael Naas. Stanford, CA: Stanford University Press, 2005.

———. *Specters of Marx: The State of the Debt, the Work of Mourning, and the New International.* Translated by Peggy Kamuf. New York: Routledge, 1994.

———. "White Mythology: Metaphor in the Text of Philosophy." In *Margins of Philosophy,* translated by Alan Bass, 207–71. Chicago: University of Chicago Press, 1982.

Díaz, Miguel. *On Being Human: U.S. Hispanic and Rahnerian Perspectives.* Maryknoll, NY: Orbis, 2001.

Dickerman, Sherwood Owen. "Some Stock Illustrations of Animal Intelligence in Greek Psychology." *Transactions and Proceedings of the American Philological Association,* no. 42 (1911): 123–30.

Dickey, James. *Staying Alive: Real Poems for Unreal Times.* Edited by Neil Astley. Northumberland, UK: Bloodaxe, 2002.

Dillard, Annie. *Pilgrim at Tinker Creek.* New York: HarperCollins, 1974.

Dunning, Benjamin. *Specters of Paul: Sexual Difference in Early Christian Thought.* Philadelphia: University of Pennsylvania Press, 2011.

Dünzl, Franz. *Braut und Bräutigam: Die Auslegung des Canticum durch Gregory von Nyssa.* Vol. 32, *Beiträge zur Geschichte der biblischen Exegese.* Tübingen: J. C. B. Mohr (Paul Siebeck), 1993.

Durantaye, Leland de la. "The Suspended Substantive: On Animals and Men in Giorgio Agamben's the Open." *Diacritics* 33, no. 2 (2003): 3–9.
Edwards, Denis. "Every Sparrow That Falls to the Ground: The Cost of Evolution and the Christ-Event." *Ecotheology* 11, no. 1 (2006): 103–23.
———. "The Redemption of Animals in an Incarnational Theology." In Deane-Drummond and Clough, *Creaturely Theology*, 103–23.
Ellverson, Anna-Stina. *The Dual Nature of Man: A Study in the Theological Anthropology of Gregory of Nazianzus*. Stockholm: Uppsala, 1981.
Endsjø, Dag Øistein. *Greek Resurrection Beliefs and the Success of Christianity*. New York: Palgrave Macmillan, 2009.
Ephraim the Syrian. *Des Heiligen Ephraem des Syrers Sermones III*. Edited by Edmund Beck. Louvain: Corpus SCO, 1972.
Fergusson, David. "Human Nature in Theistic and Evolutionary Perspectives." *Zygon* 48, no. 2 (2013): 439–53.
Finlayson, James Gordon. "'Bare Life' and Politics in Agamben's Reading of Aristotle." *Review of Politics* 72, no. 1 (2010): 97–126.
Fischer, Hermann. "Fundamentaltheologische Prolegomena zur Theologischen Anthropologie: Anfragen an W. Pannenbergs Anthropologie." *Theologische Rundschau* 50, no. 1 (1985): 41–61.
Fischer, Klaus. *Der Mensch als Geheimnis: Die Anthropologie Karl Rahners*. Freiburg: Herder, 1974.
Foucault, Michel. *Fearless Speech*. Edited by Joseph Pearson. Los Angeles: Semiotext(e), 2001.
———. *The History of Sexuality*. Vol. 1, *An Introduction*. Translated by Robert Hurley. New York: Pantheon Books, 1978.
Fraijo, Manuel. *El Sentido de la Historia: Introducción al Pensamiento de W. Pannenberg*. Madrid: Ediciones Cristiandad, 1986.
Francis (Pope), *Encyclical on Climate Change and Inequality: On Care for Our Common Home*. New York: Melville House, 2015.
Freedman, H. (Rabbi), and Maurice Simon, eds. *Midrash Rabbah*. London: Soncino Press, 1961.
Freyer, Thomas. "Inwiefern Sind Ontologische Kategorien für eine Theologische Anthropologie Unabweisbar?" *Catholica* 61, no. 1 (2007): 15–41.
Galloway, Allan. *Wolfhart Pannenberg*. London: George Allen and Unwin, 1973.
Gilhus, Ingvild Sælid. *Animals, Gods and Humans: Changing Attitudes to Animals in Greek, Roman and Early Christian Ideas*. New York: Routledge, 2006.
Grant, Robert M. *Early Christians and Animals*. New York: Routledge, 1999.
Greenberg, David. *The Construction of Homosexuality*. Chicago: University of Chicago Press, 1988.
Gregory of Nazianzus. *Festal Orations*. Translated by Nonna Verna Harrison. Crestwood, NY: Saint Vladimir's Seminary Press, 2008.

———. *Grégoire de Nazianze: Discours 27–31*. Edited by Paul Gallay. Vol. 250, *Sources Chrétiennes*. Paris: Éditions du Cerf, 1978.
———. *Grégoire de Nazianze: Discours 38–41*. Edited by Claudio Moreschini. Translated by Paul Gallay. Vol. 358, *Sources Chrétiennes*. Paris: Éditions du Cerf, 1990.
———. *Grégoire de Nazianze: Lettres Théologiques*. Edited by Paul Gallay and Maurice Jourjon. Vol. 208, *Sources Chrétiennes*. Paris: Éditions du Cerf, 1974.
———. *On God and Christ: The Five Theological Orations and Two Letters to Cledonius*. Translated by Lionel Wickham and Frederick Williams. Crestwood, NY: Saint Vladimir's Seminary Press, 2002.
Gregory of Nyssa. *Commentary on the Song of Songs*. Translated by Casimir McCambley OCSO. Brookline, MA: Hellenic College Press, 1987.
———. "De hominis opificio." In *Patrologiae Cursus Completus: Series Graece*, vol. 44, edited by J. P. Migne. Paris: Migne, 1863.
———. *Gregorii Nysseni in Canticum Canticorum*. Edited by Hermann Langerbeck. Vol. 6, *Gregorii Nysseni Opera*, edited by Werner Jaeger. Leiden: Brill, 1960.
———. *Gregorii Nysseni Opera Ascetica*. Edited by Werner Jaeger, Johannes Cavarnos and Virginia Callahan. Vol. 8.1, *Gregorii Nysseni Opera*, edited by Werner Jaeger. Leiden: Brill, 1952.
———. "On Perfection." In *St. Gregory: Ascetical Works*. Translated by Virginia Callahan, 95–122. Vol. 58, *Fathers of the Church*. Washington, DC: Catholic University of America Press, 1967.
———. "On What It Means to Call Oneself a Christian." In *St. Gregory: Ascetical Works*. Translated by Virginia Callahan, 81–89. Vol. 58, *Fathers of the Church*. Washington, DC: Catholic University of America Press, 1967.
———. *Writings and Letters of Gregory, Bishop of Nyssa*. Translated by William Moore and Henry Wilson. Vol. 5, *Nicene and Post-Nicene Fathers of the Christian Church*, edited by Philip Schaff and Henry Wace. Grand Rapids, MI: Eerdmans, 1954.
Grenz, Stanley. *Reason for Hope: The Systematic Theology of Wolfhart Pannenberg*. 2nd ed. Grand Rapids: Eerdmans, 2005.
———. *The Social God and the Relational Self: A Trinitarian Theology of the Imago Dei*. Louisville, KY: Westminster John Knox, 2001.
———. *Theology for the Community of God*. Grand Rapids, MI: Eerdmans, 1994.
Gross, Aaron. *The Question of the Animal* and *Religion: Theoretical Stakes, Practical Implications*. New York: Columbia University Press, 2015.
———. "The Question of the Creature: Animals, Theology and Levinas' Dog." In Deane-Drummond and Clough, *Creaturely Theology*, 121–37.
———. "The Study of Religion After the Animal." In Deane-Drummond, Artinian-Kaiser, and Clough, *Animals As Religious Subjects*, 59–78.

Gross, Aaron, and Anne Vallely, eds. *Animals and the Human Imagination: A Companion to Animal Studies*. New York: Columbia University Press, 2012.

Gutiérrez, Gustavo. *A Theology of Liberation*. Translated by Caridad Inda and John Eagleson. Maryknoll, NY: Orbis, 1988.

Hägglund, Martin. *Radical Atheism: Derrida and the Time of Life*. Stanford, CA: Stanford University Press, 2008.

Hall, Douglas John. *Imaging God: Dominion As Stewardship*. Grand Rapids, MI: Eerdmans, 1986.

Hallward, Peter. *Out of This World: Deleuze and the Philosophy of Creation*. London: Verso, 2006.

Haraway, Donna. *When Species Meet*. Minneapolis: University of Minnesota Press, 2008.

Harrison, Nonna Verna. "Allegory and Asceticism in Gregory of Nyssa." *Semeia*, no. 57 (1992): 113–30.

Hartman, Louis F., and Alexander A. Di Lella. *The Book of Daniel*. Garden City, NY: Doubleday and Company, 1978.

Haught, John. "Ecology and Eschatology." In *"And God Saw That It Was Good": Catholic Theology and the Environment*, edited by Drew Christiansen and Walter Grazer, 47–64. Washington, DC: United States Catholic Conference, 1996.

———. *God After Darwin: A Theology of Evolution*. Boulder, CO: Westview Press, 2000.

Heidegger, Martin. *Being and Time*. Translated by John Macquarrie and Edward Robinson. London: Blackwell, 1978.

———. *Die Grundbegriffe der Metaphysik: Welt—Endlichkeit—Einsamkeit*. Vol. 2, *Gesamtausgabe: Abteilung: Vorlesungen 1923–1944*. Frankfurt: Vittorio Klostermann, 1976.

———. *The Fundamental Concepts of Metaphysics: World, Finitude, Solitude*. Translated by William McNeill and Nicholas Walker. Bloomington: Indiana University Press, 1995.

Heine, Ronald. "Gregory of Nyssa's Apology for Allegory." *Vigiliae Christianae* 38, no. 4 (1984): 360–70.

Huyssteen, J. Wentzel van. *Alone in the World?: Human Uniqueness in Science and Theology*. Grand Rapids, MI: Eerdmans, 2006.

Irenaeus of Lyons, "Adversus haereses." In Vol. 1, *Ante-Nicene Fathers*, edited by Philip Schaff. Grand Rapids, MI: Eerdmans, 1954.

Jenson, Robert W. *Systematic Theology*. Vol. 1, *The Triune God*. Oxford: Oxford University Press, 1997.

———. *Systematic Theology*. Vol. 2, *The Works of God*. New York: Oxford University Press, 1999.

Johnson, Elizabeth. *Ask the Beasts: Darwin and the God of Love*. New York: Bloomsbury, 2014.

———. *Women, Earth, and Creator Spirit*. New York: Paulist Press, 1993.

Jordan, Mark. "God's Body." In *Queer Theology: Rethinking the Western Body*, edited by Gerard Loughlin, 281–92. Malden, MA: Blackwell, 2007.

Kafka, Franz. "A Report to an Academy." In *Franz Kafka: The Complete Stories*, edited by Nahum Glatzer, 250–59. New York: Schocken Books, 1946.

Käsemann, Ernst. "Die Anfänge Christliche Theologie." *Zeitschrift für Theologie und Kirche*, no. 57 (1960): 162–85.

Keller, Catherine. *Apocalypse Now and Then: A Feminist Guide to the End of the World*. Minneapolis: Fortress Press, 1996.

———. *Face of the Deep: A Theology of Becoming*. New York: Routledge, 2003.

———. *From a Broken Web: Separation, Sexism, and Self*. Boston, MA: Beacon Press, 1986.

Kelsey, David. *Eccentric Existence: A Theological Anthropology*. 2 vols. Louisville, KY: Westminster John Knox, 2009.

Kerr, Nathan R. *Christ, History, and Apocalyptic: The Politics of Christian Mission*. Eugene, OR: Cascade Books, 2009.

Keselopoulos, Anestis G. *Man and the Environment: A Study of St Symeon the New Theologian*. Translated by Elizabeth Theokritoff. Crestwood, NY: Saint Vladimir's Seminary Press, 2001.

Kilby, Karen. *Karl Rahner: Theology and Philosophy*. New York: Routledge, 2004.

Kotsko, Adam. *The Politics of Redemption: The Social Logic of Salvation*. New York: T. and T. Clark, 2010.

———. *The Prince of This World*. Stanford, CA: Stanford University Press, 2017.

Laclau, Ernesto. "The Time Is Out of Joint." *Diacritics* 25, no. 2 (1995): 85–96.

Lacocque, André. *The Book of Daniel*. Translated by David Pellauer. Atlanta: John Knox Press, 1979.

LaCugna, Catherine Mowry. *God for Us: The Trinity and Christian Life*. New York: Harper Collins, 1991.

Laird, Martin. "The Fountain of His Lips: Desire and Divine Union in Gregory of Nyssa's Homilies on the Song of Songs." *Spiritus: Journal of Christian Spirituality* 7, no. 1 (2007): 40–57.

———. "Under Solomon's Tutelage: The Education of Desire in the Homilies on the Song of Songs." In *Rethinking Gregory of Nyssa*, edited by Sarah Coakley, 77–96. Malden, MA: Blackwell, 2003.

———. "'Whereof We Speak': Gregory of Nyssa, Jean-Luc Marion and the Current Apophatic Rage." *Heythrop Journal* 42, no. 1 (2001): 1–12.

Lawlor, Leonard. *This Is Not Sufficient: An Essay on Animality and Human Nature in Derrida*. New York: Columbia University Press, 2007.

Linnane, Brian. "Categorical and Transcendental Experience in Rahner's Theology: Implications for Ethics." *Philosophy and Theology* 10, no. 1 (1997): 199–226.

Linzey, Andrew. *Christianity and the Rights of Animals*. New York: Crossroad, 1987.

Losinger, Anton. *The Anthropological Turn: The Human Orientation of the Theology of Karl Rahner*. Translated by Daniel Dahlstrom. New York: Fordham University Press, 2000.

Loughlin, Gerard. "Introduction." In Loughlin, *Queer Theology*, 1–34.

———. "Omphalos." In Loughlin, *Queer Theology*, 115–37.

———, ed. *Queer Theology: Rethinking the Western Body*. Malden, MA: Blackwell, 2007.

Louth, Andrew. *The Origins of the Christian Mystical Tradition*. Oxford: Oxford University Press, 1981.

Loy, David R. "The Religion of the Market." In *Visions of a New Earth: Religious Perspectives on Population, Consumption, and Ecology*, edited by Harold Coward and Daniel Maguire, 15–28. Albany: State University of New York Press, 2000.

Lucas, Ernest. *Daniel. Apollos Old Testament Commentary*, edited by David Baker and Gordon Wenham. Downers Grove, IL: Intervarsity Press, 2002.

Ludlow, Morwenna. "Theology and Allegory: Origen and Gregory of Nyssa on the Unity and Diversity of Scripture." *International Journal of Systematic Theology* 4, no. 1 (2002): 45–66.

———. *Universal Salvation: Eschatology in the Thought of Gregory of Nyssa and Karl Rahner*. Oxford: Oxford University Press, 2000.

MacIntyre, Alasdair. *After Virtue*. Notre Dame, IN: University of Notre Dame Press, 1984.

———. *Dependent Rational Animals: Why Human Beings Need the Virtues*. Chicago: Open Court, 1999.

McDermott, Brian. "The Bonds of Freedom." In *A World of Grace*, edited by Leo O'Donovan, 50–63. New York: Seabury Press, 1980.

McFague, Sallie. *The Body of God: An Ecological Theology*. Minneapolis, MN: Fortress Press, 1993.

McGuckin, John. *Saint Gregory of Nazianzus: An Intellectual Biography*. Crestwood, NY: St. Vladimir's Seminary Press, 2001.

Metz, Johann Baptist. *Faith in History and Society: Toward a Practical Fundamental Theology*. Translated by J. Matthew Ashley. New York: Crossroad, 2007.

Meyer, Eric Daryl. "The Logos of God and the End of Man: Animality as Light and Life." In Moore, *Divinanimality*, 146–60.

———. "The Political Ecology of Dignity: Human Dignity and the Inevitable Returns of Animality." *Modern Theology* 33, no. 4 (2017): 549–69.

———. "They Fell Silent When We Stopped Listening: Apophatic Theology and 'Asking the Beasts.'" In *Turning to the Heavens and the*

Earth: Theological Reflections on a Cosmological Conversion, Essays in Honor of Elizabeth A. Johnson, ed. Julia Brumbaugh and Natalia Imperatori-Lee, 26–44. Collegeville, MN: Liturgical Press, 2016.
Middleton, J. Richard. *The Liberating Image: The Imago Dei in Genesis 1*. Grand Rapids, MI: Brazos Press, 2005.
Midgley, Mary. *Beast and Man: The Roots of Human Nature*. New York: Routledge, 1995.
Moltmann, Jürgen. *God in Creation*. Translated by Margaret Kohl. Minneapolis, MN: Fortress Press, 1993.
———. *The Trinity and the Kingdom*. Translated by Margaret Kohl. Minneapolis: Fortress Press, 1993.
———. *The Way of Jesus Christ: Christology in Messianic Dimensions*. Translated by Margaret Kohl. Minneapolis, MN: Fortress Press, 1993.
Moore, Stephen, ed. *Divinanimality: Animal Theory, Creaturely Theology*. New York: Fordham University Press, 2014.
———. "Ecotherology." In Moore, *Divinanimality*, 196–209.
Mosshammer, Alden. "Disclosing but Not Disclosed: Gregory of Nyssa As Deconstructionist." In *Studien zu Gregor von Nyssa und der christlichen Spätantike*, edited by Hubertus Drobner and Christoph Klock, 99–123. New York: Brill, 1990.
Naas, Michael. *Miracle and Machine: Jacques Derrida and the Two Sources of Religion, Science, and the Media*. New York: Fordham University Press, 2012.
Nash, James. *Loving Nature: Ecological Integrity and Christian Responsibility*. Nashville, TN: Abingdon, 1991.
New Testament Apocrypha. Translated by M. R. James. Oxford: Oxford University Press, 1924.
Nicklesburg, George, and James Vanderkam, trans. *1 Enoch: The Hermeneia Translation*. Minneapolis: Fortress Press, 2012.
Nolan Fewell, Danna. *Circle of Sovereignty: Plotting Politics in the Book of Daniel*. Nashville, TN: Abingdon, 1991.
Norris, Andrew. "Giorgio Agamben and the Politics of the Living Dead." *Diacritics* 30, no. 4 (2000): 38–58.
Norris, Frederick. *Faith Gives Fullness to Reasoning: The Five Theological Orations of Gregory of Nazianzen*. New York: Brill, 1991.
Norris, Richard. *Gregory of Nyssa: Homilies on the Song of Songs*. Atlanta: Society of Biblical Literature, 2012.
———. *The Song of Songs: Interpreted by Early Christian and Medieval Commentators*. Grand Rapids, MI: Eerdmans, 2003.
———. "The Soul Takes Flight: Gregory of Nyssa and the Song of Songs." *Anglican Theological Review* 80, no. 4 (1998): 517–32.
Northcott, Michael. *The Environment and Christian Ethics*. Cambridge: Cambridge University Press, 1996.
O'Laughlin, Michael. "The Anthropology of Evagrius Ponticus and Its Sources." In *Origen of Alexandria: His World and His Legacy*, edited by

Charles Kannengiesser and William Petersen, 357–73. Notre Dame, IN: Notre Dame University Press, 1988.

Oliver, Kelly. *Animal Lessons: How They Teach Us to Be Human*. New York: Columbia University Press, 2009.

Onah, Godfrey Igwebuike. *Self Transcendence and Human History in Wolfhart Pannenberg*. Lanham, MD: University Press of America, 1999.

Origen. *Contra Celsum*. Translated by Henry Chadwick. Cambridge: Cambridge University Press, 1965.

———. *Homilies on Genesis and Exodus*. Translated by Ronald Heine. Washington, DC: Catholic University of America Press, 1982.

———. *On First Principles*. Translated by G. W. Butterworth. New York: Harper and Row, 1966.

Osborne, Catherine. *Dumb Beasts and Dead Philosophers: Humanity and the Humane in Ancient Philosophy and Literature*. Oxford: Oxford University Press, 2007.

Otis, B. "Cappadocian Thought as a Coherent System." *Dumbarton Oaks Papers*, no. 12 (1958): 95–124.

Pannenberg, Wolfhart. *Anthropology in Theological Perspective*. Translated by Matthew O'Connell. Philadelphia: Westminster Press, 1985. Originally published as *Anthropologie in Theologischer Perspektive*. Göttingen: Vandenhoeck und Ruprecht, 1983.

———. *Systematic Theology*. Vol. 2. Translated by Geoffrey Bromiley. Grand Rapids, MI: Eerdmans, 1994. Originally published as *Systematische Theologie*. Bd. 2. Göttingen: Vandenhoeck und Ruprecht, 1991.

———. *Systematic Theology*. Vol. 3. Translated by Geoffrey Bromiley. Grand Rapids, MI: Eerdmans, 1997. Originally published as *Systematische Theologie*. Bd. 3. Göttingen: Vandenhoeck und Ruprecht, 1993.

———. *What Is Man? Contemporary Anthropology in Theological Perspective*. Translated by Duane Priebe. Philadelphia: Fortress Press, 1970. Originally published as *Was Ist der Mensch: Die Anthropologie der Gegenwart im Lichte der Theologie*. 7th ed. Göttingen: Vandenhoeck und Ruprecht, 1985.

Peacocke, Arthur. *Creation and the World of Science: The Reshaping of Belief*. 2nd ed. Oxford: Oxford University Press, 2004.

———. *Theology for a Scientific Age: Being and Becoming—Natural, Divine, and Human*. Minneapolis, MN: Fortress Press, 1993.

Peterson, Christopher. "The Posthumanism to Come." *Angelaki* 16, no. 2 (2011): 127–41.

Plato. *Phaedrus*. Translated by R. Hackforth. New York: Cambridge University Press, 1952.

———. *Republic*. Translated by B. Jowett. New York: Vintage, 1991.

Plumwood, Val. *Environmental Culture: The Ecological Crisis of Reason*. New York: Routledge, 2002.

———. *Feminism and the Mastery of Nature*. New York: Routledge, 1993.

Polk, David. *On the Way to God: An Exploration into the Theology of Wolfhart Pannenberg*. Lanham, MD: University Press of America, 1989.

Porter, Jean. "Moral Language and the Language of Grace: The Fundamental Option and the Virtue of Charity." *Philosophy and Theology* 10, no. 1 (1997): 169–98.

———. "A Response to Brian Linnane and David Coffey." *Philosophy and Theology* 10, no. 1 (1997): 285–92.

Quinn, Daniel. *Ishmael: An Adventure of the Mind and Spirit*. New York: Bantam, 1992.

Rahner, Karl. "Christology within an Evolutionary View." In *Theological Investigations*, vol. 5, translated by Karl H. Kruger and Boniface Kruger, 157–92. Baltimore, MD: Helicon Press, 1966. Originally published as "Die Christologie innerhalb einer Evolutiven Weltanschauung." In *Schriften zur Theologie*, 5:182–221. Einsiedeln: Benziger, 1962.

———. *Foundations of Christian Faith: An Introduction to the Idea of Christianity*. Translated by William V. Dych. New York: Crossroad, 1978. Originally published as *Grundkurs des Glaubens*. Edited by Nikolaus Schwerdtfeger and Albert Raffelt. In *Sämtliche Werke*. Zürich: Benziger Verlag, 1999.

———. "Gnade als Mitte menschlicher Existenz." *Herder Korrespondenz*, no. 28 (1974): 157–73.

———. "Natural Science and Reasonable Faith: Theological Perspectives for Dialogue with the Natural Sciences." In Theological Investigations, vol. 21, translated by Paul Imhof, 17–55. New York: Crossroad, 1988. Originally published as "Naturwissenschaft und Vernünftiger Glaube." In *Schriften zur Theologie*, 15:24–63. Einsiedeln: Benziger Verlag, 1983.

———. "The Body in the Order of Salvation." In *Theological Investigations*, vol. 17, translated by Margaret Kohl, 71–89. New York: Crossroad, 1981. Originally published as "Der Leib in der Heilsordnung." In *Schriften zur Theologie*, 12:407–27. Einsiedeln: Benziger Verlag, 1975.

———. "Theology and Anthropology." In *Theological Investigations*, vol. 9, translated by Graham Harrison, 28–45. New York: Herder and Herder, 1972. Originally published as "Theologie und Anthropologie." In *Schriften zur Theologie*, 8:43–65. Einsiedeln: Benziger Verlag, 1967.

———. "Theology of Freedom." In *Theological Investigations*, vol. 6, translated by Karl H. Kruger and Boniface Kruger, 178–96. Baltimore, MD: Helicon Press, 1969. Originally published as "Theologie der Freiheit." In *Schriften zur Theologie*, 6:215–37. Einsiedeln: Benziger Verlag, 1965.

———. "The Unity of Spirit and Matter in the Christian Understanding of Faith." In *Theological Investigations*, vol. 6, translated by Karl H Kruger and Boniface Kruger, 153–77. Baltimore, MD: Helicon Press, 1969. Originally published as "Die Einheit von Geist und Materie im christlichen Glaubensverständnis." In *Schriften zur Theologie*, 6:185–215. Einsiedeln: Benziger Verlag, 1965.

Regan, Tom. *The Case for Animal Rights*. Updated ed. Berkeley: University of California Press, 2004.

Richard, Anne. *Cosmologie et théologie chez Grégoire de Nazianze*. Paris: Institut d'Études Augustiniennes, 2003.

Ruether, Rosemary Radford. *Gaia and God: An Ecofeminist Theology of Earth Healing*. San Francisco: Harper, 1992.

———. *Sexism and God Talk: Toward a Feminist Theology*. Boston, MA: Beacon Press, 1983.

Saranyana, Jose Ignacio. "Hacia una Antropologia Teologica: A Propósito de un Libro de Wolfhardt Pannenberg." *Scripta Theologica* 10, no. 3 (1978): 1115–37.

Schmemann, Alexander. *The Eucharist: Sacrament of the Kingdom*. Crestwood, NY: St. Vladimir's Seminary Press, 1987.

———. *For the Life of the World*. Crestwood, NY: Saint Vladimir's Seminary Press, 2004.

Schüssler Fiorenza, Elisabeth. *In Memory of Her: A Feminist Theological Reconstruction of Christian Origins*. New York: Crossroad, 1985.

———. "Karl Rahner." In *In God's Hands: Essays on the Church and Ecumenism in Honour of Michael A. Fahey, S.J.*, ed. Jaroslav Skira and Michael Attridge, 129–34. Dudley, MA: Leuven University Press, 2006.

Schweitzer, Albert. *The Quest of the Historical Jesus*. Minneapolis: Fortress Press, 2001.

Schwoebel, Christoph. "Theology in Anthropological Perspective?" *King's Theological Review* 10, no. 1 (1987): 21–25.

Scott, Peter. *A Political Theology of Nature*. Cambridge: Cambridge University Press, 2003.

Shaw, Jane. "Reformed and Enlightened Church." In *Queer Theology: Rethinking the Western Body*, edited by Gerard Loughlin, 215–29. Malden, MA: Blackwell, 2007.

Sherman, Jacob Holsinger. "No Werewolves in Theology?: Transcendence, Immanence, and Becoming Divine in Gilles Deleuze." *Modern Theology* 25, no. 1 (2009): 1–20.

Shiva, Vandana, and Maria Mies. "Decolonizing the North." In *Ecofeminism*, 264–76. London: Zed Books, 1993.

Sideris, Lisa. *Environmental Ethics, Ecological Theology, and Natural Selection*. New York: Columbia University Press, 2003.

Simondon, Gilbert. *L'individu et sa Genése Physic-biologique*. Grenoble: Millon, 1995.

Singer, *Animal Liberation*. New rev. ed. New York: Avon Books, 1990.

Smith, Anthony Paul. *A Non-Philosophical Theory of Nature: Ecologies of Thought*. New York: Palgrave MacMillan, 2013.

Smith, J. Warren. "The Body of Paradise and the Body of the Resurrection: Gender and the Angelic Life in Gregory of Nyssa's 'De Hominis Opificio.'" *Harvard Theological Review* 92, no. 2 (2006): 207–28.

———. *Passion and Paradise: Human and Divine Emotion in the Thought of Gregory of Nyssa*. New York: Herder and Herder, 2004.

Smuts, Barbara. "Response." In *The Lives of Animals*, 107–20. Princeton, NJ: Princeton University Press, 1999.

Sobrino, Jon. *Jesus the Liberator: A Historical-Theological View*. Translated by Paul Burns and Francis McDonagh. Maryknoll, NY: Orbis, 1993.

Sorabji, Richard. *Animal Minds and Human Morals: The Origins of the Western Debate*. Ithaca, NY: Cornell University Press, 1993.

Southgate, Christopher. *The Groaning of Creation: God, Evolution, and the Problem of Evil*. Louisville, KY: Westminster John Knox, 2008.

Staniforth, Maxwell, ed. *Early Christian Writings*. New York: Penguin, 1968.

Stiegler, Bernard. "Doing and Saying Stupid Things in the Twentieth Century: Bêtise and Animality in Deleuze and Derrida." *Angelaki* 18, no. 1 (2013): 159–74.

Tanner, Kathryn. *Christ the Key*. Cambridge: Cambridge University Press, 2010.

Tertullian, *De virginibus velandum*. In *Ante-Nicene Fathers*, vol. 4, edited by Philip Schaff. Grand Rapids, MI: Eerdmans, 1954.

———. *Tertullian's Treatise on the Resurrection*. Translated by Ernest Evans. London: SPCK, 1960.

Tilley, Terrence. *The Disciples' Jesus: Christology As Reconciling Practice*. Maryknoll, NY: Orbis Books, 2008.

Tillich, Paul. *The Courage to Be*. New Haven, CT: Yale University Press, 1952.

———. *Systematic Theology I*. Chicago: University of Chicago Press, 1951.

Torjeson, Karen Jo. *Hermeneutical Procedure and Theological Exegesis in Origen's Exegesis*. New York: Walter de Gruyter, 1986.

Trible, Phyllis. "Depatriarchalizing in Biblical Interpretation." *Journal of the American Academy of Religion* 41, no. 2 (1973): 30–48.

———. "Eve and Adam: Genesis 2–3 Reread." *Andover Newton Quarterly* 13, no. 4 (1973): 251–58.

Tupper, E. Frank. *The Theology of Wolfhart Pannenberg*. Philadelphia: Westminster Press, 1973.

Uexküll, Jakob von. *Streifzüge durch die Umwelten von Tieren und Menschen*. Frankfurt am Main: S. Fischer, 1970.

———. *Umwelt und Innenwelt der Tiere*. Berlin: J. Springer, 1921.

Wallace, David Foster. *Infinite Jest*. Boston, MA: Back Bay Books, 1996.

Ware, Owen. "Dialectic of the Past/Disjuncture of the Future: Derrida and Benjamin on the Concept of Messianism." *Journal for Critical and Religious Theory* 5, no. 2 (2004): 99–114.

Weheliye, Alexander. *Habeas Viscus: Racializing Assemblages, Biopolitics, and Black Feminist Theories of the Human*. Durham, NC: Duke University Press, 2014.

Weiss, Johannes. *Jesus' Proclamation of the Kingdom of God.* Philadelphia: Fortress Press, 1971.

Wennberg, Robert. *God, Humans, and Animals: An Invitation to Enlarge Our Moral Universe.* Grand Rapids, MI: Eerdmans, 2003.

Wesche, Kenneth Paul. "'Mind' and 'Self' in the Christology of Saint Gregory the Theologian: Saint Gregory's Contribution to Christology and Christian Anthropology." *Greek Orthodox Theological Review* 39, no. 1 (1994): 33–61.

Westermann, Claus. *Genesis 1–11: A Commentary.* Translated by John Scullion. London: SPCK, 1984.

White, Lynn. "The Historical Roots of Our Ecologic Crisis." *Science* 155, no. 3767 (1967): 1203–207.

Willett, Cynthia. *Interspecies Ethics.* New York: Columbia University Press, 2014.

Wolfe, Cary. *Animal Rites: American Culture, the Discourse of Species, and Posthumanist Theory.* Chicago: University of Chicago Press, 2003.

———. *Wolfhart Pannenberg on Human Destiny.* Burlington, VT: Ashgate, 2008.

Wynter, Sylvia, and Katherine McKittrick. "Unparalleled Catastrophe for Our Species? Or, to Give Humanness a Different Future: Conversations." In *Sylvia Wynter: On Being Human As Praxis*, ed. Katherine McKittrick, 9–89. Durham, NC: Duke University Press, 2015.

Zachhuber, Johannes. *Human Nature in Gregory of Nyssa: Philosophical Background and Theological Significance.* Boston, MA: Brill, 2000.

Žižek, Slavoj. *Less Than Nothing: Hegel and the Shadow of Dialectical Materialism.* New York: Verso, 2012.

Zizioulas, John. *Being as Communion: Studies in Personhood and the Church.* Crestwood, NY: Saint Vladimir's Seminary Press, 1985.

———. "Human Capacity and Human Incapacity: A Theological Exploration of Personhood." *Scottish Journal of Theology*, no. 28 (1975): 401–48.

———. "On Being a Person: Towards an Ontology of Personhood." In *Persons, Divine and Human*, edited by Christoph Schwöbel and Colin Gunton, 33–46. London: T. and T. Clark, 1991.

———. "Priest of Creation." In *Environmental Stewardship*, edited by R. J. Berry, 273–90. Edinburgh: T. and T. Clark, 2006.

Index

groundworks

ECOLOGICAL ISSUES IN PHILOSOPHY AND THEOLOGY

Forrest Clingerman and Brian Treanor, series editors

Interpreting Nature: The Emerging Field of Environmental Hermeneutics
Forrest Clingerman, Brian Treanor, Martin Drenthen, and David Utsler, Editors

The Noetics of Nature: Environmental Philosophy and the Holy Beauty of the Visible
Bruce V. Foltz

Environmental Aesthetics: Crossing Divides and Breaking Ground
Martin Drenthen and Jozef Keulartz, Editors

The Logos of the Living World: Merleau-Ponty, Animals, and Language
Louise Westling

Being-in-Creation: Human Responsibility in an Endangered World
Brian Treanor, Bruce Ellis Benson, and Norman Wirzba, Editors

Wilderness in America: Philosophical Writings
Henry Bugbee, edited by David W. Rodick

Eco-Deconstruction: Derrida and Environmental Philosophy
Matthias Fritsch, Philippe Lynes, and David Wood, Editors

Inner Animalities: Theology and the End of the Human
Eric Daryl Meyer